THUCYDIDES ON STRATEGY

'A masterful, unique and important journey through the past, that sheds truly clarifying light on the present—on current and timeless dilemmas and principles of grand strategy.'

Brigadier General (Ret.) Dr Jonathan Shimshoni, Research Affiliate, MIT Security Studies Program

'I read *Thucydides on Strategy* with considerable interest, pleasure, and care. The authors have made an original contribution to scholarship ... and have managed to synthesise a coherent whole that goes far to explain how Athens lost and the Peloponnesians won this war. In the course of doing this, they also manage to explain why Thucydides' work is "for all time". They show that the same sorts of strategic questions and problems are likely to recur, again and again, as Thucydides says, so long as human nature remains the same— e.g., defining political objectives, matching a grand strategy to meet them, integrating a military strategy with the grand strategy, interacting with an enemy, avoiding overextension, and a whole range of other themes commonly studied by strategists today.'

Karl Walling, Professor in the Department of Policy and Strategy, United States Naval War College

'An excellent companion to the History, and an aid to the essential reflection that Thucydides' work requires.'

Lieutenant General (Ret.) Sir John Kiszely, author of *General Hastings 'Pug' Ismay— Soldier, Statesman, Diplomat: A New Biography*

'*Thucydides on Strategy* provides a conclusive rebuttal to those who suspect modern strategists are guilty of anachronism when they claim that the classical world thought and acted strategically. Athanasios Platias and Constantinos Koliopoulos demonstrate convincingly why Thucydides belongs in a lonely triumvirate with Carl von Clausewitz and Sun Tzu as the truly essential authors of a general strategic theory both universally and eternally valid. The wisdom in this splendid book could save our current politics from many follies. If only our politicians, civil servants, and soldiers took the time to read and understand it.'

Colin S Gray, University of Reading

'Thucydides, as he himself anticipated, wrote not only the history of the Peloponnesian War. He wrote the history of the Napoleonic Wars, World War I, World War II, and the Cold War.'

Louis Halle

'International relations continue to be a recurring struggle for wealth and power among independent actors in a state of anarchy. The classic history of Thucydides is as meaningful a guide to the behaviour of states today as when it was written in the fifth century B.C.E.'

Robert Gilpin

ATHANASIOS PLATIAS
CONSTANTINOS KOLIOPOULOS

Thucydides on Strategy

Grand Strategies in the Peloponnesian War and Their Relevance Today

UPDATED AND EXPANDED EDITION

HURST & COMPANY, LONDON

First published in the United Kingdom in 2010 by
C. Hurst & Co. (Publishers) Ltd.,
41 Great Russell Street, London, WC1B 3PL
Copyright © Athanasios Platias and Constantinos Koliopoulos, 2010
All rights reserved.

This updated and expanded edition first published in 2026 by
C. Hurst & Co. (Publishers) Ltd.,
New Wing, Somerset House, Strand, London WC2R 1LA

The right of Athanasios Platias and Constantinos Koliopoulos to be identified as the authors of this publication is asserted by them in accordance with the Copyright, Designs and Patents Act, 1988.

Distributed in the United States, Canada and Latin America by Oxford University Press, 198 Madison Avenue, New York, NY 10016, United States of America.

A Cataloguing-in-Publication data record for this book is available from the British Library.

ISBN: 9781805264460

EU GPSR Authorised Representative
Easy Access System Europe Oü, 16879218
Address: Mustamäe tee 50, 10621, Tallinn, Estonia
Contact Details: gpsr.requests@easproject.com, +358 40 500 3575

www.hurstpublishers.com

This book is printed using paper from registered sustainable and managed sources.

I have written my work, not as an essay which is to win the applause of the moment, but as a possession for all time.

Thucydides, I 22

To my daughter Maria-Alexia
A.P.

To my parents
C.K.

CONTENTS

About the Authors	xiii
List of Maps	xv
Preface to the Second Edition	xvii
Preface	xix
Chronology	xxi
1. Grand Strategy: A Framework for Analysis	1
2. Athens and Sparta: Power Structures, Early Conflict and the Causes of War	23
3. Periclean Grand Strategy	41
4. Spartan Grand Strategy	71
5. Thucydides and Strategy in Perspective	95
Epilogue	139
Postscript	141
Appendix: Strategic Concepts in Thucydides' *History*	151
Notes	167
Select Bibliography	221
Index	229

ABOUT THE AUTHORS

ATHANASIOS G. PLATIAS is a Professor of Strategy at the University of Piraeus, the President of the Council of International Relations-Greece, an Athens-based think tank, and the Coordinator for Europe of the Mackinder Forum.

He received an MA and a PhD in international relations from the Department of Government at Cornell University. He has been a Ford Foundation Fellow at Harvard University, a MacArthur Fellow in International Peace and Security at Harvard/MIT, and a NATO Fellow.

Professor Platias has held several senior advisory positions in the Greek public sector over the last thirty-five years, and has served as non-executive director in publicly listed companies for more than three decades. He also held several senior academic positions, such as Dean of the School of Economics, Business and International Studies, and Chairman of the Department of International and European Studies at the University of Piraeus.

Professor Platias is the author of numerous books and articles. His research and teaching focus on four principal areas: grand strategy; geopolitics and geoeconomics; regional security (with an emphasis on Eastern Mediterranean); and leadership.

CONSTANTINOS KOLIOPOULOS is Professor of International Relations and Strategic Studies at the University of Piraeus, Greece. He holds a PhD in strategic studies from Lancaster University.

He has been Fulbright Scholar on the Study of the United States Institute on U.S. National Security program. Apart from his univer-

ABOUT THE AUTHORS

sity career, he has been teaching international relations and strategic studies at higher Greek military academies for more than twenty-five years. Among others, he is Professor of Strategic Studies at the Hellenic National Defense College and Honoured Lecturer therein. Professor Koliopoulos used to be a tournament chess player and has been awarded the title of master by the Greek Chess Federation.

Professor Koliopoulos has authored many books and articles, mainly in the following areas: strategic theory and practice from antiquity until the present; history and theory of international politics; European security and political integration; intelligence and strategic surprise; and Mediterranean geopolitical conflicts.

LIST OF MAPS

Map 1: Central and Southern Mainland Greece, Fifth Century
BCE   xiv
Map 2: The Athenian Alliance/Empire   27
Map 3: Sparta's Peloponnesian League   29
Map 4: Athens' Urban Fortification Complex   34
Map 5: Southern Italy, Sicily and Carthage   75

PREFACE TO THE SECOND EDITION

Map 1: Central and Southern Mainland Greece, Fifth Century BCE

PREFACE TO THE SECOND EDITION

Thucydides' *History* is more than an account of conflict between Greek city-states. It is a thoughtful analysis of one of history's earliest recorded great power rivalries, and offers enduring insights for scholars and lessons for policymakers. In the current era of intense geopolitical competition akin to Cold War 2.0, the work of Thucydides, as he himself predicted, remains an invaluable source of enduring utility (κτῆμα ες αεί/ 'a possession for all time').

Our book, first published in 2010, was designed to decipher Thucydides' approach to grand strategy and to demonstrate his contribution to strategic thought. Today, this task is even more useful. Encouraged by our publisher, Michael Dwyer, we have updated the first edition. We have also added a postscript discussing the current Sino–American geopolitical antagonism from the perspective of Thucydides' classical realism. This was deemed necessary, since Thucydides' history has once again become the epicentre of a strategic debate about the future of U.S.–China relations in an era of hegemonic power transition, as evidenced by the attention that the so-called 'Thucydides' trap' has received.

We have been delighted to see that last year our book was translated and published in Chinese by The Commercial Press, a leading Chinese academic publisher. We would like to thank Professors Tang Xiaoyang and Vasilis Trigkas of Tsinghua University for writing the preface for the Chinese edition.

A.P. and C.K.
Athens, May 2025

PREFACE

Which is the best treatise on strategy? The purpose of this book is to demonstrate the contribution of Thucydides to strategic thought. It argues that the basic concepts of strategy originated in Thucydides' *History of the Peloponnesian War*. Consequently, Thucydides' text is a masterpiece of strategic analysis that vies with Sun Tzu's *The Art of War* and Clausewitz' *On War* for the honour of the best treatise on the subject.

We should forewarn the reader that it is not our intention to provide a detailed historical description of the Peloponnesian War. Our preoccupation shall be with strategy and strategic analysis, albeit examined against the background of said war. In other words, it is our intention to use the text of Thucydides[1] to draw some pertinent conclusions with regard to the strategic choices made by the main players in world politics.

The book aims to show that although material conditions may change, the logic of conflict between organized entities remains constant throughout the millennia. The issues tackled by Thucydides have recurred through the centuries and remain relevant today. Organized entities, in their quest for security, still create and implement strategies similar to those employed twenty-five centuries ago. There is a thread of irony within this consistency, as even the blunders (e.g. overextension, underestimation of the enemy, etc.) are replicated throughout history. Indeed, there is no reason to believe that this trend will not persist into the future. Consequently, the writings of Thucydides and the grand strategies contained therein are as relevant

PREFACE

today as they were in the past, and there is no reason to believe that their relevance shall diminish with time.

Louis Halle did not exaggerate when he claimed that 'Thucydides, as he himself anticipated, wrote not only the history of the Peloponnesian War. He wrote the history of the Napoleonic Wars, World War I, World War II, and the Cold War'.[2] Despite the recent debate concerning the alleged 'discontinuities in international politics'[3] and the 'transformation of world politics',[4] it is difficult to disagree with Robert Gilpin when he states that 'international relations continue to be a recurring struggle for wealth and power among independent actors in a state of anarchy. The classic history of Thucydides is as meaningful a guide to the behavior of states today as when it was written in the fifth century B.C.'.[5]

The book assumes no prior knowledge of Thucydides' work or the politics of ancient Greece. A copy of Thucydides' *History of the Peloponnesian War* would undoubtedly be helpful to the reader but by no means necessary, even though we hope that our work will provide the reader with the incentive to further explore the text.

This book is a joint effort by its authors. By exception, Athanasios Platias retains responsibility for Chapter Three, which is based on some of his earlier work.

We wish to express our gratitude to a number of people that have positively influenced this book. The editors of the journal *Comparative Strategy* provided both encouragement and outlets for our ideas on Thucydides' contribution to strategic thought.[6] Karl Walling made a thorough review of the book and produced a great number of pertinent suggestions and corrections. Colin Gray and Panayiotis Ifestos came up with highly useful points. Of course, it goes without saying that we retain sole responsibility for the views expressed in this book, errors and shortcomings inclusive.

A.P. and C.K.
Athens, March 2009

CHRONOLOGY

Note: All dates are BCE.

490	The Persian King Darius sends an army against Greece, which is defeated by the Athenians at the Battle of Marathon.
480	The Persian King Xerxes brings a larger army against Greece.
	Battles of Thermopylae and Salamis.
479	Battle of Plataea, where the Greek allies defeat the Persian army.
478	Fortification of Athens.
477	Foundation of the Delian League.
464	Catastrophic earthquake in Sparta.
461–29	The Age of Pericles in Athens.
460	Outbreak of First Peloponnesian War.
458	The Athenians build long walls to protect the road to their seaport at Piraeus.
454	The treasury of the Delian League is transferred to Athens.
447–33	Athens builds the Parthenon.
446–5	Athens and Sparta conclude the Thirty Years' Peace.
432	The Megarian Decree is passed in Athens.
431–21	First phase of the Peloponnesian War (Archidamian War).
430	Plague breaks out in Athens.
429	Death of Pericles.
427	Surrender of Mytilene to Athens.

CHRONOLOGY

	Surrender of Plataea to Sparta and Thebes.
	Civil war in Corcyra.
425	Capture of 120 Spartan soldiers on Sphacteria.
424	Thucydides goes into exile.
421–14	Peace of Nicias.
418	Battle of Mantinea.
416	Slaughter of the Melians.
415	Athenian invasion of Sicily.
414–04	Second phase of the Peloponnesian War (Decelean or Ionian War).
413	Destruction of Athenian army and navy outside Syracuse.
412	Revolt of Athenian allies.
411	Thucydides' *History* breaks off.
404	Surrender of Athens to the Spartans.

1

GRAND STRATEGY

A FRAMEWORK FOR ANALYSIS

Introduction

It is widely acknowledged that renowned classic treatises in their respective fields provide, *inter alia*, a standard of evaluation for all other field-related work and serve as a cornerstone upon which new theories can be developed. As far as the study of strategy is concerned, Michael Handel has claimed that strategists are fortunate to have access to two enduring classic texts: Sun Tzu's *The Art of War* and Clausewitz' *On War*.[1] However, we believe that another classic masterpiece needs to be added to this short list, namely Thucydides' *History of the Peloponnesian War*.[2] The purpose of this analysis, therefore, is to demonstrate Thucydides' contribution to the study of strategy.

Undoubtedly, Thucydides ranks as both a great historian and the forefather of the discipline of international relations. For instance, Robert Gilpin has wondered whether contemporary scholars of international relations actually know anything about state behaviour that was unknown to Thucydides.[3] What has been ignored is that in Thucydides' text we encounter, for the first time in history, an outline of a complete theory of grand strategy that demonstrates how states ensure their security. Thucydides' theory incorporates the economic, diplomatic, military, technological, demographic, psychological and other factors upon which a state's security depends. It is highly interesting that Thucydides did not confine his analysis to traditional strategies that focus on the military dimension. Moreover, he also took into account grand strategies that emphasize dimensions other than the military one, pointing out that these may well provide states with a path to victory.

The main argument of this study is that Thucydides' text is a classic masterpiece of strategy that contains significant strategic insights and a wealth of strategic concepts (see Appendix). Seen in this light, Thucydides *History* has at least equal right with Clausewitz' *On War* to be considered 'the strategist's toolkit'.[4] Needless to say, Thucydides did not use contemporary strategic jargon—one has to delve into the text in order to uncover these insights and concepts. This is where our own contribution lies: to bring to the surface and translate into modern strategic parlance the aforementioned concepts and insights.

One might perhaps doubt that a book written twenty-five centuries ago retains any relevance for today's strategic issues and problems. However, it has been correctly pointed out that *'there is an essential unity to all strategic experience in all periods of history because nothing vital to the nature and function of war and strategy changes'*.[5] This is the guiding principle of the present analysis and will hopefully be demonstrated as far as Thucydides' work is concerned.

Before proceeding to the examination of Thucydides' contribution to the study of grand strategy and strategy in general, we first need to clarify and elaborate upon these concepts. The essence of strategy and grand strategy needs to be understood and the various characteristics of these two concepts outlined. Consequently, in this chapter we shall first elaborate on the nature of strategy and outline its various levels. We shall then examine grand strategy and certain aspects thereof while also making an attempt to categorize grand strategies, both according to the nature of the means employed and the general approach to be followed in the pursuit of policy objectives. The final issue touched upon in this chapter is that of the planning and evaluation of grand strategy. This analysis will help us comprehend the contribution of Thucydides to the study of strategy (discussed in Chapters Two to Five).

GRAND STRATEGY

The Nature of Strategy

There have been many definitions of the term 'strategy' throughout the ages. While strategy was initially defined as 'all military movements out of the enemy's cannon range or range of vision'[6] or 'the art of making war upon the map',[7] nowadays the term has acquired a broader meaning. Two modern definitions of strategy are 'the art of distributing and applying military means to fulfil the ends of policy'[8] and 'the art of the dialectic of two opposing wills using force to resolve their dispute'.[9] These definitions make it clear that strategy is about a state coupling means and ends in the context of international competition, both in peacetime and wartime, and both during potential as well as actual conflict.

Strategy never exists in a vacuum; it implies an opponent, a conflict, a competition, a situation where somebody is trying to achieve a goal against somebody else. Thus, strategy is always formulated against one or more opponents, who in turn develop their own strategy and try to counter the former. Each side's moves are intimately connected with those of the opponent. As Clausewitz comments, 'war is nothing but a duel on a larger scale'.[10] This interaction between the strategic designs of both belligerents has been referred to as the 'horizontal dimension' of strategy.[11] The very existence of an opposing will gives strategy a comparatively paradoxical logic of its own, which differs from the traditional definition of logic that governs one's actions when no opponent is present. Thus, while a traveller, as a rule, chooses the shortest route and the best weather conditions for their journey, the existence of an opponent will make a military commander attack through a roundabout route instead of following the shorter one of a head-on assault, launch their attack at night instead of daytime, etc. An even more striking example of the paradoxical logic of strategy is the well-known Latin aphorism '*Si vis pacem, para bellum*' ('If you want peace, prepare for war'). Even though in other areas of life similar aphorisms would be clearly absurd (e.g. 'if you want to be sober, prepare some drinks'), this aphorism is accepted as conventional wisdom in the realm of strategy.[12]

However, states in general, and military organizations in particular, sometimes 'forget' that they are facing opponents possessing an independent will and employing a strategy of their own. Overlooking this can have dire consequences. For instance, at the turn of the nineteenth century, the German army moved from Moltke's conviction that 'no plan of operations extends with certainty beyond the first contact with the enemy's main strength'[13] to the concept of 'war by timetable' as promulgated by Schlieffen. In strict adherence to this approach, the German invasion of France in 1914, the capture of Paris and the subsequent transfer of the German troops to the East in order to fight the Russians had been pre-planned down to the last detail. However, as the failure of the Schlieffen Plan revealed, strategy can seldom be subjected to such meticulous planning—the opponent, as a rule, is bound to interfere with one's plans.[14] It is certainly far more pleasant for an army during peacetime to contemplate what it will do to the enemy on D-day than what the enemy will do to it.[15]

Something that accentuates the difficulty of formulating strategy is that in strategy, as in economy, resources are normally scarce, especially as far as smaller states are concerned. Precisely due to this scarcity of resources, strategy ought to rate the objectives to be pursued and prioritize them accordingly.

The Levels of Strategy

Traditionally, 'strategy' has been distinguished from 'tactics', with the latter having more to do with the execution of the former. The rule of thumb for distinguishing between the two has been that strategy ends and tactics begins the moment the opposing forces make contact.[16] In other words, while strategy decides where, when and with what force an action will be conducted, tactics governs how this action will be deployed.[17] Consequently, the term 'tactics' refers to what takes place in the battlefield, taking into account the extension of the concept of 'battlefield' brought about by the advent of aircraft as well as medium- and long-range missiles. In general, tactics refers to 'battle' and strategy to 'war': the former to the use of the means; the latter to their impact on the achievement of the policy ends.[18]

The need to distinguish between strategy and tactics shows that strategy operates on various levels; this is the so-called 'vertical dimension' of strategy.[19] Although still relevant, the traditional distinction between strategy and tactics far from exhausts the issue. To get the full picture, one has first to examine the roots of strategy. The governing mind behind strategy is policy, which sets the aims that strategy will subsequently be called upon to achieve. As far as strategy is concerned, the process by which the aims are set and the nature of the political leadership that sets them are irrelevant. As a matter of fact, the concept of political leadership varies from country to country, depending on the country's political system. Political leadership may at times even comprise individuals who happen to be outside the official state institutions. For instance, Stalin and Deng ruled their respective countries for considerable periods of time without in fact holding any state office.[20] An individual or a group of individuals may belong to the 'political leadership' irrespective of whether they are actually 'politicians' or not. At times, the political leadership of various countries has included hereditary rulers (like the kings of Saudi Arabia and Morocco nowadays), clerics (Richelieu in France, Alberoni in Spain, Makarios in Cyprus) or military men (Napoleon, Pinochet, the Japanese army leadership during the 1930s and 1940s, and the Turkish army leadership from the 1960s until the late 2000s). In other words, as far as strategy is concerned, political leadership refers to 'those who run the country'. The leadership may be democratic or authoritarian, legitimate or illegitimate, but it is still this leadership that will set the aims that strategy will then serve.[21]

As illustrated, when policy objectives are coupled with the various means and care is taken to overcome the opponent's resistance, one enters the realm of strategy. We shall shortly examine the various levels of strategy. Despite their differences, each level is governed by the paradoxical logic of strategy. In addition, none of these levels are free from the difficulty of scarcity of resources that compels strategic planners to assign priorities among the objectives to be pursued. Finally, there is constant interaction with the opponent at every one of these levels; in other words, the horizontal and the vertical dimensions of strategy are constantly intermingled (see Table 1.1). The various levels are not conceived as rigidly separated and contrasted categories, but as successive areas of a continuum,[22] especially since they continuously interact among each other.

THUCYDIDES ON STRATEGY

Table 1.1: Horizontal and Vertical Dimensions of Strategy

State A		Opposing State B
Grand Strategy $\updownarrow$	↔	Grand Strategy $\updownarrow$
Military Strategy $\updownarrow$	↔	Military Strategy $\updownarrow$
Operational Art $\updownarrow$	↔	Operational Art $\updownarrow$
Tactics	↔	Tactics

The highest level of strategy is grand strategy. Grand strategy refers to the use of all available means (military, economic, diplomatic, etc.) at a state's disposal in order to achieve the objectives set by policy in the face of actual or potential conflict.[23] It is formulated by the political leadership, and deals with the fundamental issues of war and peace and whether a state will go to war in order to achieve the objectives set by policy. In addition, grand strategy will align the military strategy of a war with the political, diplomatic and economic strategies that form part of the war effort, making sure that they interact harmoniously and that one of these strategies does not have a detrimental impact on another.

The domain of grand strategy is chiefly the international system. A state's grand strategy is extensively (but not solely, as we will soon see) influenced by such factors as the structure of the international system, the international balance of power, the international diplomatic scene, and trends in international economy. In addition, grand strategy covers the whole of sovereign space and population. This is the case both because it makes use of all national means—both material and nonmaterial—and because a grand strategy must ensure its domestic legitimacy.

When a grand strategy is applied to a specific war, with a specific opponent and within a specific international environment, it becomes a theory of victory. A theory of victory explains how a specific war can be won.[24] Although this is by definition related to a specific context, certain theories of victory contain elements of permanent importance. A highly interesting example of such permanent elements of a theory of victory can be found in Clausewitz' analysis about how one could achieve total victory against Russia. According to him, this country could not be forcibly conquered, in contrast to the other European countries—neither Napoleon's 600,000 men in 1812 nor Hitler's 3 million in 1941 proved sufficient for a conquest. Russia can only be destroyed from within—that is, by exploiting its internal divisions. In the case of Napoleon, since the Russian leaders retained their composure and the Russian people remained loyal to the government, Napoleon's campaign could not succeed.[25] Although Clausewitz' analysis did not examine the broader international context, it had nevertheless provided the essential elements of a theory of victory against Russia, at least in the pre-nuclear era. In simple words, this theory stated that: 'If your aim is total victory over Russia and the international environment allows it, your only chance of success lies in exploiting the internal divisions of that country'. This analysis has been historically vindicated. The collapse of Russia in the First World War was caused by internal revolutionary movements that were largely assisted by the Germans.[26] On the contrary, in the Second World War, the rallying of the Soviet people behind their government and the final failure of the German invasion was precisely the result of Hitler's refusal to exploit the internal divisions of the Soviet Union (by playing either on the anti-communist sentiments of the population or on the ethnic division between Russians and non-Russians) and his insistence on treating the whole of the conquered Soviet population as 'subhumans' (*Untermenschen*).[27]

Supporting grand strategy are the military, economic, diplomatic and political strategies. The latter three will be discussed in the next section, where grand strategy will be elaborated upon. The rest of this section will deal with military strategy and the levels below that, namely the operational and tactical levels.[28]

Military strategy is the use of all military means at a state's disposal, in order to achieve the objectives set by policy in view of actual or potential conflict.[29] It is military strategy that determines the structure and the mission of a country's armed forces. Irrespective of the various administrative divisions adopted in different countries, a state's armed forces may be divided into land, naval, air and (where in existence) mass destruction forces.[30] The degree of participation of each of these branches in the state's attempts to achieve their policy objectives during peacetime and wartime is the objective of military strategy.

Military strategies may attempt either to retain or overthrow the status quo. Both of these can be achieved either by the threat or the actual use of force. Depending on this ends–means balance, military strategies may be classified as offensive, defensive, deterrent and compellent (see Table 1.2).[31]

Table 1.2: Military Strategies

		Political Objectives	
		Overthrow Status Quo	Retain Status Quo
Means	Use of Force	Offensive	Defensive
	Threat of Force	Compellent	Deterrent

An offensive military strategy aims at overthrowing the existing status quo by the use of force. A 'pure' offensive strategy is characterized by the emphasis it places on (a) the first strike; (b) territorial conquest; and (c) decisive victory over the armed forces of the enemy. An offensive military strategy may have unlimited or limited territorial aims, i.e. either complete conquest of an opponent (e.g. the Iraqi conquest of Kuwait), or seizure of a specific piece of territory (e.g. the Argentine conquest of the Falklands).

A defensive military strategy, on the other hand, attempts to retain the existing status quo by the use of force; in other words, it aims at repelling the enemy's offensive. A 'pure' defensive strategy is characterized by the emphasis it places on (a) absorbing the opponent's first strike; (b) denying the territorial objectives of the enemy by holding territory; and (c) denying the decisive victory of an adversary by limiting damage to one's armed forces. The Soviet Union followed such a strategy during the period 1941–4, replacing it with an offensive one during the period 1944–5.[32]

It is to be noted that between offensive and defensive military strategies there exists the grey area of anticipatory first strikes. An anticipatory attack aims at the destruction of a potential source of threat before the said threat actually materializes. Depending on the maturation time of the perceived threat, anticipatory attacks may be either preventive or pre-emptive.[33] Prevention deals with threats expected to mature after years, whereas pre-emption deals with threats expected to mature within weeks, days, or even hours. The logic of prevention is that of fighting early and creating a *fait accompli* while this is still possible—that is, before the balance of power tips in any decisive way and the strategic opponent becomes strong enough to be threatening (e.g. the Israeli strike against the Iraqi nuclear reactor in 1981).[34] In contrast, pre-emption does not have to do with long-term threats, but revolves around immediate crises: a state strikes against the offensive forces of another so as to blunt an attack that is assumed to be imminent—in other words, the attack is already viewed as a matter of fact rather than as conjecture about the distant future.[35] There are important legal and moral distinctions[36] between prevention and pre-emption that make pre-emption a borderline case between offence and defence. However, in our study, both strategies will be considered as offensive on the grounds of their behavioural manifestation, namely war initiation.

Deterrence is the notion of using threat to dissuade opponents from attempting to achieve their objectives. A deterrent military strategy attempts to retain the existing status quo by the threat of force. There are three types of deterrent threats: denial, retaliation/retribution, and punishment. The aim is that the opponent does not attack at all, fearing that the resulting cost will be greater than the likely benefit.[37] There are some deterrent military strategies that, although meaningful before an opponent violates the status quo (*ex ante*), it is questionable whether they constitute rational choices after an opponent violates the status quo (*ex post*). The most characteristic example is the U.S. threat of nuclear retaliation in case of a Soviet invasion of Western Europe during the Cold War. When the Soviet Union itself acquired the capability of large-scale nuclear strikes on U.S. territory, the U.S. threat of nuclear retaliation still retained its deterrent value, since it signified very serious consequences; however, the rationality of its execution if the Soviet Union did invade Western Europe was put into considerable doubt.

Finally, compellence is a strategy of using threat to persuade the opponent to perform some desired action. There are several examples of compellent military strategies, which include strategies where the aim is to overthrow the existing status quo by the threat of force; in other words, to make the opponent submit without war. In most instances, military strategies of this kind are synonymous with the offensive ones—the best way to make opponents accept an adverse change of the status quo without war is persuading them that you can bring about this change by the use of force anyway. However, as in the case of deterrent strategies, there have been some military strategies that were suitable for compellence in peacetime but unsuitable for a victory in war. One example is Germany at the turn of the nineteenth century, who launched an ambitious program of naval development that emphasized battleship construction. The aim was to create a naval threat against Great Britain so that they would make concessions to Germany. During the First World War, however, the German navy rarely used its expensive battleships and basically resorted to submarine warfare. The conclusion was clear: battleships were suitable for compellence in peacetime, but submarines were suitable for victory in war.[38]

The success of a deterrent threat is measured by it not having to be used, whereas the success of a compellent action is measured by how closely and quickly the adversary conforms to one's stipulated wishes. In compellence, as Robert J. Art explains, A is doing something that B cannot tolerate; B then initiates action against A in order to get them to stop their intolerable actions; in the end, A stops their intolerable actions and B stops theirs (or both cease simultaneously). In deterrence, A is presently not doing something that B finds intolerable; B tells A that if A changes their behaviour and does something intolerable, B will punish them; finally, A continues not to do something that B finds intolerable (see Figure 1.1).[39]

The domain of military strategy is far narrower than that of grand strategy. Military strategy covers the whole of the sovereign space, as well as the whole of the actual or potential theatre(s) of operations. Still, broader considerations are not necessarily absent from military strategy. For instance, if armaments are imported from abroad, then it is obvious that arms procurement, which constitutes an important part of military strategy,[40] can be influenced by the international environment. Military strategy used to be formulated by the commander-

GRAND STRATEGY

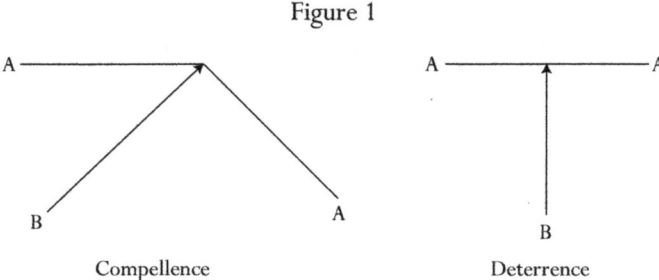

Figure 1

Compellence   Deterrence

in-chief of the armed forces, who more often than not happened to be a hereditary king. The advent of the general staff and defence ministries brought more professionalism in the making of military strategy, which nowadays is viewed as the domain of the political and military leadership of a state's defence ministry.

In the context of war, military strategy determines the role of each branch of the armed forces, as well as the relative priority of the various theatres of operations. Thus, the Schlieffen Plan assigned priority to the Western theatre of operations (France) over the Eastern one (Russia), in the same way that the military strategy of the Western allies in the Second World War gave priority to the European theatre of operations ('Germany first') over the Pacific one ('Japan first').

Immediately below the level of military strategy, but above that of tactics, lies the operational level. The concept of the operational level of war[41] has only recently entered the strategic thought of Western countries, being borrowed from the Soviets, who, in turn, had taken it from the Germans.[42] Whereas military strategy has to do with the 'war' and tactics with the 'battle', the operational level has to do with the 'campaign'. The operational level is the domain of large military units (conventionally starting from the army corps) of one or more branches of the armed forces that operate within a certain theatre of the war. Theatres of war vary in size; there are theatres as vast as the Pacific Ocean during the Second World War and as small as the Golan Heights during the Yom Kippur War (1973). Even within a particular theatre, it is possible that some smaller yet completely autonomous theatres may evolve (the Crimean theatre within the broader Russian front in 1942 was such a case).[43]

THUCYDIDES ON STRATEGY

It has, with good reason, been pointed out that the scale of operations and the variety of military units are conditions necessary but not sufficient for talking about an independent operational level; the actions of these units must constitute something more than the sum of their tactical parts.[44] In practice, however, these two conditions normally prove sufficient. For instance, while the single pikeman or the small band of pikemen stood no chance against the single cavalryman or the small band of cavalrymen, large units of pikemen could hold their own against similar bodies of charioteers or cavalrymen.

Some analysts believe that, since different operational situations may exist and different operational methods may be used within the same theatre of operations, one should discern both a separate level of 'theatre strategy', located immediately below that of military strategy and covering the activities within a theatre, and an 'operational level', located below the level of theatre strategy and dealing with the various operational methods of action.[45] The Kosovo War (1999) is a striking example of different operational conditions and methods coexisting within the same theatre. On the one hand, there was the high-tech aerial warfare, while on the other the irregular operations on the ground reminded one of the wars of the Middle Ages or the Thirty Years' War. Nevertheless, the continuum 'battle–campaign–war' is neat enough, and we see no compelling reason why it should be broken by the introduction of another level dealing with the style in which war is waged.

We have already devoted some attention to tactics, which is the lowest level of strategy.[46] Clausewitz defined tactics as 'the use of armed forces in the engagement'.[47] The tactical level is characterized by its smaller scale: the military units that operate within it can be as small as a rifle squad or a machine gun crew (there is even 'individual tactics', referring to the conduct of the individual soldier), and their actions take place in comparatively limited space. Details of weather and terrain are crucial, and the same applies to details of the order of battle.[48] Last but not least, the tactical level is the area of personal bravery.[49] Tactics is basically the domain of the officers and, where very small units are concerned, the non-commissioned officers.

When making a strategic analysis, it is very important to think in terms of the levels of strategy. This is for two reasons: first, a course of action that is feasible or advisable on a certain level may be impractical or even detrimental on another level; and secondly, since there is constant interaction among the various levels, a possible malfunction in one of them may have an adverse impact on the whole strategic structure.

Regarding the second point, both Clausewitz and Moltke have emphatically pointed out that when strategy is wrong, tactical dexterity is not enough to make up for the strategic mistake. The examples of Japan and Germany in the Second World War have often been used to make this point. Although their armed forces (especially Germany's) displayed a high degree of effectiveness at the tactical and operational level, gross blunders at the grand strategy level (namely going to war against vastly superior opponents) condemned these two countries to defeat.[50]

The Iraq War (2003–11) is another case in point.[51] Here, the U.S. not only failed to achieve one of its core political objectives in that war—namely that of creating a stable and democratic Iraq ruled by a friendly regime and serving as a model of democracy in the Middle East—but also remained entangled in a deepening and costly morass for a long time. The U.S. armed forces performed excellently in the realms of military strategy, operational art and tactics during the conventional phase of the Iraq War.[52] They also displayed high-quality performance at these levels during certain stages of the counterinsurgency phase of that war.[53] However, in the end, this war merely proved to be another example where dexterity in the lower levels of strategy could not help a flawed grand strategy achieve the policy objectives of the state.

However, the interaction of the levels works the other way round as well, whereby lower levels may influence the higher ones. As Sir Basil Liddell Hart stated, a strategy's success depends on whether it is tactically feasible. Thus, Stalin, after pushing the Germans back from the outskirts of Moscow in December 1941, launched a massive counter-offensive in the middle of winter 1941–2, aiming to shatter the German army, whose vulnerability he had correctly grasped. Despite their enthusiasm, however, the Soviet troops and their commanders had not yet reached the necessary level of operational and tactical efficiency. The result was that they suffered casualties disproportionately high compared to the meagre results of their offensive.[54] It took the Red Army less than two years to improve on its operational and tactical skills. Then, by following the same strategy that had failed in the beginning of 1942, the Red Army proved capable of achieving total victory.

We conclude the discussion of the levels of strategy by pointing out that, apart from strategies (grand and military) that are or have not been feasible at lower levels, there are also instances of strategies that are operationally and tactically feasible in principle, but which nevertheless fail because of mistakes at those levels. Xerxes' Persian invasion of Greece (480 BCE) is such a case. Here, Xerxes' grand strategy consisted of taking care to amass immense military power to ensure the achievement of his political objective (the conquest of Greece), while at the same time exploiting the divisions among the Greek city-states and winning many of them over to his side. His military strategy placed emphasis on cooperation between army and navy so as to keep his immense army supplied with wheat from Asia. Everything was going well, and Athens was eventually captured. However, the disaster came at the operational level, namely Xerxes' decision to engage in battle at the straits of Salamis (480 BCE). The narrow front neutralized Persia's numerical superiority, and the Greeks' heavier ships gave them victory. The Persians, however, could still have achieved their objectives, since their remaining forces in Greece were substantial. Nevertheless, through a tactical blunder, they contrived to lose the Battle of Plataea (479 BCE), where they had initially held the advantage. In this case, the main body of their army was moved behind the archers that had been confronting the Spartans opposite them, thus cutting the archers' line of retreat and leaving them defenceless against the determined Spartan assault; the Persian army was thrown into disarray and took to flight. In the end, a brilliant strategic design that was objectively bound to succeed was ruined by operational and tactical ineptitude.[55]

Aspects of Grand Strategy: Military and Non-Military Components

Given that the concept of grand strategy is central to our analysis, we need to elaborate on it a little further.[56] Essentially, grand strategy is a state's theory about how it can 'cause' security for itself, namely preservation of its sovereignty, territorial integrity, and relative power position.[57] Indeed, the way states choose to ensure security for themselves forms the very core of grand strategy, and their success in doing so is the crucial test of any particular grand strategy. In other words, the validity of a grand strategy can be empirically tested. Ideally, grand strategy must include an explanation of why this security-producing theory is expected to work in a given environment. It can be understood as a state's response to specific threats to its security, wherein it must identify potential threats and devise political and other remedies for them. Grand strategy should be viewed as a politico-military means–ends chain in which military capabilities are linked to military strategies that are in turn connected with political objectives. In theory, grand strategies exploit the advantages that the state possesses and aim to minimize those of the opponent. It has already been mentioned that strategy is labouring under scarcity of resources, and grand strategy is no exception. In an anarchic international environment, the number of possible threats is great and the resources to meet them are bound to be scarce; consequently, priorities must be established among both threats and remedies.

An elaborate treatment of the concept of grand strategy, containing an excellent description of the various means grand strategy employs, both in peacetime and in wartime,[58] has been given by Liddell Hart. According to him:

> [T]he role of grand strategy—higher strategy—is to co-ordinate and direct all the resources of a nation, or band of nations towards the attainment of the political object of the war—the goal defined by fundamental policy. Grand strategy should both calculate and develop the economic resources and man-power of nations in order to sustain the fighting services. Also the moral resources—for to foster the people's willing spirit is often as important as to possess the more concrete forms of power. Grand strategy, too, should regulate the distribution of power between the services and industry. Moreover, fighting power is but one of the instruments of grand strategy—which should take account of and apply the power of financial pressure, of diplomatic pressure, of commercial pressure, and, not least of ethical pressure, to weaken the opponent's will.[59]

Since we have already dealt extensively with the military component of grand strategy, let us also briefly comment on its other important, non-military components.[60] Diplomacy is a component of grand strategy that can contribute to national security by securing allies, minimizing the number of potential antagonists, negotiating with opponents or diplomatically isolating them.[61] A high premium is put on identifying and exploiting opportunities offered by the existing or evolving situation in the international (or regional) system. An eye keen on detecting such opportunities, coupled with a capacity to exploit them, may enable statesmen to achieve extraordinary results.

The Austrian Chancellor Clemens Metternich offers an excellent example. The Austrian Empire had been in decline since the mid-eighteenth century, had suffered badly during the Napoleonic Wars, and its multinational composition was a cause of major concern, especially in view of the emergence of the new concept of nationalism. Nevertheless, not only did Metternich manage to extract substantial territorial gains after Napoleon's defeat, but also ensured Austrian supremacy in both Germany and Italy for many decades to come. The secret of his success was simple: after the turmoil created by the French Revolution and Napoleon's campaigns, the watchword among the European great powers was 'stability'.[62] Metternich managed to persuade the two key players—Great Britain and Russia—that Austria was the ideal guardian of stability in Central Europe and the Italian peninsula, while it posed absolutely no threat to the existing balance of power.

The economic component of grand strategy also exercises profound influence on national security. This is done in two ways: first, by supporting military strategy (e.g. enabling arms procurement, sustaining long periods of mobilization, etc.) and diplomacy (e.g. by financing influential groups in foreign countries); and secondly, in an independent capacity, by granting economic aid to foreign countries or conducting economic warfare against them.[63]

Although possession of a strong economic base does not automatically guarantee military prowess (e.g. the Persian Empire versus Alexander, or the West Roman Empire versus the barbarians), the connection between the two is too well-known to require elaboration. Similarly, the idea of paying one's way to an alliance is probably as old as the mountains. In early modern history, Cardinal Richelieu set a pattern by offering subsidies to the Swedish king Gustavus Adolphus in order to secure the support of the mighty Swedish army against the German Emperor. In the same manner, the British subsidized Frederick the Great of Prussia so that he could preoccupy not only the Austrians, but the French as well. Economic aid is another familiar concept. The Napoleonic Wars witnessed an interesting case of reciprocal economic warfare: Napoleon forbade the Europeans from trading with Great Britain, whereas the British, by means of a naval blockade, tried to make sure that the Europeans would trade solely with them. British blockade was irksome and not altogether in compliance with international law, but trading with Great Britain carried many attractions, since the advanced British economy had many valuable goods to offer. Thus, the temptation to break with the Napoleonic 'Continental System' was too great. In fact, Russia's decision to opt for trade with Great Britain was one of the reasons that led the French emperor to undertake the disastrous Russian campaign.[64]

Apart from the military, economic and diplomatic power (alliances, etc.) that constitute so-called 'hard power', states also possess and employ in their grand strategies so-called 'soft power'.[65] This can take the form of cultural, ideological or religious affinity or influence. In addition, nowadays a state might enjoy a certain amount of influence by participating in some key international organizations (for example, the EU and NATO). Soft power is not to be underrated; in fact, it can play an important role in securing the legitimacy of a grand strategy both home and abroad. This is indeed the political component of grand strategy. The Byzantine Empire provides a textbook case of exploitation of soft power, which involved the conversion of various barbarian nations to Christianity, with a view to minimizing the number of opponents and extending the Empire's influence.[66] The exploitation of communist ideology by the Soviet Union is another case in point whereas, in the same vein, Iran's exploitation of Islamic fundamentalism enabled that state to achieve an international influence out of all proportion to its hard power.

Typologies of Grand Strategies

We have already encountered a typology of military strategies according to their ends–means mix (namely offensive, defensive, deterrent and compellent strategies). There has been no dearth of typologies of grand strategies as well. A particularly important typology that will be used extensively in our study is the one devised by the prominent German historian Hans Delbrück, based on the means that a strategy employs.

Delbrück outlined two basic forms of strategy: the strategy of annihilation (*Niederwerfungsstrategie*) and the strategy of exhaustion (*Ermattungsstrategie*).[67] The aim of the strategy of annihilation is that of the decisive battle (*Vernichtungsschlacht*),[68] whereas a strategy of exhaustion employs the battle as but one of a variety of means, such as territorial occupation, destruction of crops, blockade, etc. In general, the concept of economic damage to the enemy plays a key role in this strategy. The strategy of exhaustion is neither a variation of the strategy of annihilation, nor inferior to it. On the contrary, such a strategy can often be the only way for a state to achieve its political aims. (It must be noted that these two strategies are ideal types; in practice, one often encounters a mix between them.)

Although Delbrück referred to military strategies without necessarily mentioning grand strategies, his distinction between a strategy of annihilation and a strategy of exhaustion may be invaluable to the study of grand strategies. One must also note that in Delbrück's time, the term 'grand strategy' was used in a much more restrictive sense than at present—that is, as only covering the overall war policy of a state. Nowadays, a grand strategy by definition makes use of all available means and does not restrict itself to the traditional military ones. Nevertheless, a distinction between a grand strategy of annihilation and a grand strategy of exhaustion can still be made, depending on which means feature most prominently in a grand strategy. In a grand strategy of annihilation, the state depends mainly on military strategy; all other strategies (economic, diplomatic, etc.) are essentially subservient to it. On the other hand, a grand strategy of exhaustion makes simultaneous use of all possible means so as to achieve the aims set by state policy.[69]

The Napoleonic campaigns constitute classic examples of the strategy of annihilation. They culminated in decisive battles (e.g. Marengo, Austerlitz, Jena, Friedland, Wagram), in which the French emperor completely crushed the armed forces of his enemies, forcing them to sue for peace.[70] On the other hand, the grand strategy that Great Britain adopted from the seventeenth century onwards was a typical example of a strategy of exhaustion. The so-called 'British way of warfare' can be described as entailing several aspects, including: the blockade of continental ports; distant maritime operations directed against the colonies and the overseas trade of the rival continental powers; subsidies to allies; nominal ground forces' commitment to the continent; and peripheral raiding around the continental littoral to exploit the flexibility of sea power for surprise manoeuvre.[71]

In effect, the Napoleonic campaigns created the second typology of grand strategies that will be used in this study, namely that between the direct and indirect approach. It must be noted that these concepts are not confined to the grand strategy level, but extend to all levels of strategy; nevertheless, we will focus on their application at the level of grand strategy.

The campaigns of Napoleon formed the basis of the theory of war promulgated by Clausewitz shortly afterwards. Here, Clausewitz laid emphasis on the direct approach, namely the direction of one's war effort primarily towards the main opponent and/or the 'centre of gravity' (i.e. the strongest component of the enemy's war effort). In most instances, this centre of gravity was the armed forces of the enemy, who invariably had to be destroyed or depleted. Obviously, the strategy of annihilation occupies a central position in Clausewitz' theory, and it is no wonder that it continues to be associated with him and Napoleon to this day.[72] However, a strategy of annihilation and direct approach are not identical concepts, as shall be illustrated later.

In contrast, and throughout his work, Liddell Hart has argued in favour of the advantages of the indirect approach.[73] This term has had a turbulent history, and Liddell Hart's repeated elaborations of it have rendered it practically meaningless.[74] However, we believe that something of use can still be salvaged out of the conceptual mess. For instance, the indirect approach generally denotes the sidestepping of the enemy's strong points and the avoidance of attrition warfare. At the level of grand strategy, the indirect approach may be regarded as the evading of the main opponent by directing one's war effort against a secondary opponent (or several secondary opponents), thereby postponing the decisive strike in favour of a more suitable moment.

THUCYDIDES ON STRATEGY

Planning and Evaluating Grand Strategy

When taking into account the analysis so far, one reaches the conclusion that, in order to be considered successful at the level of grand strategy, planning needs to address the following four dimensions[75] (see Table 1.3). The first is an assessment of the international environment, so as to identify potential or actual threats to national security, as well as the various constraints and opportunities in relation to the implementation of the grand strategy that may be present in this environment. With this, the crucial test for a grand strategy in this dimension is international strategic fit.

The second dimension is the identification of the ends that the grand strategy is to pursue in view of the means available, along with the aforementioned threats, constraints and opportunities. In view of the ever-present scarcity of resources, there are certain limits to the ends pursued. As already mentioned, priorities must be established among the various aims, but one must make sure that the aims that have been set do not exceed the means available. This would lead to the phenomenon of overextension on which we shall elaborate later. The avoidance of overextension is one important indicator of the performance of a grand strategy.

The third dimension is the allocation of resources so as to achieve the objectives outlined by grand strategy. The means have to be tailored to the ends so as to avoid both wasting scarce resources and marshalling inadequate resources for the tasks ahead. Thus, the avoidance of redundancy or inadequacy of means is the critical test that a grand strategy has to meet.

The final dimension is that of shaping the 'image' of the grand strategy both at the domestic and international level. This is to ensure that the society actively supports the grand strategy of the state, all parts of the state structure work towards the same purpose; and the grand strategy of the state is viewed as legitimate by the international community. In other words, to be successful in this dimension, a grand strategy has to be accepted both at home and abroad.

We have already pointed out that grand strategy is a security-producing theory whose validity can be empirically tested. In addition, we outlined the crucial tests that this theory has to meet to

GRAND STRATEGY

Table 1.3: Planning of Grand Strategy

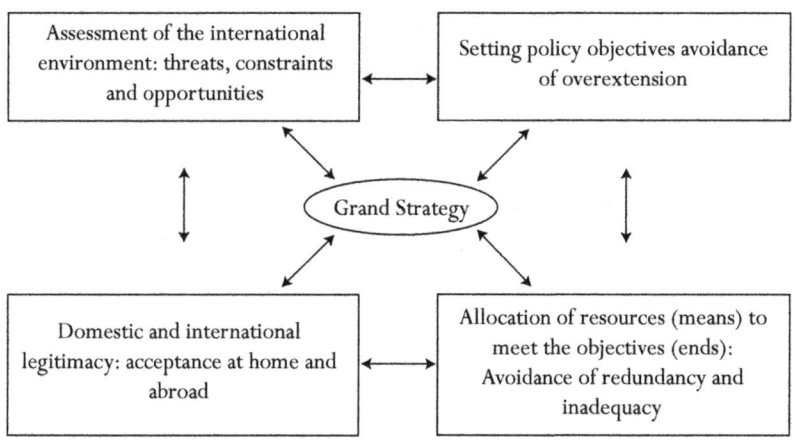

prove its validity. There are, however, five more criteria that are used for evaluating grand strategies.[76]

The first is the external fit criterion: the degree to which a grand strategy fits in with the international and domestic political environment. An example is how the advent of a bipolar world in 1945 made it difficult for small states to pursue a grand strategy by shifting their allegiance among the various great powers as they saw fit; instead, they had to choose a camp (if they were in fact allowed to) practically once and for all.[77] As far as the domestic political environment is concerned, increased public concern about foreign policy, which began with the French Revolution, has made it difficult for decision-makers to follow a policy of constantly shifting alliances, where yesterday's friend becomes today's enemy.

The second criterion is the relation between means and ends, namely the degree to which the objectives of a grand strategy correspond to the available means, and vice versa. This has to do with the traditional problem of how to avoid overextension (i.e. pursue aims beyond one's capabilities),[78] while at the same time not unduly reducing one's objectives (see Table 1.4). As noted, this is a very important criterion of grand strategy.

The third criterion is that of efficiency, which relates to whether a grand strategy makes the best use of the available resources. This leads

THUCYDIDES ON STRATEGY

Table 1.4: Linking Means and Ends of a Grand Strategy

		Political Commitments (Ends)	
		Few	Many
Available Means (Capabilities)	Few	Passivity	Overextension
	Many	Reduction of Objectives	Strategic Sufficiency

to the issue of cost–benefit assessment, whereby each of the alternative strategic designs available to a state at a given moment leads to different calculations of their costs and benefits. Thus, the task of the strategist is to hit upon the optimum strategy, the most efficacious one, the one that yields the best results in this cost–benefit analysis.

The fourth criterion is internal coherence, namely that one element or one means of the grand strategy does not hamper the function of another. Indeed, this is what happened to Israel in 1973, prior to the Yom Kippur War. Israeli military strategy, which placed emphasis on striking first, was in conflict with the state's diplomatic strategy, which emphasized enlisting U.S. support. However, if Israel, by striking first, gave the impression of being the aggressor, then it would forfeit U.S. support and thus invalidate its diplomatic strategy.[79]

Finally, the fifth criterion is durability to mistakes, which involves the ability of a grand strategy to withstand coincidental mistakes and mishaps without prohibitively high costs. The aforementioned example of the Persian invasion of Greece is a typical example of a grand strategy with low durability to mistakes. Conversely, U.S. grand strategy during the Cold War proved durable enough to sustain the mistakes and/or mishaps associated with their involvement in Vietnam (1955–75).

We shall now proceed to the examination of Thucydides' contribution to the study of strategy. In doing so, we shall be assisted by the numerous concepts outlined above.

2

ATHENS AND SPARTA

POWER STRUCTURES, EARLY CONFLICT AND THE CAUSES OF WAR

Introduction

In this chapter, we will provide an overview of the background of the strategic rivalry between Athens and Sparta. The chapter begins with an outline of the domestic structures, the strategic culture and the power bases of the two strategic opponents, where the 'hegemony' of Sparta is contrasted with the 'empire' of Athens. Then, we will briefly outline the earlier phase of the conflict between Athens and Sparta during the so-called *Pentecontaetia*—the interval of roughly fifty years between the end of the Persian Wars and the beginning of the Peloponnesian War. It must be noted that we do not intend to give a detailed account of the *Pentecontaetia*. Rather, as Thucydides himself did, we will only focus on the most salient, strategically significant events.[1] We must also point out that our analysis will not deal with the events directly leading to the Peloponnesian War.[2] As will become evident in both the present chapter and Chapters Three and Four, we wholeheartedly endorse Thucydides' view that the causes of the war were long-term structural and perceptual (notably the growth of Athenian power and Sparta's concomitant threat perception and attempt to check that growth).³ Hence, we contend that the final prewar crises over Potidaea and Corcyra played a comparatively minor role in the outbreak of the war. Those crises did influence the timing of that outbreak, but nothing more. The crucial role was played by the structure of the international system and the associated threat perceptions, which made it likely that war would break out.⁴ In fact, the overall issue of Thucydides' explanation of the causes of the war between Athens and Sparta, and his contribution to the study of the causes of war in general, will be tackled at the end of the present chapter.

Spartan Hegemony versus Athenian Empire: Domestic Structures and Strategic Culture

The clash between Sparta and Athens was a conflict between two different power structures and two societies organized in very different ways. The domestic structures of each of these two societies exerted a profound influence on what modern analysts call the 'strategic culture' or 'national style' of the two belligerents.⁵

As is well-known, Athenian polity was the archetypal democracy, and central to this was the citizen assembly (*Ecclesia*). This was the most important decision-making body, in which all Athenian adult males were eligible for participation. The *Ecclesia* convened at least forty times a year, debated openly, and took decisions by majority vote, and every state issue, even details of military planning, was decided by it. To be sure, ten generals were elected annually (and could be re-elected indefinitely) but their actions were constantly and carefully scrutinized by the *Ecclesia*, which could (and quite often did) punish the generals for actual or alleged misconduct.⁶

Although the political organization of direct democracy often resulted in inconsistent decision-making, this was more than counterbalanced by the feeling of active participation in the city affairs that every citizen experienced. This feeling ensured enthusiastic citizen support in the formulation and implementation of state policy, as well as the mobilization of all available means for the achievement of the various ends set by that policy.⁷

In contrast, the domestic structures of Sparta were completely different.⁸ Spartan polity was composed of monarchical elements (two hereditary kings), oligarchic elements (a council of elders, the so-called *Gerousia*, consisting of twenty-eight members elected for life plus the two kings) and democratic elements (a citizen assembly).[9] Another institution with immense powers and steadily increasing importance was that of the five *ephors* (overseers). These managed the daily affairs of Sparta and supervised the conduct of its populace, keeping a close eye on the Spartan kings. They were elected for a year, presumably with no right for re-election.[10] Nevertheless, despite the co-existence of all these elements, Sparta was essentially an oligarchic polity. The Spartans had developed a reputation for disdaining luxury[11] and devoted their whole life from the age of seven onwards to military training. The outcome of this long and intensive training was to turn the Spartans into arguably the best soldiers in the world.[12]

In fact, they had good reason to become such. When the Spartans originally settled in Laconia (the south-eastern part of the Peloponnese), they enslaved the indigenous population, the so-called helots. After this, the helots were forced to cultivate the land and yield part of the product to their Spartan masters. This allowed the Spartans to focus on leading a military life. Moreover, when Sparta also conquered Messenia (the south-western part of the Peloponnese), the number of the helots swelled.[13] Both Spartans and helots acted as if a state of war existed between them.[14] The helots were constantly looking for an opportunity to rebel, whereas the Spartans were continuously trying to suppress them by every conceivable means.[15] In essence, the Spartans had turned their city into an armed camp and lived accordingly.[16]

As to the 'strategic cultures' of Athens and Sparta, one may notice that in contrast to the enterprising Athenians, conservatism and caution were the fundamental characteristics of the Spartans. As their Corinthian allies put it to the Spartans:

> The Athenians are addicted to innovation, and their designs are characterized by swiftness alike in conception and execution; you have a genius for keeping what you have got, accompanied by a total want of invention, and when forced to act you never go far enough. Again, they are adventurous beyond their power, and daring beyond their judgment, and in danger they are sanguine; your wont is to attempt less than is justified by your power, to mistrust even what is sanctioned by your judgment, and to fancy that from danger there is no

release. Further, there is promptitude on their side against procrastination on yours; they are never at home, you are most disinclined to leave it, for they hope by their absence to extend their acquisitions, you fear by your advance to endanger what you have left behind.[17]

The difference in strategic culture between Athenians and Spartans was not so much a result of their different 'national characters' (although this undoubtedly played a role)[18] as of the different structures of their respective polities. The democratic polity of Athens encouraged citizen participation in the affairs of the state and fostered a spirit of innovation, which at times bordered on recklessness. On the contrary, the central role of the elders of the *Gerousia* ensured a relative stability of state policy in Sparta,[19] which at the same time led to excessive conservatism and an inability to keep up with external developments. The conservatism and caution of the Spartans were also bolstered by the continual fear of a helot revolt, which made them view external expeditions with reluctance.

These different strategic cultures were evident in the security policies of the two cities. Thucydides goes to some length to document the rise of Athenian power during the *Pentecontaetia*.[20] To start with, the low fertility of the Attic soil, coupled with demographic pressures, forced the Athenians to turn to the sea and become a seafaring nation. Thus, as early as at the time of the Persian invasion, Athens possessed a powerful navy. This naval power enabled Athens to assume the lead in pushing Persia out of the Greek coastal cities of Asia Minor (see Map 2).

In the process, the Athenians established a progressively firmer control over their allies. With this, the Athenian Empire was born, and it gradually proved to be a tremendous source of wealth for Athens, wherein tribute from their allies, imperial mines, and increased commercial activity all contributed to the growth of the economic power of the Athenian metropolis.[21] This wealth sustained the efficiency of the Athenian navy, guaranteeing the preservation of the empire and ensuring more income that would once again augment the naval power of Athens. Thucydides put it succinctly:

> For this the allies had themselves to blame; the wish to get off service making most of them arrange to pay their share of the expense in

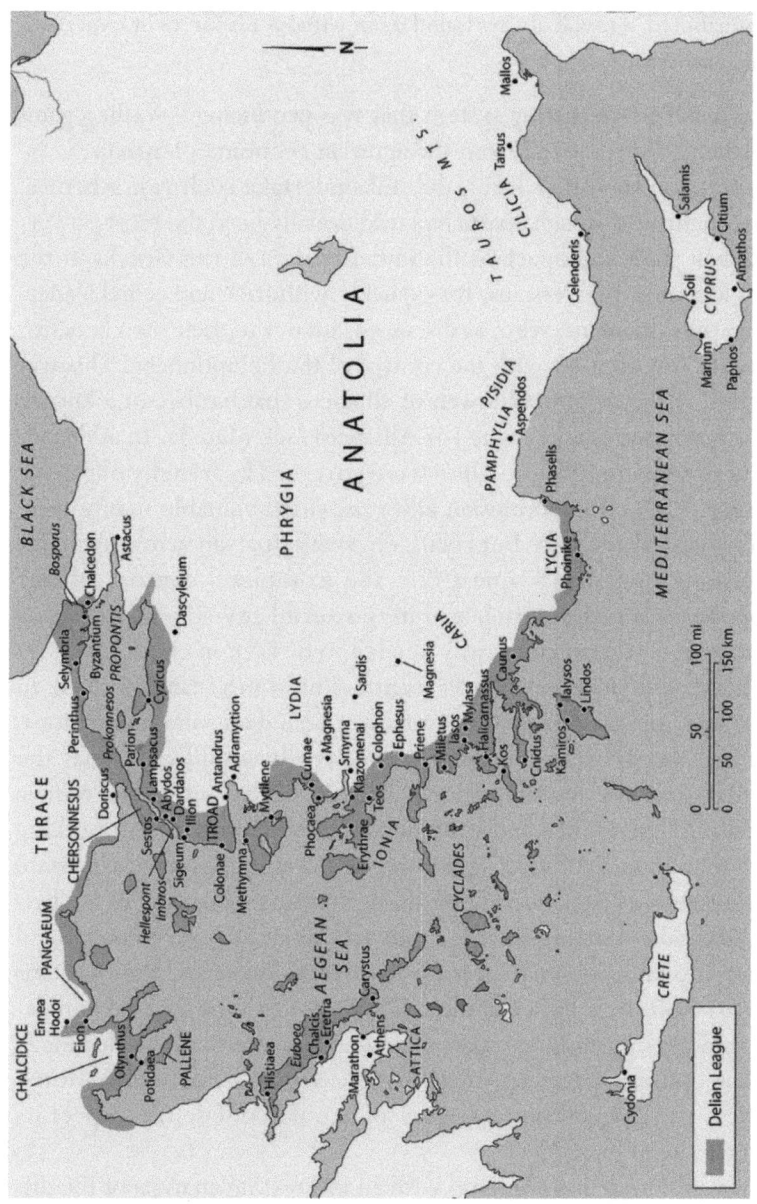

Map 2: The Athenian Alliance/Empire

money instead of in ships, and so to avoid having to leave their homes. Thus while Athens was increasing her navy with the funds which they contributed, a revolt always found them without resources or experience for war.[22]

It was a self-perpetuating system that was producing spiralling gains for Athens, far removed from the agrarian economy of Sparta.[23]

Sparta, on the other hand, did not undertake such vast schemes. Consequently, although Sparta had traditionally been the most powerful Greek state and Spartans the initial leaders of the Greeks in the struggle against the Persians, they quickly withdrew and ceded leadership to the Athenians, who, as discussed, used it to their own benefit.

Sparta was content with the control of the Peloponnese. This was ensured by the forging of a web of alliances that has become known as the Peloponnesian League (or Alliance) (see Map 3). In addition, Sparta also saw to it that its allies were governed by friendly oligarchic regimes.[24] The Peloponnesian allies provided valuable manpower, which assisted the elite but relatively small Spartan army. A major inhibition in Sparta's quest for the complete control of the Peloponnese was the existence of the powerful city-state of Argos—a permanent rival that constantly needed to be kept in check.[25]

This examination of the two contending states brings to light an important point: although Spartan power rested on solid foundations, it lacked the dynamism Athens possessed. It would seem that the peculiar Spartan system had reached its limits—it could ensure Spartan independence and control of the Peloponnese, but nothing more than that.[26] As such, Sparta remained an introverted city-state whose economy depended upon the agricultural economy of the helots. To make matters worse, in an attempt to preserve their land ownership and possibly increase it through dowries, the Spartans came to limit the number of their offspring. With the Spartan population steadily diminishing, Spartan power was also likely to decline.[27] On the contrary, Athens, by creating a commercial and maritime empire, had opened new avenues and could confidently expect its power to keep growing.

Michael Doyle has come up with an interesting analysis of the different nature of the Athenian and Spartan power structures. According to him, Athens' commercial activities enabled it to acquire

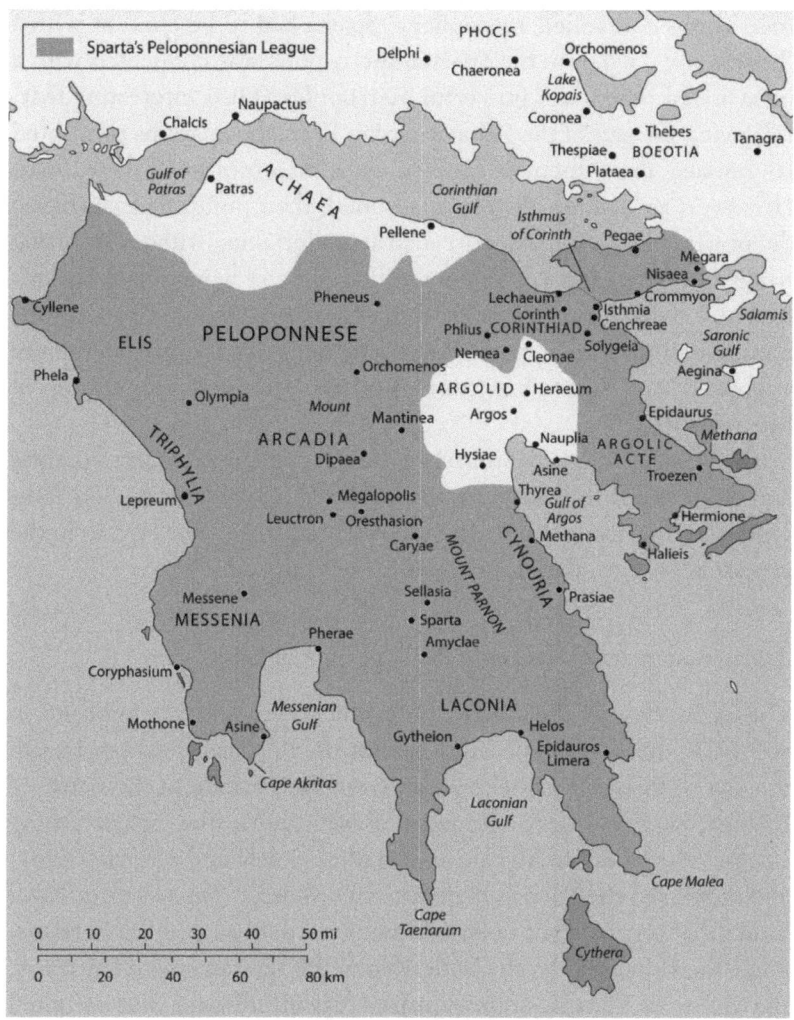

Map 3: Sparta's Peloponnesian League

immense influence beyond its borders, which created a 'periphery' that was controlled by the Athenian 'metropolis'. In contrast, the international influence of Sparta was based exclusively on its military power. The cost of military power was high for the relatively small Spartan warrior community, thus limiting Sparta's international influence. As a result, whereas Athens had created an 'empire' in which a metropolis controlled a periphery, Sparta had to be content with a 'hegemony', wherein the Spartan metropolis was connected with a network of other, less powerful metropoles.[28] It is interesting that, following the end of the Peloponnesian War, the Spartans attempted to replace the Athenian Empire with an empire of their own. However, as we have already mentioned, their political organization did not enable them to support such an undertaking without resorting to sheer military force.[29] Spartan military power being relatively limited and costly, Sparta was forced into overextension. As a result, merely four decades after the Peloponnesian War, the Spartan Empire collapsed, and Sparta lost control of the Peloponnese and then of Messenia itself.[30]

Once again, the Corinthians captured the essence of the situation and described it brilliantly to the Spartans: 'your habits are old-fashioned as compared with theirs [the Athenians]. It is the law, as in the arts so in politics, that improvements ever prevail'.[31]

Athens and Sparta: The Early Phase of the Conflict

The early phase of the conflict between Athens and Sparta begins in 479 BCE, during an expedition against the Persians (see Map 1). On the day of the great Greek victory over the Persians at the Battle of Plataea, a Greek expeditionary force under the Spartan king Leotychidas landed at Mycale in Asia Minor, defeated a Persian army, and destroyed the Persian fleet stationed there.[32] The Greek cities of Ionia (the Aegean coast of Asia Minor) revolted against the Persians, while the Greeks under the leadership of the Spartan regent Pausanias, the victor of Plataea, soon captured Byzantium and thus assumed control of the Dardanelles.[33] Suddenly, the Greeks had gone over to the offensive, which would continue for the next thirty years.

However, they would do so under new leadership. The abrasive manner of Pausanias and his treacherous contacts with the Persians had made Spartan leadership unpopular among the rest of the Greeks. In any case, it seems that the Spartans had had enough of distant expeditions. Thus, they withdrew from the alliance together with their Peloponnesian allies and ceded the leadership to the Athenians. Consequently, in 478 BCE, Athens assumed the leadership of the

ATHENS AND SPARTA

Greeks in the anti-Persian struggle, which heralded the birth of the Delian League.[34] This was a development of tremendous significance, laying the foundations of the Athenian Empire.

The Athenian power position vis-à-vis Sparta was also improved by the rebuilding of the walls of Athens, which neutralized the Spartan infantry. The Athenians started rebuilding the walls after the Persian invaders withdrew. Meanwhile, the Spartans tried to prevent the rebuilding, coming up with an ingenious arms control proposal, namely the demolition of the walls of every city outside the Peloponnese, Athens included:

> Perceiving what they were going to do, the Spartans sent an embassy to Athens. They would have themselves preferred to see neither her nor any other city in possession of a wall [...]. They begged her not only to abstain from building walls for herself, but also to join them in throwing down the remaining walls of the cities outside the Peloponnesus. They did not express openly the suspicious intention with regard to the Athenians that lay behind this proposal but urged that by these means the barbarians, in the case of a third invasion, would not have any strong place, such as in this invasion he had in Thebes, for his base of operation; and that the Peloponnesus would suffice for all as a base both for retreat and offense.[35]

The Athenians, under the direction of the brilliant statesman Themistocles, procrastinated in replying to the Spartan suggestion, until the wall had reached sufficient height.[36]

The Athenians proved worthy leaders of the anti-Persian struggle, pursuing the war with vigour. Under the leadership of the splendid Athenian general Cimon, the Delian League continued to defeat the Persians, most notably in 466 BCE, when Cimon inflicted a shattering defeat on the Persian army and navy in the Battle of the Eurymedon River, along the southern coast of Asia Minor. The Persians resorted to a military build-up, but the tide of Athenian conquest could not be stemmed; the Delian League continued to grow, chiefly at Persian expense.[37] The high point of the Athenian advance was reached in 460 BCE, when the Athenians launched a campaign against Persian-held Cyprus and then proceeded to assist an anti-Persian rebellion in Egypt.[38]

Apart from these overseas successes, Athens registered a dramatic coup in mainland Greece proper that same year: a clash between Athens' neighbouring city of Megara and Corinth, both members of the Peloponnesian League, following which they made Megara join the Athenian alliance. The Athenians promptly fortified the region, effectively barring the route of a possible Peloponnesian invasion.[39]

While Athenian power continued to grow, Sparta was experiencing great difficulties. During the 470s and 460s BCE, Sparta was in acute danger of losing its hegemony in the Peloponnese. Powerful anti-Spartan alliances emerged: first, between Argos and the Arcadian city of Tegea, and then between all the Arcadians with the exception of the Mantineans. Sparta faced a critical situation but, in traditional Spartan (and later Clausewitzian) manner, two decisive battles at Tegea and Dipaieis settled matters, and Sparta successfully defended its Peloponnesian hegemony.[40] As if these challenges were not enough, in 464 BCE there was a terrible earthquake that caused horrendous material damage and many fatalities among the Spartans. During the chaos, the helots seized the opportunity and revolted. The rebels captured and fortified a strongpoint, held their own in a ten-year siege, and finally evacuated Spartan territory under terms. The Spartans enlisted Athenian help in the siege, since the latter were considered experts at siege warfare. However, as the Athenians did not make the expected progress, the Spartans came to distrust them and finally asked them to leave. Furious, the Athenians abandoned the alliance with Sparta, which dated from the Persian invasion, and aligned themselves with Argos instead.[41]

Up to this point in history, a clear picture is emerging. Athens has started to attract former members of the Peloponnesian League into its own alliance; subsequently, the power of Athens is growing relative to the power of both Persia and Sparta. Consequently, Athens expands territorially at Persian expense and is growing continually richer than Sparta. For Sparta, the alternatives were clear: the loss of primacy in Greece or the launch of a preventive war. The die would be cast circa 460 BCE, with the start of the so-called First Peloponnesian War.[42]

With the Athenian fortification of Megara barring invasion, it took the Spartans three years to bring their land forces to bear against Athens. In order to settle a local dispute, a large Peloponnesian force moved on to central Greece by way of the Corinthian Gulf. However, the Athenian navy quickly established control there, cutting off the Peloponnesian forces. As a result, the Spartans attempted to return to the Peloponnese via Boeotia and Megarid. The Athenians, considering the situation opportune and backed by an Argive force, met them at the Boeotian town of Tanagra in 457 BCE. However, in the ensuing battle, the redoubtable Spartan infantry proved its worth once again, defeating the Athenians and securing the withdrawal of the Peloponnesians through Megarid. Nevertheless, that victory was bought at the price of heavy casualties.[43] Tanagra was not an Austerlitz, but a Borodino.

Actually, Tanagra was relatively insignificant strategically, for the remainder of 457 BCE proved nothing less than an *annus mirabilis* for the Athenian arms.[44] A mere sixty-two days after that battle, the Athenians invaded Boeotia, defeated the combined Boeotian forces at the Battle of Oenophyta, and in so doing conquered both Boeotia and Phocis. Shortly afterwards, the island of Aegina, an old naval rival of Athens, capitulated to the Athenians and became a tributary state.[45] This was the apex of Athenian expansion. To crown their triumph, the Athenians completed the 'long walls' connecting Athens with Phalerum and Piraeus (see Map 4).[46]

However, soon after this, Athenian imperialism starts producing diminishing returns. An ominous and significant development was the annihilation of the Athenian expeditionary corps in Egypt in 454 BCE.[47] The impact of this was to prompt Athens to renounce further expansion in mainland Greece, reach a compromise with Sparta, tighten control over its alliance/empire, and concentrate forces against Persia.[48] It soon became evident that equilibrium had been reached on both fronts. In 451 BCE, Athens and Sparta concluded the Five Years' Peace (in all probability an acknowledgement of the existing status quo);[49] two years later, in 449 BCE, after an unsuccessful Athenian campaign in Cyprus, Athens concluded the famous Peace of Callias with Persia.[50] The precise terms of that treaty are still a matter of controversy,[51] but it is reasonably certain that the Persian fleet could not sail in the Dardanelles and the Aegean Sea, as well as in the eastern Mediterranean waters west of Pamphylia, and the autonomy of the Greek cities in the west coast of Asia Minor was formally recognized.[52]

THUCYDIDES ON STRATEGY

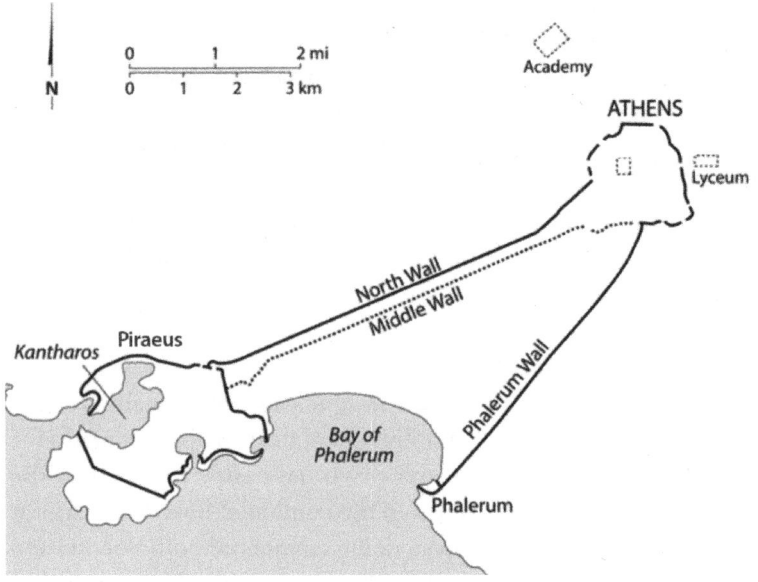

Map 4: Athens' Urban Fortification Complex

Although the Peace of Callias formalized the equilibrium between Athens and Persia, events in Greece proper were to take a turn for the worse for the Athenians. The Athenian attempt to consolidate control of Boeotia ended in failure at Coronea in 446 BCE. Consequently, Athens was forced to relinquish both Boeotia and Phocis. Shortly afterwards, the prosperous island of Euboea revolted from the Athenian alliance and, worse still, the Megarians rejoined the Peloponnesian League, slaughtering their Athenian garrison in the process.[53]

No sooner had the Megarid route opened and the Five Years' Treaty expired than the Spartan infantry entered the fray. The Peloponnesians under the Spartan king Pleistoanax invaded Attica in 446 BCE.[54] However, the invasion was brief, and the Peloponnesians withdrew before penetrating deep into Attica.[55] The Spartan political leadership obviously considered the withdrawal premature because, on returning to Sparta, Pleistoanax was accused of having been bribed by the Athenians and was forced to go into exile.[56] One cannot be certain of the actual events, but shortly afterwards, in 446/445 BCE, Sparta and Athens concluded the Thirty Years' Peace. Athenian control over Aegina was confirmed, but Athens ceded all other territories of the Peloponnesian League still under Athenian occupation.[57] To all intents and purposes, the Thirty Years' Peace put an end to Sparta's pretensions of being the sole hegemon in Greece.

Thus, by 445 BCE, all the pieces of the strategic jigsaw puzzle had been put in place. Although unable to retain the maximum gains it had achieved, Athens had freed itself from Persian occupation to create and consolidate a highly profitable maritime empire. The events of 446 BCE had ensured that the Athenian Empire would not expand further into the Greek mainland, but on the other hand, together with the Peace of Callias, they had ensured that Athenian naval and commercial supremacy within the Aegean Sea and the greater part of the eastern Mediterranean would remain unchallenged. This strategic background would remain unaltered until the eve of the Peloponnesian War (433 BCE). Then, Athens further enhanced its naval mastery by enlisting the support of Corcyra, an important maritime power which had remained neutral up to that point. Since Corcyra was a colony of Corinth, albeit alienated, this led to a dispute between Athens and Corinth. As things between Corcyra and Corinth came to a head, an Athenian naval squadron became embroiled in a victorious naval battle of the Corcyreans against the Corinthians at one of the Sybota islands.[58] Though strictly acting in defence, the Athenians had clashed with the second-most powerful member of the Peloponnesian League.[59]

This is an issue that will recur in the next two chapters in the discussion of the causes of the Peloponnesian War of 431–04 BCE. However, having examined the rise and the course of the early conflict between Sparta and Athens, this is the appropriate point to deal with the theoretical issues involved.

Thucydides on the Causes of War

Thucydides makes it clear that the growth of Athenian power which took place immediately after the Persian Wars sharply altered the political landscape of the eastern Mediterranean in general, and ancient Greece in particular. Athens continued to expand territorially and continued to grow stronger in both economic and military terms in relation to Sparta and indeed every other Greek state. Sparta felt threatened, which led to the outbreak of the First Peloponnesian War (circa 460 BCE).

This is a classic instance of what nowadays is referred to as 'power transition', which eventually led to 'hegemonic war'.[60] In these instances, the second greatest power in the system registers higher rates of growth compared to the hegemonic power in the system, eventually casting doubts on the hitherto accepted systemic hierarchy. The old hegemon not only refuses to concede its primacy without a fight, but actually launches a preventive war.

Thucydides has therefore been rightfully recognized as both the father of scientific political historiography[61] and as history's first 'power transition theorist'.[62] In the theory of international relations, power transition and hegemonic war have long occupied the epicentre of heated debates and these remain a theoretically engaging subject.[63] It is thus essential to recognize the appropriate variables, investigate the causal mechanism, and then make a more fitting comparison with contemporary international relations. This section squarely identifies Thucydides' logic and his basic theory of hegemonic war.

One can easily spot the birth of the power transition theory in the history of the Peloponnesian War. As Robert Gilpin has stated, 'Thucydides discovered the law of dynamics' in international relations, namely the unequal growth of power.[64] As Thucydides stated, the true cause of the Peloponnesian War (the one starting in 431 BCE) was the product of 'the growth of the Athenian power, which putting the Lacedaemonians [Spartans] into fear necessitated the war'.[65]

The Thucydidean power transition theory of hegemonic war naturally includes the growth of Athenian power but also fear; fear is *prima facie* evident in this much-quoted extract on the truest cause of the Peloponnesian War. Threat perception is critical in determining a state's strategic choices, both of which are shaped by the political leadership, as shown in Chapter One. The Corinthians discussed both elements—power and fear—in their arguments to mobilize the Spartans for war. For this, the Corinthians depicted the Athenians not only as powerful but also as proactive aggressors who constantly machinated to expand their empire: '[the Athenians] were born into the world to take no rest themselves and to give none to others'.[66] Thucydides describes succinctly the Spartan strategic calculus after Sybota:

ATHENS AND SPARTA

> Finally, the growth of the Athenian power could no longer be ignored as their own [the Spartans'] confederacy became the object of its encroachments. They then felt that they could endure it no longer, but that the time had come for them to throw themselves heart and soul upon the hostile power, and break it, if they could, by commencing the present war.[67]

This passage demonstrates both the structural and the perceptual elements at play. The Spartans had always been keen observers of the balance of power and were very wary of emerging powers in Greece, irrespective of those powers' initial intentions (if anything, the geographical proximity among all the major actors in ancient Greece left little time to ponder on volatile intentions). The growth of Athenian power in the aftermath of the wars with Persia was not lost to the Spartans, and they almost decided upon war with Athens around 478–7 BCE with a view to gaining hegemony in the Aegean. The war was averted due to the intervention of a member of the *Gerousia*, named Hetoimaridas, who persuaded the Spartans that this venture would not be to Sparta's interest.[68] It would be highly interesting to know the arguments with which the Spartan elder persuaded his fellow citizens against action: he might have pointed out that Athens could be a useful buffer from the Persians; he could have demonstrated Sparta's sheer inability to win a war with Athens at that moment; he might have hinted at Spartan internal difficulties (the controversial Pausanias had recently been put to death, for instance); he could have pointed out the Spartans' problems with their allies (the Battle of Tegea would be fought in the near future). Or he might have said something else entirely. What is important, however, is that Athens at that moment had not only not threatened Sparta at all, but was in fact Sparta's most valuable ally in the life-and-death struggle against the Persians—who might reappear at any moment. This is the biggest proof that the structure of the international system reigned supreme in the Spartans' mind.

Nevertheless, the First Peloponnesian War taught the Spartans a lesson: Athens had come to stay as a hegemonic power in Greece. As such, Sparta had to accept co-hegemony in 445 BCE. At first, the Spartans managed to live with this state of affairs. But as time went by, not only did Athenian power keep growing, but Athens also began to threaten the integrity of the Peloponnesian League. Corinth was not an ally to be trifled with: the Corinthians would probably find it difficult to mend fences with Athens, with both being maritime and commercial powers, but a Corinthian rapprochement with Argos, Sparta's persistent Peloponnesian enemy, was not out of the question (it did in fact happen some years after the Peloponnesian War). That could spell disaster for the Peloponnesian League and even put in jeopardy the fertile Messenia, its helots and the whole power structure of Sparta. This is what enhanced the threat perception of the Spartan leadership and, as Thucydides states, what led to war.

This Thucydidean explanation of the causes of war between Sparta and Athens broke new ground in the study of international conflict, as well as international relations in general. A mere generation earlier, Herodotus had been content to explain the Greek–Persian conflict solely on the basis of mythical incidents and human passions. The explanation of Thucydides marks a gargantuan leap in the transition from mythology and crude psychology to international relations theory. The notion that wars are the result of underlying systemic forces rather than the result of the will of the gods or the whims of individuals lies at the very core of modern international relations theory. Through Hobbes, Hegel and Marx,[69] all the way through to the modern structural theories of Kenneth Waltz and Robert Gilpin,[70] systemic explanations of international outcomes remain powerful analytical tools. The Thucydidean analytical combination of structure and perception, however, is even more nuanced.

These systemic explanations of the causes of war have not convinced everybody. A number of analysts have remained sceptical about explanations founded on the underlying causes of wars, focusing instead on the 'proximate' causes of wars, namely the handling of the very crises that immediately preceded these wars. In the specific context of the Peloponnesian War, the argument that its 'proximate' causes were more important than the 'underlying' ones will be examined in detail in Chapters Three and Four.[71] Nevertheless, we would at this point like to make some comments on the overall issue of underlying versus proximate causes, using as an example the work of the distinguished American professor Richard Ned Lebow.[72]

Lebow rejects systemic explanations of the causes of wars, such as those offered by Thucydides. He believes that international crises may well constitute important intervening variables that affect in crucial ways both the likelihood of war and the overall evolution of relations between the contending parties. He points out that, had the Cuban Missile Crisis (1962) ended up in war, as the Sarajevo Crisis did (1914), there would have been plenty of analysts ready to attribute that war to underlying causes, the foremost being the systemic antagonism and threat perceptions between the United States and the Soviet Union. The fact that there was no war in 1962, or in 1898, when Great Britain and France got embroiled in the Fashoda Crisis, shows, according to Lebow, that alternative outcomes are indeed possible and that underlying causes fail to tell the whole story, or even the most important part of it.

Though we strongly disagree with the opinion that the events directly leading to the Peloponnesian War were more important than the systemic and perceptual background of that war, we do not feel that 'proximate cause' explanations ought to be entirely dismissed. In general, specific wars are not inevitable. Nevertheless, when hegemonic rivalry is paramount, there are powerful systemic pressures towards a collision course. Sparta and Athens, like Great Britain and Germany before the First World War, were clearly bent on systemic primacy; as such, it was probable that they would end up fighting each other. On the other hand, France was not a would-be hegemon in 1898, hence it could and did back down in the Fashoda Crisis.[73]

It may be argued that the Cuban Missile Crisis seems to disprove what has just been said about the structural and perceptual causes of hegemonic war. However, by quoting an example from the nuclear age in order to disprove the conclusions of the pre-nuclear era, one may be comparing apples with oranges. States will fight for systemic supremacy through hegemonic war, provided they reckon that the cost of the war will be acceptable. Thucydides makes this clear, incidentally anticipating what nowadays is called 'expected utility theory':[74]

> No one is forced to engage in it [war] by ignorance, or kept out of it by fear, if he fancies there is anything to be gained by it. To the former the gain appears greater than the danger, while the latter would rather stand the risk than put up with any immediate sacrifice.[75]

Occasionally, this estimate proves to be a miscalculation, such as was the case with the First World War. In fact, Thucydides, anticipating

Martin van Creveld, points out that men, especially young ones, possessing an inner desire to fight, are all too prone to misjudge the costs of war.[76] However, in the nuclear age, such miscalculations are unlikely, the cost of carnage being all too clear.

In light of the above, the following conclusion emerges: the antagonism between two states for pre-eminence in an international system is a necessary condition for the outbreak of a hegemonic war. Threat perceptions impinge on this condition, either stimulating or mollifying it. After that, there comes the sheer cost–benefit analysis. When the leaders calculate that the cost of that war is acceptable (as was generally the case in the pre-nuclear case), then the combination of structure and perception becomes a condition sufficient for war.

This concludes the examination of the background to the strategic rivalry between Athens and Sparta. We shall now proceed to conduct an examination of the grand strategic designs of the two opponents during the Peloponnesian War.

3

PERICLEAN GRAND STRATEGY[1]

Introduction

It is customary to regard the Peloponnesian War as a conflict between a land power and a sea power.[2] Thucydides indeed dealt with the interplay between these two types of power, thus making himself, apart from his other credentials, the father of geopolitics as well. However, to reduce the Peloponnesian War to a fight between a land and sea power would be a highly distorting view of the issue, since the Spartans quickly understood the need to rival Athenian naval strength—and eventually did so. As such, it is much more accurate to view the war as a contest between two opposing grand strategic designs. The use of the ideal types of the strategy of annihilation and exhaustion (see Chapter One) will be particularly pertinent in this respect. One may recall that the strategy of annihilation aims at the destruction of the enemy's armed forces through decisive battle, whereas in the strategy of exhaustion, the battle goes side by side with the economic damage that ensues from territorial occupation, destruction of crops, naval blockade, etc.

In Thucydides' text, one can see both of these grand strategies at work: while Sparta employed a grand strategy of annihilation, Athens, initially at least, resorted to a grand strategy of exhaustion. The present chapter will examine the grand strategy of exhaustion that Athens employed against Sparta during the first years of the Peloponnesian War (under the direction of the leading statesman and general Pericles).[3] We shall henceforth refer to this strategy as 'Periclean grand strategy' since he not only conceived it but also supervised its implementation. The four dimensions of grand strategic planning presented in Chapter One will constitute the conceptual framework through which this grand strategy will be analysed.

Assessment of the International Environment

The Greek City-State System: Power Distribution and Future Trends

In terms of modern international relations theory, the Greek city-state system[4] has been commonly described as 'bipolar', its two opposed poles being Sparta and Athens.[5] Naturally, everything depends on where one sets the boundaries of the system. For instance, the vast Persian Empire, with its ample resources, obviously influenced the scene.[6] Nonetheless, if the system is confined to mainland Greece or the Greek world in general, then it makes sense to talk about a bipolar system with Sparta and Athens as the respective poles; this is certainly how contemporaries viewed the situation. According to W.R. Connor, at the beginning of the Peloponnesian War, there existed three additional players of importance in terms of the distribution of power: Thebes, Magna Graecia (the Greek colonies of southern Italy and Sicily), and Corcyra.[7] Although these players tried to exploit the conflict between Sparta and Athens to their own advantage, each ended up siding with one of the central protagonists of the conflict. Hence, the distribution of power was essentially bipolar. Nonetheless, one should always keep in mind that the relative position of Sparta and Athens vis-à-vis the other Greek states did not remotely resemble that of the United States and the Soviet Union vis-à-vis the rest of the world during the Cold War.[8]

Apart from the static analysis of power distribution within the Greek city-state system, the dynamic one (i.e. the identification of the various trends in the distribution of power) is of crucial importance as well. Thucydides' famous explanation of the cause of the Peloponnesian War is that 'I conceive to be the growth of the

PERICLEAN GRAND STRATEGY

Athenian power, which putting the Lacedaemonians [Spartans] into fear necessitated the war'.[9] Thucydides' statement reveals that the emerging power of Athens was growing in strength at a faster rate than Sparta, the traditional hegemon in Greece. Athens had founded an extensive empire based on naval strength and maritime trade, whereas Sparta remained an agrarian economy.

In the previous chapter, it was shown how Athens managed to create an extensive and lucrative maritime empire in the Aegean. Initially, due to its naval power (and following the withdrawal of Sparta), Athens assumed the leadership of the anti-Persian struggle of the Greeks and gradually increased its control over its allies, in effect turning them into tributary states. The obvious difference in wealth that this created would eventually become apparent. Fully aware of the economic power of Athens, Pericles, while outlining the balance of power to his fellow citizens, provided them with an extensive account of the economic resources of Athens, which were very ample indeed.[10] Notwithstanding this, Pericles confined his account to state funds and did not mention the immense private wealth that was amassed in the city. With trade and allied revenues continually adding to this wealth, it was evident that Athenian power would soon reach frightening proportions. Since economic power constitutes the enabling force behind military power (and especially naval power),[11] the picture that emerged for the opponents of Athens was a highly alarming one.

In view of these developments, the claim of the distinguished American historian Donald Kagan that 'Athenian power did not grow between 445 and 435 [BCE]'[12] is hard to understand. Kagan has been led astray by the territorial losses the Athenian Empire sustained in the last phase of the First Peloponnesian War, and by the fact that Athens did not acquire any new allies until the conclusion of the defensive alliance with Corcyra in 433 BCE. At the same time, however, he does not appear to have taken into account the continuous growth of the Athenian economic power during that period. Relative economic power is an extremely important dimension of state power.[13] Even in the absence of territorial acquisitions, changes in the economic power of states may bring about profound shifts in the balance of power over time. In fact, Thucydides pointed out precisely this, namely that the growth of Athens' economic power enabled it to more than counterbalance its recent territorial losses:

> Athens, on the contrary, had by degrees deprived hers [its allies] of their ships, and imposed instead contributions in money on all except Chios and Lesbos. Both found their resources for this war separately to exceed the sum of their strength when the alliance flourished intact.[14]

Thucydides shows an incisive grasp of the link between wealth and power.[15] In this respect, he must be regarded as the originator of a long political realist tradition that paid due attention to the economic sources of national power.[16]

Athens and Sparta: Bilateral Balance

As previously demonstrated, Sparta and Athens were the two strongest states of ancient Greece, although the prospects in terms of distribution of power were clearly balanced in favour of Athens. However, what was the correlation of forces between the two combatants at the time of the outbreak of the war? It seems that Athens was at worst invulnerable to Sparta and its allies, and at best superior to them. Three elements of Athenian power accounted for this assessment: its navy, their financial power, and the alliance/empire. This was highlighted by Pericles and acknowledged by the Spartan king Archidamus. Their statements are of particular interest and well worth citing. Pericles, trying to persuade the Athenians that they did not need to fear the outcome of a war against the Peloponnesians, stated the following:

> As to the war and the resources of either party, a detailed comparison will not show you the inferiority of Athens. Personally engaged in the cultivation of their land, without funds either private or public, the Peloponnesians are also without experience in long wars across sea, from the strict limit which poverty imposes on their attacks upon each other. Powers of this description are quite incapable of often manning a fleet or often sending out an army: they cannot afford the absence from their homes, the expenditure from their own funds; and besides, they have not command of the sea. Capital, it must be remembered, maintains a war more than forced contributions. [...] In a single battle the Peloponnesians and their allies may be able to defy all Hellas, but

PERICLEAN GRAND STRATEGY

> they are incapacitated from carrying on a war against a power different in character from their own [...]. But the principal point is the hindrance that they will experience from want of money. The slowness with which it comes in will cause delay; but the opportunities of war wait for no man. [...] Familiarity with the sea they will not find an easy acquisition. [...] It must be kept in mind that seamanship, just like anything else, is a matter requiring skill, and will not admit of being taken up occasionally as an occupation for times of leisure; on the contrary, it is so exacting as to leave leisure for nothing else. [...] If they march against our country we will sail against theirs, and it will then be found that the desolation of the whole of Attica is not the same as that of even a fraction of the Peloponnesus; for they will not be able to supply the deficiency except by a battle, while we have plenty of land both on the islands and the continent. The rule of the sea is indeed a great matter.[17]

Pericles' speech reveals his confidence in the outcome of the war. The economic and naval power of Athens guaranteed that it would not lose, save through errors of its own making.[18] Peloponnesian land power was largely inadequate against a maritime power, while lack of economic resources would impede Peloponnesian operations.

This was no empty boasting on Pericles' part. A surprisingly similar picture emerged at the other side of the hill. Shortly before Pericles had made the speech cited above, in an attempt to dissuade his compatriots from voting in favour of war with Athens, the Spartan king Archidamus had made an identical outline of Athenian power at the Spartan Assembly. According to him:

> In a struggle with Peloponnesians and neighbors our strength is of the same character, and it is possible to move swiftly on the different points. But a struggle with a people who live in a distant land, who have also an extraordinary familiarity with the sea, and who are in the highest state of preparation in every other department; with wealth private and public, with ships, and horses, and hoplites [heavy infantry], and a population such as no one other Hellenic place can equal, and lastly a large number of tributary allies—what can justify us in rashly beginning such a struggle? Wherein is our trust that we should rush on it unprepared? Is it in our ships? There we are infe-

rior; while if we are to practice and become a match for them, time must intervene. Is it in our money? There we have a far greater deficiency. We neither have it in our treasury, nor are we ready to contribute it from our private funds. Confidence might possibly be felt in our superiority in hoplites and population, which will enable us to invade and devastate their lands. But the Athenians have plenty of other land in their empire, and can import what they want by sea. Again, if we are to attempt an insurrection of their allies, these will have to be supported with a fleet, most of them being islanders. What then is to be our war?[19]

The strategic deadlock is apparent in Spartan strategy. To put it metaphorically, in a contest between a lion and a shark, the lion cannot force a decision, since it cannot reach the sources of the shark's strength.

Thus, the net assessment of the relative balance of power indicated that the situation was not unfavourable to Athens, to say the least. The famous motto 'we have the ships, we have the men, we have the money too' could well have been uttered by the Athenians, twenty-five centuries before it was coined by the British jingoists.[20]

Policy Objectives

Policy Objectives and Grand Strategic Designs

The next important step in the formulation of a grand strategy is that of setting political objectives. For Athens, these objectives were simply the maintenance of the status quo. The preserved existence of the empire guaranteed the prosperity and power of Athens, both in absolute terms and in comparison to the other Greek states. Moreover, the Thirty Years' Peace of 446/5 BCE acknowledged the equal status of Athens and Sparta. For the Athenians, it was perfectly satisfactory to be placed on an equal footing with what had traditionally been the leading Greek state.[21] This does not necessarily mean that Athens did not aim at achieving primacy in Greece. In fact, considering the fast growth of Athenian power, one may well argue that a status quo policy on behalf of Athens was the best vehicle for establishing Athenian hegemony over the Greek world. Simply put, Athens merely had to wait and allow the law of uneven growth to work in its

PERICLEAN GRAND STRATEGY

favour.[22] These differential rates of growth would eventually produce significant shifts in the balance of power. For Athens, a particularly welcome eventual change to the territorial status quo would be the reacquisition of Megara; as we saw in Chapter Two, the possession of this town conferred enormous strategic advantages to the Athenians.

In view of the above, it is clear why Sparta did not have any particular reason to be happy with the status quo. Consequently, it initiated preventive war in order to dissolve the Athenian Empire and thus cripple Athenian power, precisely as it had unsuccessfully attempted to do thirty years earlier. Earlier on, Sparta had revealed its intentions by presenting the Athenians with an ultimatum: as war was approaching, a Spartan embassy informed the Athenians that 'Sparta wishes the peace to continue, and there is no reason why it should not, if you would let the Hellenes be independent'.[23] This amounted to saying that the Spartan aims were unlimited, as acceptance of the Spartan ultimatum would have clearly led to the dissolution of the Athenian Empire. Since the Spartans could not hope to achieve their aims by peaceful means, they had obviously decided to initiate war.

An important point emerges here. Thucydides' analysis of the Spartan motives and their relation to the outbreak of the war makes it evident that he was fully cognizant of the relation between war and politics. Obviously for Thucydides, the Peloponnesian War was an act of force on behalf of Sparta to compel Athens to comply with its will. Sparta's political objectives could not be attained by peaceful means, therefore, to use Clausewitzian terms, war came as 'the continuation of policy by other means'. Bernard Brodie has stated that the idea expressed in this famous dictum by Clausewitz must really be an old one.[24] It would seem that the first detailed expression of this idea is to be found in Thucydides.[25]

The grand strategies of the two competing states were shaped by their respective political objectives. Athens, the status quo power, formed a defensive grand strategy whose aim was to dissuade its opponent from attempting to change said status quo. This would be achieved by convincing the enemy that Athens was unbeatable militarily and that the state possessed ample resources to continue the struggle long after the opponent would be exhausted. In other words, Athens formulated a grand strategy of exhaustion in which non-military dimensions such as economic strength played a crucial role.[26]

THUCYDIDES ON STRATEGY

On the other hand, Sparta, the revisionist power, resorted to an offensive, more Clausewitzian grand strategy, based on the Spartan military might. Initially, the Spartans attempted to persuade the Athenians to make concessions under the threat of military defeat (in other words, compellence). Following the failure of forceful persuasion, they resorted to actual warfare, attempting to secure victory through a decisive land battle.

The respective grand strategic designs of both Sparta and Athens correspond remarkably to the model types that Sir Basil Liddell Hart denoted as acquisitive and conservative states. According to Liddell Hart:

> The acquisitive State, inherently unsatisfied, needs to gain victory in order to gain its object—and must therefore court greater risks in the attempt. The conservative State can achieve its object by merely inducing the aggressor to drop his attempt at conquest—by convincing him that 'the game is not worth the candle.' Its victory is, in a real sense, attained by foiling the other side's bid for victory.[27]

In other words, Athens did not have to beat Sparta in military terms. If the Spartans were made to abandon their quest for overthrowing the Athenian Empire, this would signify the victory of the Athenian grand strategy. It is amazing that Liddell Hart's analysis, perceptive though it is, has in fact added nothing novel to the one produced by Thucydides twenty-five centuries earlier. Apart from anticipating Liddell Hart, Thucydides may be said to operate on the same wavelength as his younger contemporaries, the authors of *The Art of War*.[28] Simply put, instead of defeating the might of Sparta, Athens chose to foil the Spartan plan for victory—what Sun Tzu called the highest form of strategy.[29]

To reiterate, Athens was satisfied with the status quo, whereas Sparta was bent on overthrowing it. Consequently, Athens formulated a grand strategy of exhaustion, aiming to make Sparta acknowledge the futility of trying to change the status quo, while the latter formulated a strategy of annihilation in which they tried to force a land battle where its powerful infantry would prove decisive.

PERICLEAN GRAND STRATEGY

Athenian Grand Strategy: Two Underlying Principles

An underlying principle of the Athenian grand strategy was rejection of appeasement, whereby Pericles insisted on securing equal status between Athens and Sparta. Any unilateral Athenian concessions, no matter how trivial they might seem, would erode this status. Thus, immediately before the outbreak of the war, the Spartans stated that peace could be preserved, provided the Athenians revoked the famous Megarian Decree, which excluded the citizens of Megara from the ports of the Athenian Alliance and the agora (marketplace) of Athens.[30] Even on this relatively minor issue, Pericles was not prepared to make unilateral concessions. For him, this Spartan request was nothing except a test of the Athenians' determination and will. If Athens conceded on that issue, then Sparta was sure to come up with further demands. As Pericles himself put it:

> There is one principle, Athenians, which I hold to through everything, and that is the principle of no concession to the Peloponnesians. [...] Now it was clear before that Sparta entertained designs against us; it is still more clear now. [...] [T]hey conclude with an ultimatum warning us to leave the Hellenes independent. I hope that you will none of you think that we shall be going to war for a trifle if we refuse to revoke the Megara decree [...]. Why, this trifle contains the whole seal and trial of your resolution. If you give way, you will instantly have to meet some greater demand, as having been frightened into obedience in the first instance; while a firm refusal will make them clearly understand that they must treat you as equals. [...] For all claims from an equal, urged upon a neighbor as commands, before any attempt at arbitration, be they great or be they small, have only one meaning, and that is slavery.[31]

Consequently, Pericles asked the Spartans to offer a quid pro quo for the revocation of the Megarian Decree, namely that they would abandon their practice of periodic expulsion of foreigners from their territory (*xenelasia*), which was hampering the trading activities of Athenians and their allies.[32] These terms were rejected by the Spartans and thus war became inevitable. Rather than submit to coercive demands, Pericles chose war.

49

THUCYDIDES ON STRATEGY

Here we are provided with as good an analysis of the dangers of appeasement as any in modern literature. From this, we can see the lessons that the Western democracies had to painfully learn while dealing with Hitler in the 1930s[33] had already been understood by Thucydides several centuries earlier. Naturally, this does not conclude the discussion about appeasement, which had negative connotations in the West because of the Munich Pact (1938), but which can sometimes actually be a very useful instrument. (The Byzantines, for example, often resorted to appeasement in order to close secondary fronts and deal with the primary threat unhindered.)[34] However, when a state, especially a hegemonic power, utilizes the tool of appeasement, it runs two risks: first, that its behaviour may invite further demands and challenges by its adversary; and secondly, that it may be perceived as a sign of weakness by its own allies and thus jeopardize the hegemonic supremacy. It was precisely for these reasons that Pericles rejected appeasing the Peloponnesians.[35]

Another underlying principle of Periclean strategy was the avoidance of overextension. Pericles advised that Athens should not try to expand its dominions. During a period of competition with one's principal adversary, war with a third party ought to be avoided.[36] The fact that Pericles rejected the opportunity of further territorial aggrandizement is clear evidence that he had grasped what has now become widely accepted, namely that the collapse of great powers can be brought about by overextension.[37] Under this practice, a state sets objectives and undertakes commitments beyond the means available to it. Consequently, the costs it incurs in pursuing these objectives and sustaining these commitments are often greater than the benefits it extracts from its endeavours (e.g. a costly war in a far-off place that produces little in return), and in the long run, its power diminishes.

We have examined the international situation prior to the outbreak of war, the political objectives of Athens and Sparta, and the grand strategic plans these objectives generated. Let us now turn our attention to the means employed by the grand strategy of Athens under the direction of Pericles.

PERICLEAN GRAND STRATEGY

The Means of the Periclean Grand Strategy

Periclean grand strategy made use of a variety of means. Apart from the traditional military means, it employed economic, diplomatic, technological and psychological ones. The particular combination of these means (policy mix) was guided by the following principles:

a. Balance the power of the enemy.
b. Exploit competitive advantages and negate those of the enemy.
c. Deter the enemy by the denial of their success and by the skilful use of retaliation.
d. Erode the international power base of the enemy.
e. Shape the domestic environment of the adversary to your own benefit.

a. Balance the Power of the Enemy

The first aim of the Periclean grand strategy was the balancing of the power of Sparta and its allies. Balancing can be done either by utilizing power from abroad (external balancing) and/or by mobilizing and exploiting domestic resources (internal balancing).[38] External balancing is achieved primarily through alliances, which Athens did by drawing upon the collective resources of its free allies: Chios, Lesbos, and Corcyra.[39] These allies provided ships in wartime.[40] In one instance, Thucydides mentions that in the first year of the war, an expedition around the Peloponnese by an Athenian fleet consisting of 100 ships was assisted by a powerful squadron of fifty ships from Corcyra.[41]

Athens was also drawing financial support from within its empire. If the free allies provided Athens with ships, the subordinate ones— or, as Thucydides put it, 'tributary cities'[42]—supported Athens financially and provided a pool of trained sailors in addition to those possessed by Athens itself.[43]

Athenian internal balancing drew upon the resources of both its imperial holdings and the city of Athens. Thus, the Athenians created a financial and naval reserve to be used only in extreme emergency:

> They also resolved to set apart a special fund of a thousand talents from the moneys in the Acropolis. This was not to be spent, but the current expenses of the war were to be otherwise provided for. If anyone should move or put to the vote a proposition for using the

money for any purpose whatever except that of defending the city in the event of the enemy bringing a fleet to make an attack by sea, it should be a capital offense. With this sum of money they also set aside a special fleet of one hundred triremes, the best ships of each year with their captains. None of these was to be used except with the money and against the same peril, should such peril arise.[44]

One cannot fail to grasp the link between wealth and power (in this case, naval power). The decision to create this iron reserve is significant because it suggests that the Athenians had begun mobilization for a long war and wanted to hedge against the possibility of serious depletion of their reserves.[45]

Finally, Pericles also paid attention to the ongoing training of the Athenians in maritime affairs, which provided the city with a constant number of sailors, whose mastery of their craft was superior to that of their enemies.[46]

In sum, in order to achieve its goals in wartime, balancing within the Periclean grand strategy basically consisted of the mobilization and deployment of both Athenian wealth and manpower together with that of their free allies and imperial subjects.[47]

b. Exploit Competitive Advantages and Negate Those of the Enemy

A second principle of Pericles' grand strategy was to exploit the competitive advantage of Athens and to diminish that of Sparta. One such advantage was provided by the existence of a comprehensive urban fortification complex, namely the walls around Athens (see Map 4). The story of the rebuilding of these walls at the suggestion of Themistocles after the Persians withdrew, and their subsequent expansion to cover the ports of Phalerum and Piraeus, was mentioned in the previous chapter. These walls were to have a significant impact on the relations between Athens and Sparta in general, and the conduct of the Peloponnesian War in particular, by neutralizing the advantage the Spartans derived from their highly trained land forces. As Josiah Ober observed, 'Pericles' strategy radically altered the use of force in Greek international relations. The physical obstacle represented by stone and brick fortifications effectively stymied the deployment of military force by human agents who lacked the technological means to overcome the obstacle'.[48] Essentially, these walls

PERICLEAN GRAND STRATEGY

made Athens a safe haven, an island, which was indeed what Pericles himself suggested: 'Suppose that we were islanders: can you conceive a more impregnable position? Well, this in future should, as far as possible, be our conception of our position'.[49]

This brings us to the second source of Athenian competitive advantage that the Periclean grand strategy put in good use, namely the navy.[50] In essence, Pericles suggested that instead of fighting a pitched battle with the Spartan infantry, the Athenians should use their navy for launching commando raids on enemy territory. Thus, they would make the war costlier for the Spartans without suffering serious casualties themselves. We have already seen Pericles (and Archidamus) highlighting the importance of the Athenian navy in the forthcoming war. At a later stage, Pericles gave his fellow citizens a more general account of the importance of sea power. His statement has retained its validity throughout history:

> You perhaps think that your empire extends only over your allies; I will declare to you the truth. The visible field of action has two parts, land and sea. In the whole of one of these you are completely supreme, not merely as far as you use it at present, but also to what further extent you may think fit: in fine, your naval resources are such that your vessels may go where they please, without the King [of Persia] or any other nation on earth being able to stop them.[51]

Interesting analogies may be drawn with later eras. For instance, one may easily argue that the maritime strategy of Athens is a direct predecessor to the similar and renowned strategy that was used many times by Great Britain to such good effect.[52] Paul Kennedy has given the following definition of naval mastery:

> [A] situation in which a country has so developed its maritime strength that it is superior to any rival power, and that its predominance is or could be exerted far outside its home waters, with the result that it is extremely difficult for other, lesser states to undertake maritime operations or trade without at least its tacit consent.[53]

Great Britain enjoyed such a fortuitous situation from the end of the seventeenth century until the end of the First World War. Athens was certainly in such a situation from the end of the Persian Wars until the destruction of its expeditionary force at Sicily in 413 BCE. The only problem with the Athenian maritime strategy was that the financial costs were considerable.[54] A strategy that focused upon naval warfare was much more demanding upon resources than a strategy that was reliant upon the traditional methods of a land campaign. Nonetheless, Athens proved that it could quite easily sustain the relevant cost.

c. Deter the Enemy by the Denial of Their Success and by the Skilful Use of Retaliation

The third principle of the Periclean grand strategy envisaged the use of what in modern terminology we call deterrence (see Chapter One). Athenian deterrence had two dimensions. The first was what would nowadays be referred to as 'deterrence by denial'. The formidable walls of Athens plus the easy supply of the city by sea ensured that Athens would not be conquered, no matter how powerful Sparta and its allies were on land. In the meantime, the Athenians would avoid decisive battle with the enemy, irrespective of how much damage an invasion of Attica might cause—a strategy that later became known as the 'Fabian strategy'.[55] Pericles argued that it would be suicidal for the Athenians to abandon their walled defences and offer battle on land against the invading Peloponnesians. To begin with, the Spartans and their allies were more numerous; moreover, the superior quality of the Spartan infantry was only too well-known.[56] Simply put, the Peloponnesians were invincible (or, as the Spartan defeat at Sphacteria revealed, near invincible) on land, a point that Pericles repeatedly emphasized.[57] Even if by a miracle the Athenians managed to win a land battle, the war would still not be over; the following year would once again feature a Peloponnesian invasion. If, alternatively, the outcome was the likely one of an Athenian defeat, then Athens would lose both the war and the empire at a stroke, since it would be unable to retain control of its allies. In Pericles' words:

> Dismissing all thought of our land and houses, we must vigilantly guard the sea and the city. No irritation that we may feel for the former must provoke us to a battle with the numerical superiority of the Peloponnesians. A victory would only be succeeded by another

battle against the same superiority: a reverse involves the loss of our allies, the source of our strength, who will not remain quiet a day after we become unable to march against them. We must cry not over the loss of houses and land but of men's lives; since houses and land do not gain men, but men them.[58]

In Periclean strategy, the distinction between deterrence by denial and defence was a clear-cut one. For him, defence is directed against the enemy's hostile actions. Pericles rejected this and suggested instead a strategy addressing Sparta's aims, which was its motivation in undertaking offensive action. Furthermore, defence seeks to prevent harm to oneself, whereas denial seeks to prevent enemy gains. While these two strategies are frequently similar, they are not synonymous.[59]

With the hindsight of history, Pericles' rationale may appear sound, but one has to understand that it ran counter to the prevailing Greek *ethos* from Homer onwards, namely the glory of war.[60] Having the Spartans outside the walls destroying the land while suggesting that nothing should be done about it, leaves one open to accusations of cowardice—an accusation far more potent in ancient Greece than in our era. In this respect, the post-heroic strategy suggested by Pericles was an extremely difficult one to expound. However, Pericles stuck to his strategy, for he sincerely believed that it was the only one that could bring victory. In the meantime, the Athenian navy would keep the empire together, thus enabling Athens to continue the war indefinitely, precisely as Pericles (and Archidamus) envisaged, yet in contrast to those in Sparta who were thinking in terms of a short war.[61]

There is an interesting psychological aspect in the deterrence by denial as encountered in Periclean grand strategy. Since the avoidance of battle implicitly consented to the destruction of the Attic mainland, it constitutes an interesting variation of the 'scorched-earth policy' that is generally construed as an indication of determination to continue the struggle without sparing any sacrifices.[62]

The second dimension of Athenian deterrence—'deterrence by retaliation'—is a more familiar one. As Pericles had made clear, any Peloponnesian invasion of Attica would provoke reprisal raids on the Peloponnesian coast by the Athenian navy. This was of particular importance to the credibility of the Athenian deterrence, since it carried the threat of imposing costly retribution on Sparta and its allies. Such a powerful threat was lacking in the case of pure defence behind the walls, for although such a strategy guaranteed the impregnability of Athens, it did so without inflicting any punitive costs on the invading Peloponnesians. This is precisely what Liddell Hart had in mind when he rejected static defence as a military strategy for conservative states and instead stated that 'economy of force and deterrent effect are best combined in the defensive-offensive method, based on high mobility that carries the power of quick riposte'.[63]

As to the retaliatory dimension of Athenian deterrence, it is interesting to note that this was of relatively moderate proportions at the beginning of the war. As we will see later on, this has led to accusations of weakness and lack of strategic purpose that persist to this day. In reality, Athenian retaliation was foreboding and progressively escalating. Thus, in the second year of the war (430 BCE), Pericles, in what was an important organizational innovation, transferred about 300 cavalry to the Peloponnese by sea on special horse-transports: 'These horsemen had virtually free rein for the Spartans possessed no mounted force to impede them'.[64] Even more important, that Athenian expedition featured the storming and sack of the Laconian coastal town of Prasiae.[65] This escalation threatened the already fragile stability of Sparta's social order, since it encouraged a revolt of the restless helots. If Sparta did not comply with the Athenian desire but persisted with the war, retaliation was bound to escalate further.

In this respect, the capture and fortification of Pylos and the subsequent Spartan defeat at Sphacteria in 425 BCE, far from constituting deviations from the Periclean grand strategy,[66] were in fact its logical corollary. As was demonstrated at Prasiae, Pericles was willing to attack and seize anything located on a coast, but does not seem to have been bent on permanent conquest and fortification, which he felt could wait until later. When the progressive Athenian escalation reached that point, and Pylos was seized and fortified, the Spartans were thrown out of balance and were induced to commit the blunder of sending a force to the small island of Sphacteria, opposite Pylos. This presented the Athenians with a golden opportunity that they were quick to

PERICLEAN GRAND STRATEGY

exploit—to blockade and then capture the Spartan force. As Pericles himself had stated: 'the opportunities of war wait for no man'.[67]

One might ask why Sparta would ever be compelled by retaliation to yield when it had not been deterred by the threat of retaliation in the first place. Pericles, however, was determined to demonstrate to the Spartans that the marginal benefits of their aggression were bound to decline over time, whereas the marginal costs of retaliation were bound to increase over time. This was clearly demonstrated by events at Prasiae, Pylos, and Sphacteria: Sparta could not defeat Athens while continuing to haemorrhage losses and incur costs in the war. As a result, the Spartans sued for peace—a clear vindication of the Periclean strategy.[68]

d. Erode the International Power Base of the Enemy

Another principle of the Periclean grand strategy was the erosion of the international power base of the enemy. The primary weapon in promulgating economic warfare and intimidation was the use of the Athenian navy. The damage inflicted by its deployment was twofold: it inflicted damage on the Peloponnesian coast; and it hampered the trading activities of the Peloponnesians. This was particularly damaging for such states as Corinth and Megarid, which depended considerably on maritime trade.[69] Thus, the Peloponnesians were forced to cope with the means provided by the agricultural sector of their economies—in other words, with financial means inferior to those possessed by Athens.[70] In addition, the international power base of Sparta was weakened by intimidating both its actual and potential allies. Among the various instances of this policy, the most famous one occurred after Pericles' death, namely the Melian Dialogue. Even neutral states that were leaning towards Sparta had to be intimidated in disproportion to what they were doing.[71]

e. Shape the Domestic Environment of the Adversary to Your Own Benefit

Finally, a further principle of the Periclean grand strategy was that Athens should try to shape the domestic environment of Sparta in a way that would benefit Athenian interests. For this to happen, Athens needed to wage psychological warfare on its enemy. Pericles intended to convince the Spartans that war against Athens was futile. Although they might ravage Attica at will, it would become evident to them that they could not force a decision, while in the meantime, the Peloponnesian coasts would lie at the mercy of the Athenian navy.[72] This situation would eventually bring about a shift in the domestic balance of power in Sparta; moderate leaders would emerge who would understand that the war did not make any sense, and they would sue for peace. This was actually how the two opponents reached peace after the tenth year of the war, when King Pleistoanax, the commander of the invading force of 446 BCE and a supporter of peace, became the principal figure in Sparta.[73]

In terms of modern strategic theory, this attempt of Pericles to influence the domestic balance of power in Sparta by the controlled use of Athenian offensive forces constitutes an example of environment-shaping strategy. Such a strategy enables a state to cope with the reality that its decisions affect the political environment. Environmental shaping entails using power to help create security conditions that render it unnecessary to fight in order to protect one's interests.[74]

These were the principles that governed the policy mix of the various means (military, economic, diplomatic, technological and psychological) employed by the Periclean grand strategy in order to attain Athens' political objectives. Thus, a pretty clear outline of the Periclean grand strategy emerges. By aiming at the maintenance of the status quo, it attempted to dissuade the opponent through a strategy of exhaustion. In military terms, this grand strategy rested upon the deterrent effect that impregnable fortifications and naval commando raids would have on the enemy (see Table 3.1). It now remains for us to deal with the important dimension of legitimacy, both domestic and international.

The Issue of Legitimacy

It is fundamentally important that the grand strategy of a state must be perceived to be grounded in legitimacy, both at home and abroad. The U.S. experience in Vietnam should suffice to prove this point, as the loss of domestic legitimacy exercised a crippling effect on American grand strategy. How, then, did Pericles cope with the problem of ensuring domestic legitimacy for his grand strategy?

PERICLEAN GRAND STRATEGY

Table 3.1: The Grand Strategies of Athens and Sparta

	Athens	Sparta
Political Objectives	Limited aims—maintenance of the status quo preservation of the Athenian Empire	Unlimited aims—change of the status quo dissolution of the Athenian Empire
Grand Strategy	Dissuasion by exhaustion	Persuasion by threatened or actual military annihilation
Military Strategy	Deterrence by denial and retaliation	Offence, decisive land battle

Domestic Legitimacy

One may recall that the Periclean grand strategy was inherently unpopular. The fact that Pericles actually managed to persuade the Athenian public to adhere to an unpopular policy speaks volumes of his talent as a statesman. It is for this reason that Hans Delbrück has called Pericles one of the greatest statesmen and military leaders in history.[75] Nevertheless, even Pericles himself did not find this persuasion easy. The Athenians, who had felt that moving behind the walls and thus abandoning their property to the mercy of the enemy was difficult enough, were shattered to see this property being destroyed in front of their eyes:

> The territory of Athens was being ravaged before the very eyes of the Athenians, a sight which the young men had never seen before and the old only in the Persian wars; and it was naturally thought a grievous insult, and the determination was universal, especially among the young men, to sally forth and stop it.[76]

Pericles became a convenient scapegoat and a fine was imposed on him—a characteristic example of the erratic decision-making of the Athenian polity.[77] Nevertheless, the Athenians remained true to the strategy devised by Pericles and did not seriously depart from it until long after his death.[78] To put the matter differently, domestic legitimacy is a *conditio sine qua non* for the success of a grand strategy. All strategic designs will collapse unless there is domestic legitimacy, and this is particularly true for democracies. In this respect, Pericles' *Epitaph*, his speech in memoriam of those who fell during the first year of the war, deserves special attention. This speech is a tribute to the Athenian way of life, aiming to persuade the Athenians to rally round the war effort of their city.[79]

The question of domestic legitimacy also included another dimension in the Athenian grand strategy: the attempt to undermine the domestic power base of Sparta by efforts to foment a revolt of the helots. The raids of the Athenian navy were providing the helots with excellent opportunities to wreak havoc on their Spartan masters and the visible possibility of achieving liberation.[80]

International Legitimacy

International legitimacy can also be helpful to a cause. Obviously, under conditions of international anarchy (i.e. in the absence of a supreme authority that regulates interstate antagonism), relations between states are fundamentally conflictual.[81] Consequently, one cannot expect much goodwill from the international environment. Nevertheless, if the grand strategy of a state is internationally acknowledged as legitimate, this might at least spare that state some potential enemies and thus enable it to economize on its resources.

Unfortunately for Periclean Athens, things were not promising in this respect. What had begun as the Delian League, an alliance wrought to defend against the Persian threat, had turned into the Athenian Empire, which, as demonstrated earlier, was primarily a source of revenue for Athens. All legitimacy had disappeared, and the coercive power of the Athenian navy was the sole factor responsible for holding the alliance together. The Athenians were all too cognizant of this fact. Athenian ambassadors that had visited Sparta shortly before the outbreak of the war had no trouble acknowledging that the Athenians faced 'extreme unpopularity with the Hellenes, not at least unpopularity for our empire'.[82] Pericles himself went as far as calling the Athenian Empire a tyranny, yet a tyranny that it would be unsafe to abandon:

> [Y]ou cannot decline the burdens of empire and still expect to share its honors. You should remember also that what you are fighting against is not merely slavery as an exchange for independence, but also loss of empire and danger from the animosities incurred in its exercise. Besides, to recede is no longer possible [...] For what you

hold is, to speak somewhat plainly, a tyranny; to take it perhaps was wrong, but to let it go is unsafe.[83]

Here, what was weakness for Athens constituted strength for Sparta. The Spartans presented themselves as the liberators of the Greeks from Athenian oppression, thus gaining considerable support.[84]

This point concludes the examination of the Periclean grand strategy. A more or less complete picture of the relative strengths and weaknesses of each side has been gained (see Table 3.2), as has the way in which Athens tried to exploit its strengths and minimize the impact of its weaknesses. Let us now attempt to evaluate the Periclean grand strategy.

Table 3.2: Athens and Sparta: Relative Strengths and Weaknesses

Athenian Strengths	Spartan Strengths
• Naval Mastery • Economic Strength • Overseas Empire • Impregnable Fortifications	• Powerful Land Forces • International Legitimacy • Low-Cost Strategy
Athenian Weaknesses	**Spartan Weaknesses**
• Weak Land Forces • Lack of International Legitimacy • High-Cost Strategy • Erratic Decision-Making and Precarious Domestic Legitimacy	• Weak Naval Forces • Limited Financial Resources • Danger of Internal Revolt • Difficulty of Long and Distant Campaigns

Evaluation of the Periclean Grand Strategy

In Chapter One, it was pointed out that grand strategy—the theory of how a state produces security—is empirically tested against political outcomes, namely the survival and well-being of the state. Given that Athens lost the Peloponnesian War, how should the Periclean grand strategy be rated? Was it a failure? Literature is divided. We have already cited Delbrück's statement about Pericles being one of the greatest statesmen and military leaders in history. Conversely, some analysts have called the Periclean strategy 'a form of wishful thinking that failed'[85] and have stated that 'as a strategist he [Pericles] was a failure, and deserves a share of the blame for Athens' great defeat'.[86] Clearly, this calls for a more detailed evaluation of the Periclean grand strategy.

As aforementioned, there are five criteria used for the evaluation of grand strategies: external fit; relation between means and ends; efficiency; internal coherence; and durability to mistakes and mishaps. Undoubtedly, the Periclean grand strategy did remarkably well according to these criteria. To start with, it fitted in properly with the international environment. The territorial and political status quo was perfectly satisfactory for Athens, while at the same time Athenian power was continually growing. Consequently, Athens had no need for an offensive strategy; after all, it had already alienated many states and there was no reason to increase its considerable list of enemies.[87] If anything, with the Aegean Sea being solidly under Athenian control, the targets of an offensive strategy could only be directed towards the mainland, and that meant dealing with the Spartan infantry. Rather than doing this, the Athenians chose a competitive strategy, one in which their strengths were applied over the enemy's weaknesses (for example, naval raids directed against the delicate Spartan domestic structure). Pericles explicitly analysed the comparative strengths and weaknesses of each side (see Table 3.2) and prepared a strategy to exploit them in favour of Athens. As to the domestic political environment, the Periclean grand strategy did not run counter to any of the norms or premises of the Athenian polity per se.

The Periclean grand strategy also scored well in terms of the relation between means and ends. For while the important Athenian objectives were achieved, overextension was carefully avoided; the resources of Athens were certainly considerable, but not unlimited. Pericles understood both sides of the link between economic resources and political ends: 'First, not by downplaying but by accurately emphasizing the great expense at war; and second by implying that such expense was not unanticipated and that Athens had ample funds to meet it'.[88]

It is obvious that under the leadership of Alcibiades, the Athenians abandoned the Periclean principle of balancing means and ends in order to avoid overextension.[89] The outcome was the costly Sicilian expedition that aimed at extending Athenian control to the remote and populous lands of Sicily (and even beyond), which ended in an

PERICLEAN GRAND STRATEGY

unmitigated disaster for Athens.[90] This expedition changed the whole course of the war and, according to Thucydides, was the very reason for the Athenian defeat.[91]

Regarding the criterion of efficiency, one can see that the Periclean strategy once again performed well. First, all available means were utilized; in other words, the strategy was total. What is striking is that, although Athens was in the midst of a great war, the military element did not dominate its grand strategy. In addition to military strategy, the Athenian grand strategy featured economic strategy, diplomacy, psychological pressure, and domestic legitimacy. Secondly, without suffering undue casualties, the Athenians were able to beat off the challenge of the Peloponnesians (as well as some of their own allies) and retain their empire in Greece, at least until the disaster in Sicily. The destruction of Attica was insignificant in comparison, and it was only in financial terms that the costs were appreciable. However, this was intrinsic to the capital-intensive maritime strategy that Athens had followed since the days of the Persian Wars, in contrast to the labour-intensive continental strategy of Sparta. Moreover, Athenian resources were equal to the task of sustaining the war effort.

Furthermore, the Periclean grand strategy had no difficulty at all in meeting the criterion of internal coherence. All the components of this grand strategy reinforced each other and none of them restricted the influence of another. For instance, the military dimension (naval commando raids) was never allowed to interfere with the diplomatic one (tacit bargaining with the enemy).

Finally, the Periclean grand strategy proved startlingly durable to mishaps, though these mishaps were uncommonly severe. In 430 BCE, Athens was hit by a plague that raged for two years, then subsided, and then, in the winter of 427–6 BCE, flared up again for one more year. According to modern estimates, this epidemic wiped out one third of the Athenian population.[92] Even though Thucydides finds it impossible to ascertain the total number of fatalities, he makes it clear that it was a major calamity.[93] A disaster of this magnitude would normally suffice to undermine any grand strategic design; indeed, even coping with such an eventuality seems too much to ask of a grand strategy. Nevertheless, Periclean grand strategy proved durable enough to overcome these impediments.

THUCYDIDES ON STRATEGY

A grand strategy that scores so well against these criteria can be expected to score well when put into operation, and this is indeed what happened with the Periclean grand strategy. All the components of this grand strategy coalesced into the main objective: victory through the exhaustion of the enemy. After ten years of war, the Spartans admitted that they had had enough and abandoned their quest for victory. In fact, Athens could have achieved even more. According to Arther Ferrill:

> In the first six years of the war (431–426) Periclean strategy had worked to Athens' advantage. To be sure, Platea had fallen to Thebes and Sparta, and Attica had been at the mercy of the Spartan army, while the plague took a heavy toll; but around Corcyra and the Corinthian Gulf Athens had held its own and inflicted losses on the Peloponnesians. [...] Athens remained strong, and the Spartans seemed unable to use their land power effectively against the naval giant.[94]

Then, in 425 BCE, there followed the astonishing Athenian success in Sphacteria. Had the Athenians been more astute in exploiting this triumph, they would have emerged victorious, since the Spartans were clearly willing to make concessions:[95] 'In the first six years Periclean strategy had very nearly worked, but the Athenians refused to negotiate'.[96] As if this were not enough, the Athenians suffered two serious defeats on land: the first at Delium in 424 BCE against the Boeotians, and then at Amphipolis in 422 BCE against a Peloponnesian expeditionary force under the Spartan general Brasidas.[97] Nonetheless, even the Peace of Nicias in 421 BCE can be regarded as favourable to Athens, as it retained its profitable empire and discouraged further Spartan attacks (until Alcibiades decided upon the Sicilian expedition).[98]

Critiques of the Periclean Grand Strategy

Finally, we must examine the specific criticisms directed against the Periclean grand strategy. Pericles' grand strategy has been primarily criticized on four counts.[99] The first is that by rejecting even minor concessions to the Peloponnesians, the grand strategy brought about war, which meant it was a high-cost strategy. The second criticism is that it was unforeseen by the enemy, hence it lacked credibility and, consequently, its deterrent value was low (in other words, the strategy provoked war, which again can be seen as a high-cost manoeuvre). Third, it was considered too feeble to exploit any opportunities and increase the cost the enemy had to bear (that is, misuse of available means). And finally, it is seen as being too dependent on Pericles for its execution and thus was bound to be abandoned after his death (in fact, this criticism does not question the soundness of the strategy itself). Let us deal with each of these criticisms in turn.

The first criticism—that Pericles' rejection of appeasement (that is, his refusal to revoke the Megarian Decree) brought about the Peloponnesian war[100]—brings us once again to the issue of underlying versus proximate causes of the war (see Chapter Two). As far as this criticism is concerned, it should be noted that it is unjustified to put all of the blame on Pericles. The international situation at the time was very tense, and no one can say with confidence that the war could have been avoided. David Baldwin presents a more balanced view:

> Although Pericles' action failed to deter war, the probability of war was fairly great to begin with; and perhaps nothing he could have done would have avoided it. Given the tense and complex situation, the imposition of economic sanctions may well have been the policy option with the highest probability of success—even though it was very low. Taking into consideration the difficulty of the task, the policy alternatives available, and the complexity of the situation, it seems as plausible to say that the Peloponnesian War occurred *despite* Pericles' prudent—perhaps even ingenious—attempt to head it off via the Megarian Decree as it does to say that the decree 'precipitated' the war.[101]

In addition, refusal by Sparta to give the quid pro quo asked for by Pericles (that is, to stop applying *xenelasia* to Athenians and their allies) is an indication that Pericles' assessment of the true nature of the Spartan request may have been correct. It seems that Sparta had unlimited objectives and was essentially impossible to appease. Given this, had the Athenians backed down in the face of the Spartan demand, they would probably have faced more pressure from Sparta in the future.

With regard to the second criticism—that the Periclean grand strategy was unforeseen by the enemy and thus could not deter him—

we have seen that the avoidance of battle, a core principle of the Periclean strategy, was in sharp contrast to the prevailing Greek *ethos* of the era. Donald Kagan has made much of the contrast between the prescriptions of Periclean strategy on the one hand and the predominant Greek culture on the other, arguing that this contrast made it unlikely in the eyes of the enemy that the Athenians would actually follow such a strategy. Consequently, this strategy, though reasonable, lacked credibility as a deterrent.[102]

Nevertheless, Kagan has overstated his case. To start with, Archidamus had thought it improbable that 'the Athenian spirit will be the slave of their land'.[103] As such, Spartan policymakers had no difficulty in anticipating that the Athenians would avoid battle. In addition, there had been an even more striking precedent in the past where the Athenians had behaved similarly: in 480 BCE, during the Persian invasion, not only did the Athenians avoid battle with the Persians, but they in fact abandoned their city and continued the war with their navy. It is true that the Periclean grand strategy was a difficult one to envisage, let alone implement. However, this is a long way from saying that it was completely unanticipated by the enemy and therefore of limited deterrent value. Furthermore, the strategy of avoiding battle in Attica was never seriously questioned, even after the death of Pericles. Clearly, it had been endorsed by the Athenians, precisely as Archidamus had predicted.

In order to counter the third criticism—that the Periclean grand strategy was too feeble to exploit any opportunities and inflict additional costs on the enemy[104]—one needs to elaborate upon the deterrent dimension of the Periclean grand strategy, which, for all its importance, has often been misunderstood. Deterrence is a form of coercion that attempts to influence the enemy's behaviour in a manner conducive to the interests of the coercer.[105] Coercion involves affecting the relative attractiveness of the various courses of action open to an opponent. This is precisely what the Athenians under Pericles did: they manipulated the threat of negative sanctions (retaliation) that Athens could impose on Sparta. The threat of retaliation is the threat to inflict pain unrelated to the non-desirable activity of the opponent until the opponent complies.[106] Recall Pericles: 'If they march against our country we will sail against theirs, and it will then

PERICLEAN GRAND STRATEGY

be found that the desolation of the whole of Attica is not the same as that of even a fraction of the Peloponnesus'.[107]

The strategy of Pericles threatened Sparta with the certain prospect of greater pain in the event of Spartan invasion. The infliction of this pain, however, was not a once-and-for-all administration; instead, it was part of an ongoing bargaining process, a gradual turning of the screw. This explains Athenian relative moderation in inflicting damage during the first year of the war and its escalation thereafter.[108] In modern strategic jargon, Pericles was using a strategy of graduated escalation in inflicting pain as a bargaining tool.[109]

Obviously, badly designed, impulsive retaliation (e.g. massive raids and immediate occupation of outposts) might have had the exact opposite impact—that is, moving the Spartan political leadership from a cool and rational calculation of marginal costs and benefits to impulsive conduct permeated by revanchism. As an author otherwise critical of Pericles admits:

> The offensive actions were deliberately unimpressive, for they were intended only as evidence that an extended war would be damaging to the Peloponnesians. To engage in offensive actions which were more vigorous would, in fact, conflict with the plan. Offensive actions, while unable to bring about victory, might enrage the enemy.[110]

As to the fourth criticism—that the Periclean grand strategy depended solely on Pericles for its execution[111]—one must recall that Athenian reliance on fortifications and naval power existed long before Pericles.[112] In formulating his grand strategy, Pericles built upon past experience and took into account the geopolitical realities (structural imperatives). Consequently, it is wrong to attribute this particular element of Athenian strategy solely to his influence and to conclude that with Pericles gone this strategy would necessarily be abandoned. In contemporary parlance, Athens' maritime strategy was a core strategy—a state strategy consisting of all elements of policy that remain constant regardless of the international environment in which the state finds itself.[113]

To reiterate, the Periclean grand strategy cannot be blamed for the outbreak of the war: in actual fact, the war was not at all unforeseen, and the approach taken thus constituted a sound strategy of deterrence.

THUCYDIDES ON STRATEGY

Moreover, it coerced the enemy with escalating retaliation as a part of a bargaining process, and therefore it was neither weak nor lacking in strategic intent. Finally, to a large extent it reflected structural imperatives that coexisted with or without the presence of Pericles.

Why Athens Lost

In evaluating the Periclean grand strategy, it might be pertinent to quote the opinion of Thucydides, who would have been well positioned to make an accurate judgement. Thucydides asserts that Athens lost the war because it abandoned the strategy devised by Pericles. He goes on to say that had Athens kept following that strategy, it could have beaten the Peloponnesians.

> He [Pericles] told them [the Athenians] to wait quietly, to pay attention to their marine, to attempt no new conquests, and to expose the city to no hazards during the war, and doing this, promised them a favorable result. What they did was the very contrary [...]. So excessively abundant were the resources from which the genius of Pericles foresaw an easy triumph in the war over the unaided forces of the Peloponnesians.[114]

Colin Gray has summarized the anatomy of the Athenian failure in the Peloponnesian War as follows:

> For Sparta to succeed, Athens had to be weakened by plague, had to suffer irreparable losses in men and prestige in the expedition to Sicily (415–413 B.C.) and, having effected a partial recovery from these calamities, then had to commit major errors in lack of vigilance in the naval campaign for control of the Dardanelles. No less important, massive financial subsidies from Persia were required for Sparta to acquire the naval power that it needed.[115]

Persia, it must be said, did not dare subsidize Sparta's naval build-up against the powerful state of Athens before the Athenians ruined themselves by overextension in Sicily (see the next chapter).

It therefore becomes evident that the Athenians lost the war only when they dramatically reversed the Periclean grand strategy, which had explicitly disdained further conquests. Pericles had not only

PERICLEAN GRAND STRATEGY

outlined a theory of victory to his fellow citizens, but had also laid down the conditions under which his grand strategy was *not* expected to work:

> I have many other reasons to hope for a favorable outcome, if you can consent not to combine schemes of fresh conquest with the conduct of the war, and will abstain from willfully involving yourselves in other dangers; indeed, I am more afraid of our own blunders than of the enemy's devices.[116]

The fact that the Athenians chose to bring about these very conditions is not Pericles' fault. We have seen that in Thucydides' opinion the Periclean grand strategy would have brought victory to Athens if meticulously followed. This is an important tribute to Pericles, who not only devised it but made sure that it was followed, albeit less than wholeheartedly, by the Athenian public. The present study is in complete agreement with Thucydides' praise of Pericles.

4

SPARTAN GRAND STRATEGY

Introduction

As repeatedly illustrated, strategy is never conducted in a vacuum; it is always directed against one or more opponents who in turn formulate their own strategy. Consequently, no strategic analysis of the Peloponnesian War—or in fact any other war—can be complete without examining the interaction between the strategic designs of both belligerents, i.e. the 'horizontal' dimension of strategy. Therefore, it is necessary to examine not only the grand strategy of Pericles and Athens in general, but also the grand strategy of Sparta in particular.[1] As was pointed out in the previous chapter, Sparta followed a grand strategy of annihilation whereas Athens, under the direction of Pericles, initially followed one of exhaustion. However, the Sicilian expedition (415–13 BCE) marked Athens' turn to a grand strategy of annihilation, which it would follow until the end of the war.

The analysis in the previous chapter ended with the Peace of Nicias (421 BCE), which represented the victory of Periclean grand strategy. In this chapter, our examination will span the whole duration of the war. Naturally, bearing in mind what has been mentioned above, we will not be confined to a static analysis of the Spartan grand strategy, but we will also analyse its constant interaction with the grand strategy of Athens.

THUCYDIDES ON STRATEGY

Sparta and Athens: The Bilateral Balance of Power

This bilateral balance of power between Sparta and Athens has been extensively analysed in the previous chapter. The case presented was that Sparta and Athens were the two most powerful states in Greece, that the power of Athens was growing faster than that of Sparta's (chiefly because of its more advanced economic system), and that at the time of the outbreak of the war, the economic power, the navy and the empire of Athens made it at worse immune to Sparta and its allies and at best superior to them. As made evident by Archidamus' speech to the Spartan Assembly, Spartan grand strategy had reached a deadlock: whereas Athenian power was growing and Athens was encroaching upon Sparta's allies,[2] thereby undermining a basic element of Spartan security, Sparta lacked the means to strike at the centre of gravity of Athenian power, namely the navy.

For Archidamus, the problem of the growth of Athenian power and the threat that this created for Spartan security could not be immediately solved. Sparta needed to redress the balance with Athens first. Apart from internal mobilization (marshalling their domestic resources), Sparta and its allies needed to resort to external balancing, namely securing allies (Greeks or Persians) that could provide the two things the Peloponnesian League lacked—a navy and money:

> I do bid you not to take up arms at once, but to send and remonstrate with them in a tone not too suggestive of war, nor again too suggestive of submission, and to employ the interval in perfecting our own preparations. The means will be, first, the acquisition of allies, Hellenic or barbarian it matters not, so long as they are an accession to our strength naval or financial—I say Hellenic or barbarian, because the odium of such an accession to all who like us are the objects of the designs of the Athenians is taken away by the law of self-preservation—and secondly the development of our home resources. If they listen to our embassy, so much the better; but if not, after the lapse of two or three years our position will have become materially strengthened, and we can then attack them if we think proper.[3]

Unfortunately for Sparta, it was not Archidamus' counsel, but the belligerent speech of the *ephor* Sthenelaidas that carried the day with the Assembly. Sthenelaidas did not counter any of Archidamus' arguments. Instead, he concentrated on the injuries that the Athenians had inflicted on the Peloponnesian League. The closing sentences of his speech are characteristic: 'Vote therefore, Spartans, for war, as the honor of Sparta demands, and neither allow the further aggrandizement of Athens, nor betray our allies to ruin, but with the gods let us advance against the aggressors.'[4]

This shows that although both Archidamus and Sthenelaidas agreed that Athens' power was growing in relation to Sparta's, they differed in their assessment of the existing balance of power. While Archidamus considered Athens to be stronger, Sthenelaidas considered Sparta to be more powerful (as did the majority of the Spartans).[5] This misperception was to remain evident in Spartan grand strategy for the next ten years. It seems that Sthenelaidas and his followers expected a short war, believing that a Spartan invasion of Attica would lead to a quick victory,[6] while also thinking that Sparta could wage a low-cost war without suffering much itself. Events were to prove them wrong on both counts: the destruction of Attica did not bring about the capitulation of Athens, whereas Sparta was far more vulnerable to Athenian sea power than previously thought.

Thus, the net assessment of the relative balance of power indicated that the situation was not unfavourable to Athens. However, the majority of Spartans thought otherwise. The enormous disparity between the (unlimited) political objectives assigned to it and the (inadequate) means available was to the serious detriment of the Spartan grand strategy.

A change in the balance of power occurred only after the destruction of the Athenian expeditionary force in Sicily in 413 BCE. At that point, apart from its traditional advantage on land, Sparta had also obtained parity at sea; the Athenian Empire, meanwhile, was collapsing. Furthermore, the Persians had started giving financial aid to Sparta.[7] The only hope for Athens was a change in Persian policy. As the Athenian statesman Pisander put it to his fellow citizens in 411 BCE:

> In the face of the fact that the Peloponnesians had as many ships as their own confronting them at sea, more cities in alliance with them, and the King and Tissaphernes to supply them with money, of which the Athenians had none left, had he [the fellow citizen] any hope of

saving the state unless someone could induce the King to come over to their side?[8]

As we shall see, the Persians, far from changing policy, actually intensified their aid to the Spartans. The massive Persian support had dramatically tilted the balance in favour of Sparta. With the continuation of this support, Sparta's victory was, for the most part, a matter of time.

Political Objectives

As mentioned in the previous chapter, under Pericles' direction, Athens had limited political objectives, merely aiming at the preservation of the status quo; this was in contrast to Sparta, who had unlimited objectives, namely the destruction of Athenian power and the dissolution of the Athenian Empire. Nevertheless, bearing in mind the strategic culture of Sparta, resorting to a war with unlimited objectives must have been a novel experience for the Spartans. As already pointed out, Athens, the status quo power, formed a defensive grand strategy of exhaustion aiming to convince the enemy that Athens was an unbeatable military power and thus make the enemy abandon the effort of overthrowing its empire. On the other hand, Sparta, the revisionist power, resorted to an offensive grand strategy of annihilation, based on the Spartan military might. The Spartans initially attempted to achieve their policy objectives through compellence and, failing that, to secure victory through a decisive land battle.[9]

Archidamus favoured a strategy of complete annihilation, both on land and at sea.[10] Nevertheless, he believed that Sparta lacked the means to pursue such a strategy and therefore recommended that it make preparations for war and secure allies. Sthenelaidas too favoured annihilation, but, in contrast to Archidamus, he thought that Sparta did have the means to implement it, at least on land.[11] However, a grand strategy of this kind was highly demanding: whereas Athens had merely to make the Spartans abandon their quest for overthrowing the Athenian Empire, nothing short of a complete victory would suffice for Sparta in order to achieve its policy objectives.[12]

The political objectives of the Athenian grand strategy underwent a dramatic change in 415 BCE when the Athenians, at the instigation

SPARTAN GRAND STRATEGY

of Alcibiades, undertook the Sicilian expedition. All of a sudden, Athens had set unlimited aims, namely the domination of the entire Hellenic world plus the western Mediterranean (see Map 5).

Alcibiades himself, after defecting to Sparta, gave the Spartans the following account of the Athenian war aims:

> We sailed to Sicily first to conquer, if possible, the Sicilians, and after them the Italians also, and finally to assail the empire and city of Carthage. In the event of all or most of these schemes succeeding, we were then to attack the Peloponnesus, bringing with us the entire force of the Hellenes lately acquired in those parts, and taking a number of barbarians into our pay [...], and building numerous triremes in addition to those we had already (timber being plentiful in Italy); and with this fleet blockading the Peloponnesus from the sea and assailing it with our armies by land, taking some of the cities by storm, and besieging others, we hoped without difficulty to defeat them completely and after this to rule the whole of the Hellenic world.[13]

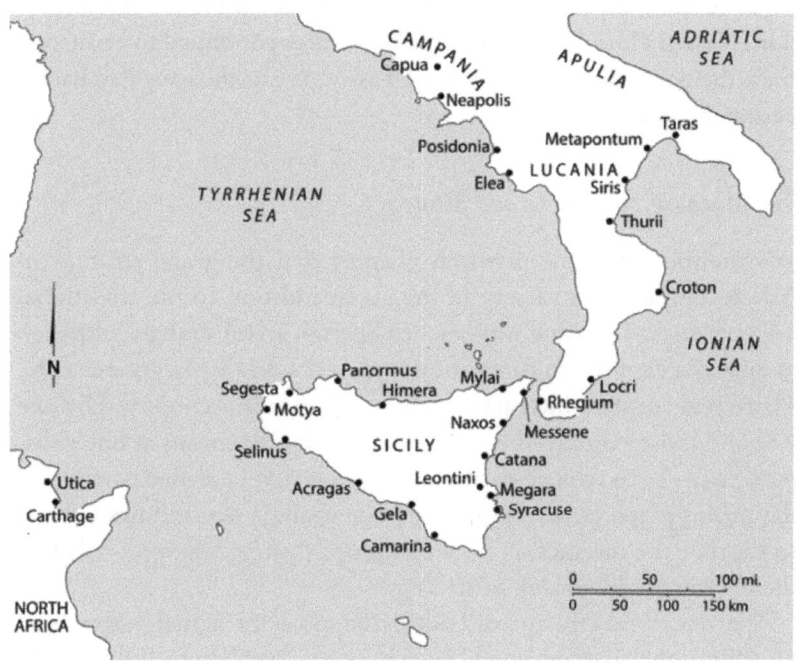

Map 5: Southern Italy, Sicily and Carthage

As a result, Athenian grand strategy was readjusted based on the revised objectives set by policy. To achieve these objectives, Athens had to revert to a grand strategy of annihilation: crushing its enemies on the battlefield and then conquering them. In addition, Athens followed a direct grand strategic approach by turning against Syracuse, the strongest city in Sicily.

The Sicilian expedition ended in complete disaster for Athens, with its expeditionary force totally annihilated in 413 BCE (see next chapter). At the same time in Greece, the Spartans had reopened hostilities, and some of the Athenian allies had revolted. In its attempt first to retain what had not been lost from its empire (and then to recover what had been), Athens relied on a strategy of annihilation. Since Sparta's challenge of the Athenian maritime empire had to be repelled, the Athenians were seeking decisive encounters at sea. Consequently, a war that had started as a clash between a status quo and a revisionist power employing a grand strategy of exhaustion and one of annihilation, respectively, ended with both combatants pursuing unlimited objectives and employing grand strategies of annihilation. Nonetheless, the approach of both sides continued to be direct: since the navy was the enemy's chief asset, it was the navy that had to be sought and destroyed.

The Means of Spartan Grand Strategy

We mentioned in the previous chapter that the grand strategy of Athens employed a variety of means in addition to the traditional military ones. The same was true for Spartan grand strategy, although in Sparta's case the military means played a relatively greater role. There was constant interaction between the means employed by one side and those employed by the other. Using the means at one's disposal in order to achieve one's political objectives entailed countering the means at the enemy's disposal. The analysis that follows will try to capture the interaction between those strategic designs—that is, the horizontal dimension of strategy.

Spartan grand strategy did not presuppose the actual outbreak of hostilities; the Spartans would have been perfectly happy if they could have achieved their objectives by the mere threat of war. Archidamus especially had a masterly understanding of the workings of coercive diplomacy and consistently tried to achieve Spartan objectives through the threat of force, holding its actual use in reserve. As he urged his fellow citizens:

> For the only light in which you can view their [the Athenians'] land is that of a hostage in your hands, a hostage the more valuable the better it is cultivated. This you ought to spare as long as possible, and not make them desperate, and so increase the difficulty of dealing with them.[14]

Spartan coercive diplomacy featured the issuing of a series of demands towards the Athenians. The revocation of the Megarian Decree was one of these, while the final Spartan ultimatum asking the Athenians to 'let the Hellenes be independent' was nothing but a blunt demand for the dissolution of the Athenian Empire.

What made the Spartans so confident that they could achieve their aims through ultimata? As already mentioned, the majority of Spartans believed that they were holding a trump card, namely that of their ability, through their superiority in land forces, to invade Attica at will. This ability entailed two potential evils for Athens: the first was a crushing defeat in a major land battle were the Athenians to take the customary step of marching to oppose the invading Peloponnesians; the second was the devastation of Attica. Spartan conventional wisdom had it that these two threats would be enough to cow the Athenians into submission. In fact, as was seen in Chapter Two, there had been a precedent in the First Peloponnesian War when a similar advance of a Peloponnesian army to Attica in 446 BCE had quickly made the Athenians sue for peace.[15]

The aforementioned incident and the lessons the Spartans drew from it are extremely interesting. To start with, it illustrates that the past behaviour of a state determines to a very great extent the other states' expectations about its future behaviour. Thus, the majority of the Spartans expected that the Athenians would be cowed by the threat of a Peloponnesian invasion of Attica, in exactly the same way as they had done previously. This clearly shows how important it is for a state to have a reputation for displaying determination and behaving uncompromisingly in any issue of vital importance to it.[16] It is precisely in a failure to retain such a reputation that we can trace the greatest danger of appeasement. If an adversary gets accustomed to securing concessions from one side, they will not believe that at some point the conceding side will be determined not to back down, and such a miscalculation may result in war.[17] It is highly probable that Sthenelaidas and the majority of the Spartans made this error of judgement.

The flawed analysis of the Spartans also illustrates the difficulty of extracting 'lessons from the past'. It is true that in 446 BCE Athens sought a compromise in light of the Peloponnesian invasion, but the international situation in 432 BCE was different. In 446 BCE, Athens had suffered a serious military defeat in Boeotia, had lost Megara, and was faced with a revolt in Euboea. Athens' attempt to create a land empire in the Greek mainland had failed, and the compromise reached in 446–5 BCE acknowledged the fact that the Athenian Empire would from then on be exclusively confined to the maritime domain.[18] In 432 BCE, however, Athens had no reason at all to back down, since its imperial territories were immune to Spartan land power. This important change of the situation was overlooked by the majority of the Spartans.

Consequently, as shown in the previous chapter, in rejecting appeasement, Pericles did not submit to the Spartan demands and thus did not allow the Spartans to gain any advantage from their powerful land forces. No such advantage was to be gained in wartime either, since the walls of Athens completely neutralized the Peloponnesian infantry and the Athenians did not come out to offer battle. At the same time, Athens was drawing freely upon the resources of the empire and the rest of its allies, while continually escalating its reprisals against Sparta, culminating in the incidents of Pylos, Sphacteria and Cythera. As a result, Sparta sued for peace.

This makes it evident that the Spartan compellent military strategy could only work in peacetime—that is, by threatening devastation of Attica and thus cowing the Athenians into submission without resorting to actual hostilities. If the Athenians chose to disregard the Spartan compellent threat, then the execution of that threat, although undoubtedly damaging to the Athenians, could not bring about victory in war. In other words, the Spartan military strategy constitutes

SPARTAN GRAND STRATEGY

another example of a military strategy suitable for compellence in peacetime but unsuitable for victory in war (see Chapter One).

The adoption of such a strategy does not mean that Sparta had merely stood and watched the Athenians' naval and financial power increasing. Rather, Sparta kept conscientiously trying to thwart the effective employment of these means possessed by Athens. One may recall that Archidamus advised the Spartans that they needed to restore the balance of power with Athens before attempting to go to war by seeking allies that could provide the Peloponnesians with money and a navy. He also pointed out that the Peloponnesians would have to tap into their own resources as well, but that alone would be inadequate.[19] Archidamus had just provided the universal theory of victory over a maritime power: creating an economic unit that can afford to build a navy equal or superior to that of this power.[20]

Despite this, the premature start of the war by Sparta rendered that plan unlikely to succeed. Simply put, Sparta's chances at sea were not rated particularly highly; consequently, few third parties were prepared to risk their naval and financial assets by backing a Peloponnesian navy. For instance, the Spartans tried to secure naval and financial aid from the Greek colonies in southern Italy and Sicily,[21] yet no help came from that quarter.[22] The Persians, who alone could tilt the balance, were also unhelpful.[23] Even worse, the Persians concluded a treaty of friendship with Athens in 424–3 BCE that acknowledged the bilateral status quo as it stood following the Peace of Callias. The Athenians, true to the Periclean grand strategy, avoided war with a third party while the Peloponnesian War was still raging. At the same time, the recently established Persian king, Darius II, had more pressing problems at home, where he faced a series of revolts, and thus had no taste for hostilities with an evidently unbeatable Athens.[24] Only rebel subjects of the Athenian Empire were willing to provide resources for the Peloponnesian navy.[25] Clearly, Sparta's attempt to match Athens' sources of strength in terms of naval strength and financial wealth had failed.

However, this was not the only way that Sparta used the various means at its disposal. A central element of Spartan grand strategy was to try and make the war as costly as possible for the Athenians. It was pointed out in the previous chapter that the Athenian maritime strategy was capital-intensive; in contrast, the Peloponnesian land forces were relatively cheap to maintain. Spartan society being continually prepared for war, actual warfare made but little difference.[26] For the rest of the Peloponnesian allies, sending their armed contingents to an excursion in Attica for some two to six weeks a year also incurred little cost.[27]

The aim, however, was to increase the cost Athens had to incur. This attempt had three dimensions: the destruction of Attica; the dissolution of the Athenian Empire; and exploitation of every secondary front opened by the Athenians. The destruction of the Attic land, apart from the immediate financial cost, would also inflict some social cost to the Athenians; the whole social fabric of Athens would be upset, as the farmers and the social strata associated with the land would be displaced and forced to seek refuge behind the city walls.[28]

The second dimension of Sparta's cost-raising strategy was the attempt to cause the dissolution of the Athenian Empire. This would be done through either encouraging defection or aiding revolts of the Athenian allies. The Spartans had been working toward this long before the outbreak of the war.[29]

The revolt of Mytilene, an island allied to Athens, in 428–7 BCE provides an excellent example of Sparta's attempt to raise the cost of war for Athens and exploit the situation. After the Mytilenians revolted, the Spartans prepared to attack Athens both by land and by sea, while also preparing a fleet to help the rebels. They obviously believed that the Athenians could not simultaneously sustain the blockade of Mytilene, the costly siege of the city of Potidaea, the raids on the Peloponnesian coast, and at the same time be able to take care of the defence of their city. According to Thucydides:

> Meanwhile the Athenians, who were aware that the preparations of the enemy were due to his conviction of their weakness, wished to show him that he was mistaken, and that they were able, without moving their fleet off Lesbos, to repel with ease the one with which they were menaced from the Peloponnesus. They therefore manned a hundred ships by embarking the citizens of Athens, except the knights and pentecosiomedimni, and the resident aliens; and putting

out to the Isthmus, displayed their power and made descents upon the Peloponnesus wherever they pleased.[30]

Obviously, Athens' resources were yet to be depleted. Nevertheless, a Peloponnesian fleet did eventually sail for Mytilene. Although the island had capitulated before the fleet arrived, there were still plenty of opportunities either to recapture it or to spread revolt along the Asia Minor coast. However, Alcidas, the Spartan commander of the fleet, must have been extremely ill at ease at sea and declined to exploit these opportunities.[31] Nonetheless, the message was obvious: Sparta was keen on undermining the Athenian Empire.

A much more vigorous attempt at this was undertaken by the Spartans in 424 BCE, when they sent a force under the valiant general Brasidas to Macedonia and Thrace. Brasidas, using a blend of military prowess and diplomatic skill, proceeded to dismantle the Athenian Empire in that area. The Spartans embarked upon this horizontal escalation of the war in order to create a diversion that would make the Athenians more amenable to peace proposals. Not only was this successful, but it also created the preconditions for the eventual ousting of the Athenians from Macedonia and Thrace.[32]

Finally, the third dimension of the Spartan cost-raising strategy was the exploitation of every secondary front the Athenians had opened. True to the adventurous and sometimes reckless spirit that their strategic culture promoted, the Athenians were eager to exploit opportunities, actual or perceived, in various places. However, wherever the Athenians appeared, the Spartans would soon follow; they would simply not let the Athenians claim easy gains.[33]

The greatest of these Athenian ventures was the expedition in Sicily. For this, Athens was using its financial and naval power not only to deter the enemy as it had been doing up to that point, but also to expand territorially. This expedition also involved, for the first and last time during the Peloponnesian War, a major Athenian commitment of land forces.

Sparta's attempt to counter this aggressive employment of Athenian means did not take long. The Spartans once again resumed their attempt to make the war costlier for the Athenians, albeit in a more systematic fashion. Thus, instead of periodically invading Attica, they established a permanent garrison there by fortifying Decelea in 413 BCE. This had disastrous consequences for Athens.

> Indeed since Decelea had been first fortified [...] it had been causing great harm to the Athenians. In fact this occupation, by the destruction of property and loss of men which resulted from it, was one of the principal causes of their ruin. Previously the invasions were short, and did not prevent them from making use of their land during the rest of the time: the enemy was now permanently fixed in Attica; at one time it was an attack in force, at another it was it was the regular garrison overrunning the country and making forays for its subsistence, and the Spartan King Agis, was in the field and diligently prosecuting the war; great damage was therefore done to the Athenians. They were deprived of their whole country: more than twenty thousand slaves had deserted, a great part of them artisans, and all their sheep and beasts of burden were lost. [...] Besides, the transport of provisions from Euboea, which had before been carried on so much more quickly over land by Decelea from Oropus, was now effected at great cost by sea round Cape Sunium; everything the city required had to be imported from abroad, and instead of a city it became a fortress.[34]

A frequently asked question is why it took the Spartans so long to establish a permanent fort in Attica. The fortification of Decelea is often attributed solely to the advice of Alcibiades,[35] whereas some scholars go as far as to claim that this delay in the creation of a permanent fort proves that Sparta did not have a strategy during the Peloponnesian War.[36] We consider both these claims to be wrong. The idea of establishing a permanent fort in Attica pre-existed in Spartan strategy. The Corinthians had mentioned it in their speech at the assembly of the Peloponnesian League in 432 BCE, long before the outbreak of hostilities. Moreover, during the negotiations that led to the Peace of Nicias, the Spartans threatened the Athenians with the creation of a permanent fort in their territory.[37] The Spartans did not embark upon this scheme earlier simply because they had not felt the need for it; as previously mentioned, the majority of them believed that the war would be short. In contrast to the annual invasions that lasted only a few weeks, the establishment of a fort in Athens and its manning on a permanent footing was an action entailing serious costs. The commitment of a substantial part of their workforce had important consequences for the economies of the Peloponnesian states (with the exception of Sparta), whereas the logistical support of a multitudinous army permanently stationed on enemy territory was impossible with the means of that time. It was precisely for this reason that the Peloponnesian force kept 'overrunning the country and making forays for its subsistence'. The fortification of Decelea was a highly costly measure, suitable for a long war, and since the majority of Spartans expected the war to be short, they did not initially feel the need to undertake it.[38]

Furthermore, the Spartans counterbalanced the Athenians in Sicily by offering aid to the city of Syracuse, Athens' chief enemy on the island. According to Thucydides, this aid was instrumental in preventing Athenian victory and allowing Syracuse to recover from its initial reverses.[39] From then on, the Athenians were forced to conduct a strategy of 'two-and-a-half wars': one war against Syracuse, another against Sparta, plus a possible allied revolt. As a result, they were soon faced with spiralling financial costs.[40]

The disaster in Sicily put an end to Athenian ventures and, consequently, to Spartan countermoves. However, the other two dimensions of Sparta's cost-raising strategy were working at full force: Decelea was depleting Athenian strength, and the Athenian Empire was all but liquidated. Athens had reached the limit of its resources; it only had to sustain a single great defeat at sea for the final collapse to come.

Furthermore, the Athenian disaster in Sicily enabled the Spartans to put into practice the Archidamian theory of victory that called for securing allies who could help them match Athenian naval and economic strength. All of a sudden, everybody rushed to help Sparta.[41] Ships and money were finally forthcoming. The Peloponnesian League embarked on an ambitious ship-building program; a powerful contingent of fifty-five ships came from Sicily to assist the Peloponnesians, and the Spartans forcibly collected money from various states of central Greece.[42]

The real game-changer, though, was Persia. Around this time, the Spartans entered into valuable agreements with the Persian satraps Tissaphernes and Pharnabazus. Although the relationship with them was not strewn with roses (especially the one with Tissaphernes), it marked an important turning point in the war.[43] Finally, in 407 BCE, the Spartans found a staunch ally in the Persian court through Cyrus, son of the Persian king, who was given an extensive command in Asia Minor.[44] Persian money started flowing freely, enabling Sparta to make up for various naval reverses.[45] Archidamus' strategic design had finally been implemented and would be resolved at the Battle of Aegospotami.

The Athenians did try to hang on to their empire after the defeat in Sicily, rebuilding their fleet and reducing public expenses.[46] In addition to these traditional means of Athenian grand strategy, they also utilized diplomacy, attempting to win the Persians over to their side.[47] (Thucydides points out that both sides tried to enlist Persian support, even before the outbreak of the hostilities.)[48] However, although the Persians were willing to reach a compromise with the Athenians initially (for example, with the Treaty of Epilycus), following the Sicilian expedition, a Persian alliance could be secured— either by Sparta or by Athens—only at the price of abandoning the Greek cities of Asia Minor to Persian control. Since most of these cities were part of the Athenian Empire, it was easier for Sparta and more difficult for Athens to pay this price. Athenian and Persian interests were clearly conflicting and, as a result, Athens' attempt to coax the Persians was doomed. The continuation of Persian support to Sparta ensured that, ultimately, Athens could not avoid defeat.

Here we conclude the examination of the means utilized by the two competing grand strategies. One realizes that the employment of the various means was not a static process set in stone within one's grand strategy. Conversely, interaction with the opponent and adaptation was continuous, influencing and shaping the means employed.

The Issue of Legitimacy

International legitimacy played a central role in Sparta's grand strategy during the Peloponnesian War. It has already been demonstrated that the one-time allies of Athens had become tributary states and were looking forward to an opportunity to revolt. Athens' considerable weakness as far as international legitimacy was concerned constituted one of the advantages of Spartan grand strategy. Sparta had built a reputation of being an enemy of tyranny and had often overthrown tyrants of Greek cities, Athens included.[49] In addition, Sparta had been the leader of the Greeks against the Persians during the crucial, defensive phase of the Persian Wars. Consequently, at the outbreak of the Peloponnesian War, it was easy for the Spartans to present themselves as the liberators of the Greeks from Athenian oppression, thus gaining widespread support. According to Thucydides: 'Men's feelings inclined much more to the Spartans, especially as they proclaimed themselves the liberators of Hellas. No private or public effort that could help them in speech or action was omitted [...]'.[50]

One may recall that the Spartans had presented the Athenians with an ultimatum that demanded they give the Hellenes their freedom. Apart from a statement revealing Sparta's unlimited aims, this was also a shrewd propaganda ploy; Sparta had just gone on record demanding the liberation of Hellas and, most importantly, was willing to fight for that cause. This was a ploy the Spartans would skilfully use throughout the war. Brasidas, for instance, during his brilliant campaign in northern Greece, repeatedly emphasized his role as a liberator; this, coupled with his just and moderate behaviour, created a most favourable attitude towards Sparta in that area.

> [T]he present valor and conduct of Brasidas, which was known by experience to some, by hearsay to others, was what mainly created an esteem for the Spartans among the allies of Athens. He was the first [Spartan] who went out and showed himself so good a man at all points as to leave behind him the conviction that the rest were like him.[51]

Besides exploiting the lack of international legitimacy of the Athenian grand strategy, Sparta also tried to undermine Athens' domestic legitimacy. Apart from (or even in contrast to) the direct approach favoured by Archidamus, namely that of matching Athenian financial and naval strength, the Spartans also adopted an indirect approach to further their political objectives. Ravaging Attica constituted this indirect approach, which was aimed—apart from the economic and social cost that has already been mentioned—primarily against

THUCYDIDES ON STRATEGY

Athenian morale. Archidamus, showing a remarkable knowledge of the domestic structure of the enemy, tried during his expedition in Attica to exploit the internal divisions of the Athenians so as to undermine the internal legitimacy of the Athenian grand strategy.[52] His conduct during the first invasion is characteristic:

> The reason why Archidamus remained in order of battle at Acharnae during this incursion, instead of descending into the plain, is said to have been this. He hoped that the Athenians might possibly be tempted by the multitude of their youth and by their unprecedented preparedness for war to come out to battle and attempt to stop the devastation of their lands. Accordingly, as they had not met him at Eleusis or the Thriasian plain, he tried to see if they could be provoked to a sally by the spectacle of a camp at Acharnae. He thought the place itself a good position for encamping; and it seemed likely that such an important part of the state as the three thousand hoplites of the Acharnians would refuse to submit to the ruin of their property, and would force a battle on the rest of the citizens. On the other hand, should the Athenians not take the field during this incursion, he could then fearlessly ravage the plain in future invasions, and extend his advance up to the very walls of Athens. After the Acharnians had lost their own property they would be less willing to risk themselves for that of their neighbors; *and so there would be division in the Athenian counsels.* These were the motives of Archidamus for remaining at Acharnae.[53]

The blow to Athenian morale was tremendous. Given the erratic decision-making of the democratic Athenian polity, where everything depended on the shifting attitudes in the *Ecclesia*, the indirect approach of the Spartans might have been successful. In fact, Thucydides mentions that after the second Peloponnesian invasion and the total devastation of Attica, the Athenians sent ambassadors to Sparta to sue for peace. Spartan demands must have been excessive (or so they must have appeared to the Athenians) because the ambassadors did not achieve anything.[54]

However, Pericles did manage to persuade the Athenian public to stand by the unpopular strategy of withdrawing behind the walls. The Athenians remained true to this strategy and neither attempted to offer battle to the Peloponnesians[55] nor sued for peace again. Moreover, as shown in the previous chapter, Pericles counterattacked and tried to shape the domestic environment of Sparta in a way compatible with the Athenian interests: if the Spartans could be convinced that war against Athens was futile, the grand strategy that prescribed war with Athens would lose its domestic legitimacy and moderate leaders would emerge. This was in fact the way the two opponents reached peace after the tenth year of the war, when Pleistoanax became the key figure in Sparta.[56]

The two opponents, apart from attempting to shape the domestic environment of each other to serve their own interests, also tried to exploit the divisions that existed between democrats and oligarchs in most Greek cities.[57] However, Sparta was in the unique position to be able to exploit such divisions in Athens itself, while Athens enjoyed no similar opportunity.[58] The Spartans tried to capitalize on the oligarchic sentiments of some prominent circles in Athens: when an oligarchic coup took place in Athens in 411 BCE, the Athenian oligarchs tried to reach an agreement with Sparta; it is even possible that they might have conspired to lead the Peloponnesian army into the city.[59] This internal strife aggravated an already difficult strategic situation and, according to Thucydides, drove the final nail into Athens' coffin.[60]

To summarize, Sparta formulated a grand strategy of annihilation,[61] aimed at the destruction of the Athenian power and the dissolution of the Athenian Empire. The threat of a decisive land battle was central to the Spartan grand strategy, while at the same time there was a continuous effort to make the war as costly as possible for Athens. Great importance was placed on international legitimacy, with Sparta appearing as the liberator of the Greeks from the Athenian oppression, while at the same time the Spartans attempted to undermine the domestic legitimacy of the enemy's grand strategy. Finally, diplomacy played a decisive role, enabling Sparta to conclude an alliance with the Persians and thus balance the naval and financial power of Athens. Although the military dimension was clearly central to the Spartan grand strategy, none of the other dimensions were ignored. What remains is to examine how this grand strategy actually worked in practice.

THUCYDIDES ON STRATEGY

Athenian and Spartan Grand Strategies: Results

An evaluation of the Spartan grand strategy during the first phase of the Peloponnesian War—the so-called Archidamian War (431–21 BCE)—against the criteria outlined in Chapter One would reveal glaring weaknesses. We have repeatedly pointed out that, as far as the relation between means and ends was concerned, the Spartan grand strategy was highly problematic: the ends pursued were unattainable with the means at hand. Additionally, there was remarkable inefficiency in the use of the available resources. The Spartans neglected establishing a permanent fort in Attica, resorting to the comparatively ineffectual annual invasions instead, while their attempts to stir trouble within the Athenian Empire were either belated (Brasidas' expedition) or half-hearted (Alcidas' Mytilenean adventure). Finally, the mistake/mishap at Sphacteria was enough to deliver a crushing blow to Spartan grand strategy.

However, turning to its positive elements, the Spartan grand strategy possessed internal coherence, and performed well in terms to the external fit criterion: since Sparta could not conceivably be content with the status quo, it would sooner or later have to resort to compellence and, failing that, war. In fact, the difference between the policy recommendations of Sthenelaidas and Archidamus was specifically in the timing of the war. The Spartan grand strategy also fitted well with Sparta's domestic political environment; the idea of preventive war may nowadays be ethically unacceptable to the public opinion and decision-makers in quite a few countries,[62] but the Spartans of the fifth century BCE found nothing wrong with it.[63] Be that as it may, the positive aspects of the Spartan grand strategy were unable to salvage it; its weaknesses were so prominent, that it was bound to fail.

This was indeed what happened. The Spartans did invade Attica and wreak havoc in their path, but the Athenians did not submit. In the meantime, Athenian retaliation progressively escalated, culminating in the events of Pylos, Sphacteria and then Cythera. These events were enough to throw the conservative Spartan leadership off balance, make it abandon its bid for victory, and try to obtain peace at almost any cost. By turning against their primary opponent, the Athenians achieved decisive results. However, as was pointed out in the previous chapter, the Athenians misused their successes and refused to negotiate, thus missing the chance to extract substantial profits.

The Athenian refusal to negotiate made the Spartans embark upon two ploys they had not felt the need to use up to that point: first, the attempt to dismantle the Athenian empire in northern Greece (Brasidas' expedition); and second, the threat to establish a fort in Attica.[64] These developments did temper the Athenian attitude and bring about peace, albeit a favourable one to Athens.[65] The Spartans failed to achieve their war aim of overthrowing the status quo, did not dare resume aggression against Athens, and by and large ignored the grievances of their allies.[66] Ten years of futile war, accompanied by terrible setbacks both in terms of morale and material losses, was the price Sparta paid for the mismatch between means and ends in its grand strategy.

During the Peace of Nicias (421–15 BC), the most important development was the re-emergence of Argos as a player in the international arena, following the expiration in 421 BCE of the Thirty Years' Treaty with Sparta. According to Thucydides, 'the Argives were in a most flourishing condition, having taken no part in the war against Athens, but having on the contrary profited largely by their neutrality'.[67] Since Sparta had been forced to ignore the grievances of its allies during the conclusion of peace with Athens, a great number of these allies defected and sought security through an alliance with the Argives. Obviously, Argive power was on the rise. Moreover, Athens seized the opportunity to develop a 'continental strategy' by aiding Argos and its allies against Sparta. This proxy war represented an increase in the efficiency of the Athenian grand strategy, while Sparta could be harmed at limited expenditure to Athenian resources.

All of a sudden, the situation became critical for the Spartans, who found themselves in danger of losing control of the Peloponnese. To counter this threat, they once again resorted to the combination of the strategy of annihilation and direct approach. In a truly Napoleonic/Clausewitzian fashion, Sparta crushed the Argive army in the Battle of Mantinea in 418 BCE, regaining its pre-eminence in the Peloponnese.

> The imputations cast upon them [the Spartans] by the Hellenes at the time, whether of cowardice on account of the disaster in the island, or of mismanagement and slowness generally, were all wiped out by

this single action: fortune, it was thought, might have humbled them, but the men themselves were the same as ever.[68]

The Battle of Mantinea provides us with the opportunity to further elaborate on the concept of the decisive battle, which occupies a central position in the Napoleonic/Clausewitzian concept of war. It has been persuasively argued that this concept has its origins in ancient Greece, where in order to cause the greatest possible damage to the enemy, an offensive campaign had to be conducted during the limited period of the year when the wheat crops were vulnerable to arson. This, combined with the fact that the armies of the Greek city-states consisted of farmers that would soon have to return to their fields, made the ancient Greeks seek a quick settlement of the issue in a single, decisive battle.[69] Probably the most important of the decisive battles of the ancient Greeks was the Battle of Plataea, already discussed in Chapter One.

However, one significant problem with battles of this kind is that their outcome is often determined by minor details or unforeseen developments, thus exponentially increasing the risk incurred by those who resort to them.[70] Hence, many of history's decisive battles could have had different outcomes from the actual ones.[71] It is probable that the same could have happened in Mantinea, provided the Athenians and the Eleans had intervened in a timely manner on the Argives' side. In general, decisive battles are 'high-risk ventures'.[72]

The year 415 BCE proved to be the turning point of the war, when Athens embarked on an attempt to conquer Sicily. It was clear to the Spartans that Athens had overextended, and they were quick to perceive this window of opportunity.[73] Consequently, the Spartans abandoned their earlier caution and renewed hostilities in Greece while sending aid to Athens' enemies in Sicily. To a great extent, these actions contributed to the Athenian disaster there, which changed the whole course of the war. This way, Sparta showed its ability to exploit the enemy's mistakes.

An evaluation of the Spartan grand strategy during the final phase of the war, the so-called Decelean War (413–04 BCE), shows that the Spartans had learned their lesson. The new grand strategic design doubtless satisfied the external fit criterion, as indeed the previous one had done. However, marked improvements were registered regarding the relation between means and ends. After Sicily, it was clear that the balance of power had shifted, and this new balance made it possible for the Spartans to successfully pursue their initial aim of overthrowing the status quo.[74] Now, for the first time, the means at their disposal matched their policy objectives. It is interesting to note that the final phase of the war was chiefly naval, conducted in the eastern Aegean. In other words, the Spartans were now capable of challenging Athens in its own element and striking at the centre of gravity of the Athenian power, namely its navy. Thus, the indecisive clash between the 'lion' and the 'shark' turned into a clash between two 'sharks' in which decisive results could be obtained.

In addition, the Spartans came to display ruthless efficiency in using their assets. The fortification of Decelea showed that this time they meant business, while their very willingness to turn against the Athenian navy, the centre of gravity of the Athenian power, made it evident that they would not squander their resources in 'sideshows'.

A particular problem that arose in the Spartan grand strategy was that there was a fundamental incoherence between Sparta's proclaimed role as liberator of Greece and the Persian alliance, which effectively meant abandonment of the Greeks of Asia Minor to Persian control. This would lead to friction between the Spartans and the Asian Minor Greeks, but the Spartans somehow managed to keep the issue subdued until the end of the war.[75]

Finally Spartan grand strategy displayed remarkable durability to mistakes/mishaps. The Peloponnesian navy sustained severe defeats at Cyzicus in 410 BCE and Arginusae in 406 BCE (in actual fact, at Cyzicus it was completely annihilated).[76] However, Persian aid enabled the Spartans to make good these losses. Consequently, the situation augured well for Sparta.

The Athenians, for their own part, immediately understood that they had to cut down on spending, maintain a decent navy, and secure the allegiance of their allies.[77] In all this, they did quite well. Thus, the Athenian grand strategy post-Sicily performed well in terms of efficiency. It also fitted well with the highly threatening international political environment and not contrary to the domestic one, while at the same time was internally coherent. As a result, though the greater part of the empire had gone for good, Athens managed to preserve some important places like Samos and Euboea, while inflicting severe defeats on the Peloponnesian navy at Cyzicus and Arginusae.

These naval battles provide an illuminating insight into the interaction between the various levels of strategy. Although the situation at the levels of grand and military strategy was clearly favourable to Sparta, the Spartans still could not achieve their objectives due to persistent failure at lower levels. This becomes even more striking if one considers that the Peloponnesian navy had come to enjoy an advantage at the tactical level. High pay, provided by Persian funds, had attracted the best seamen to the Peloponnesian navy, while the Athenians, having lost the elite of their naval personnel in Sicily, were increasingly dependent on raw recruits. Therefore, the Peloponnesian ships were 'sailing better' than the Athenian ones.[78] Nevertheless, until the arrival of Lysander, the Spartan admirals were plainly incompetent in the handling of fleets. Thus, ineptitude at the operational level blunted both grand strategic dexterity and tactical excellence.

What the Spartan admirals could not achieve, the Athenian strategic culture handed over to Sparta on a silver plate. It seems that, in spite of the difficult strategic situation, the Athenian aims were once again unlimited. This is evident since Athens twice rejected Spartan peace proposals. The story of these proposals is highly interesting, and came after Cyzicus and Arginusae, respectively. Both events called for recognition of the status quo as it stood at the time: Athenian recognition of the losses their empire had sustained and abandonment of the forts each combatant had on the other's territory, namely Pylos and Decelea.[79] In fact, at the time of the second peace proposal, the Athenians had abandoned their fort in Pylos; in other words, the Spartans were unilaterally willing to abandon Decelea, something that is highly indicative of the conservatism of the Spartan political leadership. In the same vein, Athens' rejection of the Spartan proposals speaks volumes of the Athenian adventurism.

Actually, as far as Athens was concerned, everything was hanging by a thread; one major defeat of the Athenian navy would spell the end. In other words, Athenian grand strategy had extremely low durability to mistakes/mishaps. The day of reckoning came when the Spartan admiral Lysander captured the Athenian fleet at Aegospotami in 405 BCE.[80] Athens was now blockaded by sea as well as by land. It capitulated the following year, signifying the final triumph of Spartan grand strategy.

The terms imposed on Athens were relatively generous: the long walls and the fortifications at Piraeus would be destroyed, Athens would retain no more than twelve ships, receive back the oligarchic fugitives, and join the Peloponnesian League. Interestingly enough, despite Corinthian and Theban outcries for the total destruction of Athens, the Spartans did nothing of the sort. Clearly, with the Athenian threat eliminated, Athens could be a useful tool in Spartan hands for manipulating the balance of power in Greece.[81]

5

THUCYDIDES AND STRATEGY IN PERSPECTIVE

Introduction

In this chapter, we shall proceed to review the contribution made by Thucydides to the study of strategy, and we shall examine the conclusions that can be drawn from his analysis and their possible relevance today. In addition, we will trace how some key strategic concepts that were first analysed by Thucydides have developed through history and how they are likely to endure into the future. We open the chapter with an examination of some general conclusions and then we will proceed to explore how the analysis of Thucydides can shed light on the determinants of a grand strategy. We will then explore the concepts of the strategy of annihilation and exhaustion, before finally examining the enduring theme of underestimating the enemy.

Athenian and Spartan Grand Strategies: Conclusions

Thucydides asserts that the Athenians lost a war they could have easily won, since the balance of power was in their favour.[1] Obviously, Athens courted defeat by making some flawed strategic choices. On the contrary, Sparta, despite the initial unfavourable balance of power, managed to achieve total victory by eventually choosing a strategy that maximized its advantages and minimized those of its opponent. Thus, the choice of strategy can be seen to make the difference between victory and defeat.[2]

The text of Thucydides contains the first detailed presentation of a theory of grand strategy. This has been acknowledged, but only insofar as the Periclean grand strategy is concerned. In effect, Pericles is credited with the first detailed grand strategic plan in history, and Thucydides with the presentation of this plan.[3] However, this only tells half of the story. Thucydides did not present only one but two detailed grand strategic designs; moreover, these two strategies clashed with each other. Athens was not alone in having formulated a grand strategy; Sparta had its own. The task facing Athens was twofold: first, Athens had to implement its own grand strategy; secondly, it had to contend with the Spartan grand strategy. Thucydides was fully cognizant that strategic implementation involves the interaction of two opposing wills—that is, the horizontal dimension of strategy.

The fact that this aspect of Thucydides' analysis has not been adequately understood is reflected in the publicity that some of the protagonists of his *History* have received. Pericles has rightly been praised for the grand strategy he designed and formulated, and has been acknowledged as one of the greatest statesmen and military leaders in history.[4] Archidamus, meanwhile, a remarkable general and statesman in his own right, has been ignored by contemporary scholars.[5] This is unwarranted, since he too had a profound understanding of strategy, as evidenced by both his outline of a theory of victory in dealing with a maritime power and the ingenuous way in which he used coercive diplomacy. It was Sparta's loss that Archidamus had less influence on the formulation of Spartan grand strategy than Pericles had on the formulation of the Athenian one. Whereas Pericles managed to achieve the domestic legitimacy of his grand strategy, Archidamus could not achieve the same for the grand strategy he had contemplated.

Another conclusion is that a grand strategy must adapt to the existing balance of power. It has been acknowledged that strategy is always addressed against one or more opponents. The means that can be used against an opponent are determined by the relative balance of power with the said opponent; if the means are lacking, certain ends are beyond achievement and must not be pursued. The above analysis

THUCYDIDES AND STRATEGY IN PERSPECTIVE

demonstrates that both Sparta and Athens at certain instances misjudged the balance of power, setting policy objectives (dissolution of the Athenian Empire; conquest of Sicily; recovery of the Athenian Empire) that they could not achieve with the means available to them. This overextension virtually condemned their grand strategies to failure, despite the fact that those grand strategies scored well when measured against the other criteria of evaluation. On the contrary, grand strategies that set objectives not at variance with the balance of power (for example, Periclean grand strategy, Spartan grand strategy after the Sicilian expedition) were generally successful (see Table 5.1).

Table 5.1: Evaluation of Athenian and Spartan Grand Strategies

Grand Strategy/ Criteria	External Fit	Means-Ends	Efficiency	Internal Coherence	Durability to Mistakes	Result
Athens, 431–421	+	+	+	+	+	Success
Sparta, 431–421	+	–	–	+	–	Failure
Athens, 415–404	+	–	+	+	–	Failure
Sparta, 415–404	+	+	+	–	+	Success

Nevertheless, an analysis of Athenian and Spartan grand strategies can still offer valuable lessons to the modern strategist. The increasing relevance of the Periclean grand strategy of exhaustion will become evident in ensuing sections. As to the Spartan grand strategy, it is an excellent example of the Clausewitzian approach to war, evidencing direct approach and destruction of the armed forces of the enemy. Archidamus knew, and the rest of the Spartan political leadership eventually came to understand, that decisive results could be obtained only by turning against Athens and focusing on the strongest point of the Athenian power structure (what Clausewitz called the 'centre of gravity'). In this case, this was the Athenian navy. The indirect approach of ravaging Attica could not enable Sparta to strike at this centre of gravity; only an alliance with Persia made this possible. The fact that the Spartans consciously turned against the centre of gravity of the Athenian power as soon as they obtained the means necessary to strike against it demonstrates that they had a clear belief in the advantages of the direct approach. Interestingly enough, Athenian grand strategy also demonstrates the merits of the direct approach. It was only by hurting Sparta itself (at Pylos, Sphacteria and Cythera) that Athens could secure its objectives, while at the last stage of the war, it was only by striking at the Peloponnesian navy that the Athenians could hope to beat off the grave threat facing their city and salvage what they could from their empire.

Sir Basil Liddell Hart has argued extensively in favour of the indirect approach (see Chapter One), going so far as attributing virtually every successful military action to the adoption of an indirect approach, and every unsuccessful one to the adoption of a direct approach.[6] Numerous are the criticisms levied against his theory,[7] and one might think that by criticizing it we are flogging a dead horse. Conversely, our criticism intends to highlight the very merits of Liddell Hart's thesis. One of the weaknesses of his argument is that he usually neglects the interplay between the various levels of strategy, within which he contrasts the direct and indirect approach. Thus, he cites the fact that the indirect approach was employed at the tactical or the operational level as evidence for the superiority of this approach, while at the same time ignoring the fact that the approach adopted at the strategic level was direct. For instance, he has called Lysander's victory at Aegospotami 'a tactical indirect approach at sea, which was itself the sequel to a fresh indirect approach in grand strategy'.[8] The second part of this statement is, of course, mistaken; we have repeatedly pointed out that Sparta's turn against the Athenian navy is a characteristic case of the direct approach. Demonstrably, Liddell Hart's attempt to 'usurp' all the military successes in history on behalf of the indirect approach seriously weakens his analysis. However, the first part of the statement is correct: Lysander did use an indirect approach at the tactical level.[9] Generally, the grand strategies of Sparta and Athens seem to provide arguments in favour of a direct approach at the levels of grand strategy and military strategy, whereas an indirect approach may be used (and in fact may even be advisable) at lower levels, namely at the operational or tactical levels of war.

THUCYDIDES AND STRATEGY IN PERSPECTIVE

The Determinants of Grand Strategy

An examination of Thucydides' text offers valuable insights regarding the determinants of grand strategy. It appears that one can find in the analysis of Thucydides at least the rudiments of a theory of the 'causes' of grand strategic choices, based on a combination of both structural and perceptual factors.[10]

It has been pointed out that grand strategy aims at producing security for the state (see Chapter One). Consequently, the formulation of a state's grand strategy is bound to be determined by two factors: first, the balance of power between the state and its strategic opponent; and secondly, the severity of the threats posed to the state by its strategic opponent. Thucydides was clearly cognizant of this, paying great attention to both power and fear.[11] These two factors will be examined in turn.

Obviously, an assessment of the existing balance of power with a strategic opponent is an important determinant of a state's grand strategy. However, apart from appraising the existing balance of power, states also attempt to forecast what the future balance of power will resemble. As such, their appraisal of the trends in the distribution of power is highly likely to influence their choices at the grand strategic level. As a general principle, they will try to arrest and reverse unfavourable trends while attempting to accelerate and exploit favourable ones. In other words, the trends in the distribution of power (i.e. the dynamic analysis of the balance of power) are another determining factor in deciding a state's grand strategy, and can be seen as being at least as important as the current distribution of power (i.e. the static analysis of the balance of power).[12]

The combination of static and dynamic analyses of the balance of power may lead to two possible assessments: the state growing stronger relative to its strategic opponent; or the state growing weaker relative to its strategic opponent.[13] These two possibilities form the 'structural background' against which a state's grand strategy is formulated.

A warning is in order here. Although we have found it convenient to say that states 'examine' the balance of power, it is obviously the political leadership of a state that makes that appraisal; hence one might argue that what is relevant is not the structure of the international system per se, but how the political leadership perceives it to be. Without examining at length the complex issues of perception in international politics,[14] let us point out that although perceptions of the balance of power are significant and often feature within the analysis of Thucydides (for example, the Spartans' belief in a quick victory prior to the war), structural realities cannot be ignored or misperceived for long. As both the Spartans and the Athenians discovered, the actual balance of power will eventually make itself felt.

The other determinant of grand strategy—the threat posed by a state's strategic opponent—is primarily perceptual in character. What chiefly matters here is how a state's political leadership perceives the hostile intentions of its rival. It has been pointed out that the very issue of treating separately the capabilities and the intentions of a strategic opponent implies we feel safe enough to do so; if the capabilities of a specific strategic opponent appear considerable, states normally do not pause to analyse its intentions.[15] Be that as it may, foreign intentions, as they are perceived by a state's political leadership, do matter.[16] For instance, although Egypt is more powerful than Syria, Israeli decision-makers have for decades been much more concerned about the latter; this is because Egypt is perceived as relatively benign, whereas Syria is perceived as threatening. There have even been instances where threat perception was almost completely divorced from the other side's capabilities. Thus, by 146 BCE, Carthage could by no stretch of the imagination possess the capability to challenge Rome. Defeated in three wars in succession, the once mighty Carthaginian Empire had been reduced to a tributary state. Nevertheless, the Romans still felt threatened, a perception that resulted in the total destruction of Carthage, the extermination of its adult male population, and the enslavement of its women and children.[17]

The emphasis placed upon the perception of threat does not mean that foreign threats are merely a matter of perception, lacking any foundation. Still, while the balance of power is bound to become apparent sooner or later, perceived threats may or may not actually exist—and even if they do, they may not necessarily materialize. That is why primary importance is given to how a political leadership perceives foreign intentions; regardless of the actual Athenian intentions, the Spartans felt threatened, and that is what mattered. Still, it is clear that a state is better off if the threat perceptions of its political leadership correspond to reality, as erroneous threat perception results either in waste of resources and unnecessary provocation (if one is making preparations to ward off non-existent threats) or strategic surprise (if an unanticipated threat materializes).[18]

Since strategy by definition deals with situations of actual or potential conflict, it has to estimate the degree of threat posed by various strategic opponents. Depending on the extent of the national interests threatened, the impact of a foreign threat may be perceived as high or low. These two possibilities constitute the perceptual background of grand strategy. This background is more volatile than the structural one, as perceptions change more quickly than capabilities. This occasionally results in violent fluctuations in a state's grand strategy. For instance, the sudden abandonment of appeasement by Great Britain after Hitler occupied Prague in March 1939 came as a result of a shift in the perception of the threat posed by Germany.[19]

The combination of the structural and perceptual determinants of grand strategy is given in the following matrix (see Table 5.2).

Table 5.2: The Determinants of Grand Strategy

		Balance of Power	
		Rise	Decline
Threat	High	I	III
	Low	II	IV

I: Expansion, Intransigence
II: Expansion, Benevolence
III: Buck-Passing or Balancing or Preventive War or Appeasement
IV: Buck-Passing or Appeasement

This framework can be applied to strategic relationships among any powers, irrespective of their size and power.[20] In the latter case, however, given that the power gap is normally huge, differential rates of growth often have little relevance, even if they favour the small power. For the framework to be applicable, unequal growth must be significant enough to influence bilateral relations, without necessarily threatening to alter the overall balance of power. Thus, although Athens had no chance of overpowering the Persian Empire, the relative growth of its power enabled it to gain the upper hand over Persia in the western coast of Asia Minor and the waters west of Pamphylia (see Map 2). Let us now examine the grand strategic outcomes of the combination of the balance of power and the threat perceptions of the political leadership.

Intransigent and Benevolent Expansion

It has been persuasively argued that whenever a state's power rises compared with that of its strategic opponent, that state will seek to change the status quo until the costs of doing so exceed the benefits, at which stage an equilibrium will be reached. This does not necessarily imply that the rising powers are necessarily intent on territorial expansion; the change of the status quo may take various other forms, such as extension of one's influence (for example, the enlargement of NATO) or establishing advantageous rules in the international economy (such as British and later U.S. emphasis on free trade).[21] Occasionally, it takes some time before the relative rise of a state's power versus a strategic opponent produces a significant enough shift in the bilateral balance. In such cases, we may expect the rising state to basically mark time, proceed cautiously in relation to that particular strategic opponent, and instead concentrate its efforts on other, more manageable strategic opponents.

Thus, the structural determinant of grand strategy would prompt a rising state to expand until it reaches a point of diminishing returns,[22] irrespective of the threatening environment that it finds itself in. Nevertheless, the intensity of the threats faced by that state is bound to influence the pattern of its expansion. Rising powers facing high threats have no incentive to compromise, but as a rule will try to weaken the source of a threat as much as possible or eliminate it altogether. On the other hand, a rising power operating in a low-threat environment normally does not feel the need to exert itself. For certain, rising powers facing low threats may prove as expansionist as any, especially if they feel the need to restore a favourable status quo *ante* or are simply bent on achieving 'greatness'. Nevertheless, the threat environment does make a difference.[23]

THUCYDIDES AND STRATEGY IN PERSPECTIVE

Buck-Passing, Balancing, Preventive War, and Appeasement

The greatest challenge to a grand strategy comes when a state is growing weaker relative to its strategic opponent. In these cases, the adverse shift in the balance of power is a harsh reality that requires remedial action. Once again, the perceptual determinant of grand strategy plays a key role. While rising states are likely to expand irrespective of what the threat environment looks like, the grand strategic choices of declining states depend heavily on the magnitude of the threats perceived by their political leadership. To begin with, the preferred course of declining states against rising strategic opponents, regardless of the magnitude of the perceived threat, is buck-passing (i.e. trying to get another state or states to check the rising power while they remain on the sidelines).[24] However, buck-passing is often impossible (e.g. in a bipolar international system), and even when it is possible, it may not guarantee the desired outcome.

Declining states facing low threats have a rather strong incentive to appease their strategic opponents, with appeasement defined as neutralization or at least reduction of a threat by concessions.[25] In this particular instance, assuming that buck-passing is impossible or ineffective, this is the least risky as well as the least costly grand strategic course. An intransigent policy may simply provoke the rising adversary to adopt a similar stance and possibly increase their demands. In the same vein, the low threat posed by the strategic opponent means that appeasing them is not likely to have any dire consequences in the future (see, for instance, Hans Morgenthau's classic recommendation to compromise on one's peripheral interests and staunchly defend the core ones).[26] On the contrary, compromise reached in a low-threat environment may lay the seeds for bilateral cooperation.[27]

Thus, when a declining state faces low threats, appeasement seems to provide a comparatively risk-free and cost-free grand strategic choice. However, events are much more difficult when a declining state faces high threats; in other words, times are hard when vital national interests are perceived to be under threat, and the state's power is diminishing relative to that of its strategic opponent. In this case, appeasement does not provide an easy solution, since states (particularly great powers) normally do not compromise on what they regard as their vital national interests.

Normally, the preferred course of action is the aforementioned buck-passing. Assuming that buck-passing is impossible or ineffective, another course of action is balancing behaviour. As was pointed out in Chapter Three, balancing can be done either by utilizing power from abroad (external balancing) and/or by mobilizing and exploiting domestic resources (internal balancing). Internal reform with a view to the more effective utilization of available means has been a popular course of action for old and declining empires. On the other hand, external balancing is chiefly done through alliances, either formal or informal. As a rule, a declining power welcomes new allies, whereas a rising power is generally in lesser need of them.

Buck-passing and balancing behaviour are not the only grand strategic options available to a declining state facing high threats. Preventive war is another option as well, provided that the declining state still perceives itself as being stronger than its strategic opponent (see Chapter One). It may or may not actually be stronger, but in this case, it is perception that matters. One may recall that prevention entails fighting early and creating a *fait accompli* while it is still possible—that is, before the balance of power tips in any decisive way and the strategic opponent becomes strong enough to be threatening. A grand strategy of preventive war implies the choice of the lesser evil: war today against destruction tomorrow.

Nevertheless, a declining state facing high threats may perceive itself so irreparably weak relative to its strategic opponent that neither preventive war nor balancing are an option. The balance can no longer be redressed, and the power gap grows to the detriment of the declining state. In such instances, appeasement is probably the most rational option: the declining state is inclined to concede what, in view of the increasing power differential, it is likely to lose anyway. Obviously, appeasement in a high-threat environment as a rule entails higher costs than in a low-threat one; hence, it is encountered less often as a grand strategic option. Still, as Thucydides made apparent in the Melian Dialogue, concessions, however huge, are preferable to destruction.[28]

THUCYDIDES AND STRATEGY IN PERSPECTIVE

Thucydides and the Determinants of Grand Strategy

Returning to the analysis of Thucydides, an examination of the turning strategic points of the period 479–04 BCE will confirm what has been said so far (see Table 5.3).

To begin with, the expansion of the Greek cities and later Athens at Persian expense fits with the profile of what rising states facing high threats are likely to do. The Persian invasion united the Greek city-states and persuaded them to effect a massive military (chiefly naval) build-up. On the other hand, as far as the Persians were concerned, the disaster in Greece was an enormous blow for two reasons: first, it led to a significant diminution of military power, since a considerable part of the Persian armed forces was decimated;[29] secondly, the Persian king suffered a great loss of prestige that weakened his authority and destabilized his rule.[30] Thus, Persia was unmistakably in decline compared with the Greek cities in general and Athens in particular. As outlined in Chapter Two, the Persians did attempt to check their decline and stave off the high threat by resorting to a military build-up, but this attempt at internal balancing failed.[31]

The Athenian expansion in Greece proper constitutes another example of a rising power facing high threats and, as a result, expanding without compromise. The Athenians knew that the creation and expansion of their empire was not likely to gain them anything but 'immoderate hostility' among the other Greeks. However, since Athenian power was in ascendancy, Athens could beat off the challenges and continue its expansion.

The Spartan resort to preventive war around 460 BCE is also consistent with what we have come to expect of a declining power perceiving a high threat, having no opportunity of buck-passing (that is, the bipolar ancient Greek city-state system), but also believing it is still strong enough to eliminate the source of threat by force. However, as was seen in Chapter Two, Sparta was unable to check Athenian expansion (such as the Athenian conquest of Boeotia and Aegina) and equilibrium was reached, resulting in the Five Years' Peace.[32]

In the meantime, as the reverses in Egypt and later in Cyprus demonstrated, Athenian expansion vis-à-vis Persia had reached the point of diminishing returns. The interaction between expansion to the

THUCYDIDES ON STRATEGY

Table 5.3: Strategic Turning Points, 479–404 BCE.

Date	Event	Strategic Player(s)	Balance of Power Threat	Grand Strategic Choice(s)
479	Greeks defeat Persians at Plataea and Mycale.	Greek cities–Persia	RH–DH	Expansion–Balancing
478	Athenians assume Greek leadership. Creation of the Delian League.	Athens	RH	Expansion
466	Battle of Eurymedon—Persians routed.	Athens	RH	Expansion
ca. 460	Athenian expedition to Cyprus and Egypt.	Athens–Persia	RH–DH	Expansion–Balancing
ca. 460	Megara joins Athenian Alliance.	Athens	RH	Expansion
ca. 460	Outbreak of First Peloponnesian War.	Sparta–Athens	DH–RH	Preventive War–Expansion
457	Athenian conquest of Boeotia and Aegina.	Athens	RH	Expansion
ca. 454	Athenian expeditionary corps destroyed in Egypt.	Athens	RH	Diminishing Returns
451	Five Years' Peace.	Athens–Sparta	RH–DH	Equilibrium
449	Peace of Callias.	Athens–Persia	RH–DH	Equilibrium
446	Athenian defeat at Corneia. Megarian revolt.	Athens	RH	Diminishing Returns
446	Thirty Years' Peace.	Athens–Sparta	RH–DH	Equilibrium
431	Outbreak of the Peloponnesian War.	Sparta–Athens	DH–RH	Preventive War–Intransigence
425	Battle of Sphacteria–Spartans surrender. Spartan peace offer.	Athens–Sparta	RH–DH	Expansion–Appeasement
424	Battle of Deliurn–Athenians defeated.	Athens	RH	Diminishing Returns

THUCYDIDES AND STRATEGY IN PERSPECTIVE

423	Treaty between Athens and Persia.	Athens–Persia	RL–DL	Benevolence–Appeasement. Cooperation
422	Battle of Amphipolis–Athenians defeated.	Athens	RH	Diminishing Returns
421	Peace of Nicias.	Athens–Sparta	RH–DH	Equilibrium
418	Battle of Mantinea–Spartans defeat the Argives.	Argos–Sparta	RH–DH	Expansion–Balancing
415	Athenian Expedition to Sicily.	Athens–Syracuse	RL–DH	Expansion–Balancing
413	Athenian expeditionary corps destroyed in Sicily.	Athens	RH	Diminishing Returns
412–411	Alliance between Sparta and Persia.	Sparta–Athens Persia–Athens	RH–DH RL–DH	Expansion–Balancing. Expansion–Appeasement
410	Battle of Cyzicus–Spartans annihilated. Spartan peace offer.	Sparta	RH	Diminishing Returns
407	Massive Persian help to Sparta.	Persia	RL	Expansion
406	Battle of Arginusae–Spartans defeated. Spartan peace offer.	Sparta	RH	Diminishing Returns
405	Battle of Aegospotami–Athenian fleet captured.	Sparta	RH	Expansion
404	Athens capitulates. Spartans do not destroy the city.	Sparta	RL	Expansion, Benevolence

R=Rising Power D=Declining Power H=High Threat L=Low Threat

point of diminishing returns on the one hand and balancing on the other resulted in the equilibrium reflected in the Peace of Callias.

The same process was repeated in mainland Greece, after the Athenian mishaps in Coronea and Megara in 446 BCE. Of course, Athens had safely retained its empire and consequently was still growing stronger relative to its Greek adversaries, but further expansion on land was simply unprofitable, or even unattainable. This was the state of affairs codified in the Thirty Years' Peace.[33]

The process of Sparta's resorting to preventive war in 431 BCE has been the subject of detailed analysis earlier in this book: declining in power and perceiving a high threat, but considering the combination of itself and its allies stronger than Athens, Sparta chose war (see Chapters Three and Four). The Athenian reaction is interesting, since it constitutes the only example in Thucydides' analysis where a rising power did not resort to outright territorial expansion and remained content to maintain the status quo. In all probability, Pericles estimated that Athens, the growth of its power notwithstanding, was not strong enough to engage in profitable expansion, especially since, as was pointed out in Chapter Three, the targets of this expansion could be located only in the mainland. In other words, in Pericles' mind, the equilibrium of 446/5 BCE had not shifted decisively in Athens' favour. However, Athens retained the intransigence expected from rising powers facing high threats, as was shown by its rejection of even minor concessions to the Spartans.[34]

The Battle of Sphacteria made it evident to both belligerents that Athens could now pursue an expansionist grand strategy. The Spartans accepted the fact that their attempt to check the growth of Athenian power had failed and that the situation could only worsen. Hence, willing to make huge concessions, they resorted to appeasement (see Chapter Three). However, by now the Athenians were even more intransigent and refused to enter into any negotiations.[35]

The point of diminishing returns for Athenian expansion was not far off, however. The defeats at Delium and Amphipolis drove the point home, and the Peace of Nicias codified the equilibrium reached between the two belligerents.[36]

The treaty between Athens and Persia in 423 BCE provides the only instance in Thucydides' analysis where both parties in the strategic relationship perceived the other side as presenting a low threat. Both Athens and Persia had more important things to do than attack each other, and both understood that. This treaty may be interpreted as displaying benevolence on the part of the Athenians, who satisfied themselves with the gains registered with the Peace of Callias, and appeasement on the part of the Persian king, who acquiesced to those gains. Obviously, once this issue was settled, a genuine pattern of bilateral cooperation emerged.

The grand strategy of Argos after 421 BCE and the subsequent defection of some of Sparta's allies to Argos provide yet another example of a rising power facing high threats from a traditional rival and expanding at its direct expense.[37] In defence, Sparta attempted to check the decline by securing the loyalty of its remaining allies and enlisting their support against Argos. The outcome of the Battle of Mantinea bears testimony to the success of the Spartan grand strategy.[38]

The Athenian expedition in Sicily proves that a rising power will tend to expand, even when faced with a low threat from its strategic opponent. The Athenians did not embark on the Sicilian expedition because they felt threatened by the Syracusans, but simply because they wanted to conquer Sicily (see Chapter Four and the discussion below). The Syracusans, in response, resorted to both internal and external balancing by making war preparations and enlisting Spartan support, respectively. The situation soon became critical for the Athenians, as their enormous expeditionary corps in Sicily found itself under serious threat, while they were simultaneously facing renewed and efficiently conducted hostilities in Greece proper. The annihilation of the Athenian expeditionary corps in Sicily showed that, once again, Athenian expansion had reached the point of diminishing returns.[39] However, this time, in contrast to what had happened previously, Athens could not recover and was condemned to permanent decline in contrast to its two great strategic opponents—Sparta and Persia.

Spartan grand strategy after Sicily completely conforms to the expectations of what a rising power is likely to do when perceiving high threats, namely expand uncompromisingly until it reaches the point of diminishing returns. In the mind of the Spartan political leadership, this point was reached twice: first after the Battle of

Cyzicus and then after the Battle of Arginusae. As a result, the Spartans came up with peace proposals to codify the existing equilibrium (see Chapter Four).

Persian grand strategy after Sicily presents the second instance in Thucydides' analysis where a rising power facing low threats chooses to expand.[40] In their quest to restore the status quo *ante* in western Asia Minor, the Persians were intransigent in their demand for re-incorporation of the Greek cities of the area to the Persian Empire.[41]

Athens responded differently to each of the two challenges it faced. The Spartan challenge was met with an Athenian attempt at internal balancing; in the face of a high threat, the declining state was not prepared to compromise.[42] However, in relation to Persia, Athens was willing to compromise. As was highlighted in the previous chapter, the Athenians after Sicily made strenuous efforts to win the Persians over to their side. Those efforts were certain to entail some concessions. In other words, since Athens could not hope to improve its power position vis-à-vis Persia, it resorted to appeasement.[43] The threat posed by Persia was high and appeasement was bound to entail important concessions, but these paled in comparison to the Spartan threat and its possible consequences; while the Persians only wanted the Greek cities of Ionia, the Spartans and their allies could conceivably go as far as razing Athens to the ground and selling its inhabitants to slavery.

Finally, the relatively generous terms Sparta granted Athens in 404 BCE also conform to the pattern of 'benevolent expansion' expected from rising states facing low threats. The elimination of the Athenian threat meant that, although the Spartans would definitely expand at Athens' expense, they would also exercise some restraint. Much like the United States after 1945, Sparta had switched to post-war mode and devoted itself to concerns other than Athens.

Applicability of the Theory

The above demonstrates that Thucydides' analysis of the determinants of grand strategy is able to explain the events of the period (479–04 BCE). But is this analysis universally applicable? A number of other examples would seem to validate it. Let us begin with the grand strategic outcomes of a rising power within a high- and low-threat environment, namely intransigent and benevolent expansion respectively. The previously cited example of Rome vis-à-vis Carthage shows what a rising power can do when perceiving high threats; Great Britain from the end of the seventeenth century until the defeat of Napoleon offers another such example. The British responded to this strategic situation—favourable trends in the distribution of power plus high threats—by ruthlessly expanding at the expense of the sources from where the threat emanated, first the Netherlands and then France. Hard-nosed and aggressive, the British had little taste for compromise. The War of American Independence (1775–83) signified the fact that British expansion had reached the point of diminishing returns, but with the advent of the Industrial Revolution, British power continued to rise. After a long struggle with a resurgent France, Great Britain finally emerged victorious, powerful and safe in 1815. A long period of intransigent expansion was crowned with success.

At this stage, a remarkable change took place. Since it took some time for other countries to match the developments of Great Britain during the Industrial Revolution, British power kept growing compared with that of the other great European states for some time after Waterloo. Operating in a low-threat environment, British grand strategy lost the element of intransigence that characterized it up to that point. Great Britain continued to effect favourable changes on the status quo, such as the liberalization of international trade, but at the same time showed greater willingness to compromise: the British ceased to usurp the colonies of the other European powers while playing a conciliatory role in the Concert of Europe.[44]

The United States offers a similar example of a rising state that expands yet modifies the pattern of its expansion according to the intensity of the threat it faces. Americans have repeatedly proved ferocious strategic adversaries, bent on securing the unconditional surrender of their defeated opponents. If the American public can be persuaded that a situation is threatening enough, the United States is able to exert tremendous effort to achieve unlimited objectives. The fate of Imperial and Nazi Germany, as well as that of Japan, testify to that. However, as soon as the source of threat was eliminated, American grand strategy adopted a benevolent stance. Although the

Americans generally continued to change the status quo (for example, the 'recasting' of the domestic structures of West Germany and Japan after 1945), they dropped their earlier intransigence and proved magnanimous victors.

The evolution of American strategic rivalry with Moscow seems to confirm this pattern. By the second half of the 1980s, the United States clearly had the upper hand over the Soviet Union. The existence of nuclear weapons notwithstanding, Washington missed no chance to obliterate the Soviet threat. Unequal arms' control agreements, intensive propaganda aimed at delegitimizing the Soviet model, and the encouragement of secession of the non-Russian nationalities were all employed to this end. However, after the Soviet collapse, the U.S. stance towards the newfangled Russia became markedly different. Even so, American expansion did not stop: NATO enlargement, including the Baltic states, and military action in the Balkans, coupled with increased American presence in other former Soviet territories, testified to this. However, this went side by side with financial assistance to Russia, plus recognition of certain Russian interests, such as Moscow's right to combat secession within the Russian Federation. Obviously, what made the difference was the low threat posed by Russia, at least until the late 2000s. By then, Russia's authoritarian consolidation under Vladimir Putin had led to an increase of its power relative to the 1990s. In turn, this has made Russia adopt the behaviour of a rising power facing supposedly high threats, i.e. intransigent expansion, such as the wars in Georgia and Ukraine. U.S. perceptions oscillate between considering Russia either a high threat (the Biden administration) or a low threat (the Trump administrations, especially the second one). In the former case, Washington opted for balancing; in the latter case, U.S. policy looks rather like appeasement, aiming at concentrating force and effort against who it perceives to be the main threat—China.[45]

Concerning buck-passing as a response to declining power, regardless of the magnitude of the perceived threat, the response of both Great Britain and the United States to the rise of Germany before both world wars provides a characteristic example. In each case, the 'offshore balancers' tried to shift the burden of checking Germany to others (i.e. France and Russia/Soviet Union), committing themselves to balancing Germany only when the buck-catchers failed to accomplish their mission.[46]

Regarding appeasement as the outcome of declining power in a low-threat environment, the grand strategies of a number of declining great powers help illustrate the point. One of the earliest examples is that of Spain and France at the turn of the seventeenth century. Spain was a great power of long standing, whose hegemony in Europe and tremendous expansion overseas endured for more than a century, beginning in the 1490s and formally ending with the Treaty of the Pyrenees in 1659. Although Spanish arms had repeatedly proved victorious against the French during that period, by the mid-seventeenth century France had become stronger than its opponent. However, after a series of victories and territorial acquisitions at Spain's expense, the French turned their attention elsewhere and stopped posing as grave a threat to Spain. The impact of this course of action was understood in Madrid, and thereafter the Spaniards changed strategic course vis-à-vis France, becoming a virtual French satellite (for example, the accession of a French prince on the Spanish throne in 1700).[47]

British policy towards the United States at the turn of the nineteenth century constitutes an important case of a declining state choosing to appease a strategic opponent deemed to present a low threat. From the 1890s, the burgeoning United States started following an assertive if not high-handed policy towards British interests on the American continent. The Americans, invoking the Monroe Doctrine, insisted on mediating in a border dispute between Venezuela and British Guyana, effected a favourable modification of the border between Canada and Alaska, and established exclusive control over the Panama Canal Zone, which they then fortified, despite an earlier Anglo-American treaty (1850) having called for common construction and control. The British chose to accede to the American demands on these issues, ignoring the American naval expansion program, and in due course made a 'complete strategic abandonment' of Central and North America, leaving Canada defenceless in the process.[48] Apart from a mystical belief in 'Anglo-American racial brotherhood' that had been prevalent in certain circles of British society, there were sound reasons why Great Britain opted for a grand strategy of appeasement against the United States at the time. Simply put, the British could ill afford to engage with the Americans about what were after all minor interests, while at the same time facing a dangerous threat close to home with the rise of Germany.[49]

It has been argued that declining states facing high threats will often resort to internal and external balancing (see above). Diocletian's administrative division of the Roman empire into four parts in the late third century CE, the reform of the Ottoman Empire promulgated in 1856, the transformation of the Austrian Empire into Austria-Hungary in 1867, and the proposed scheme for connecting all the 'white' subjects of the British Empire into a federation all constitute attempts at reversing decline by means of internal balancing.

In the same context, one can find numerous examples of external balancing as well. Post-1871 France was a typical case of a state growing weaker relative to its chief strategic opponent, the German Empire, who was also perceived as posing a high threat to French national security. The defeat at Prusso-German hands and the loss of Alsace-Lorraine in the war of 1870–1 were painful enough; the continued hostility of the German Empire and the tremendous growth of its power were nothing short of alarming. France responded by resorting to both internal and external balancing: the former came through the reorganization of the French army, while the latter took the form of alliances with Russia, Great Britain and eventually the United States.[50] Although in bilateral terms France itself continued to grow weaker in relation to Germany, the French balancing effort proved ultimately effective, and the First World War was won.[51]

The desperate strategic situation in which Great Britain found itself in 1940–1 was the result of a long period of decline. By 1941, Great Britain's chief strategic opponent, Nazi Germany, had won European supremacy and was making a credible bid to become the strongest power in the world, while at the same time posing a mortal threat to Great Britain itself. Although the British managed to rally their domestic resources, the situation could only be reversed through external balancing.[52] The Lend-Lease Bill, passed by the U.S. Congress on 11 March 1941, enabled Britain to draw from vast American resources, while Hitler's invasion of the Soviet Union on 22 June 1941 provided London with the opportunity to enlist Soviet support, ideological differences with Moscow notwithstanding.[53] As had been

THUCYDIDES AND STRATEGY IN PERSPECTIVE

the case with France (and Great Britain itself) in the First World War, the grand strategic choice of balancing the power of its strategic opponent enabled Great Britain to cope successfully with the challenge of decline coupled with high threats.[54]

History is littered with examples of preventive war by a declining power that still considers itself stronger than its rising and highly menacing strategic opponent. Austria vis-à-vis Prussia in 1756 provides a case in point. Austria had every reason not to welcome the arrival of Prussia to the club of great European powers, as its rise posed a grave threat to Austria's position in Germany, a point driven home by the Prussian seizure of the rich Austrian province of Silesia in 1740. Consequently, the Austrians managed to forge a great continental coalition comprising Austria, France, Russia, Sweden, and eventually Spain, in a clear attempt to check Prussian power before it reached unacceptable proportions. However, although Prussia came close to disappearing from the map during the ensuing Seven Years' War (1756–63), the failure of the Austrian grand strategic plan did not augur well for Austria's future position.[55]

It must also be mentioned that preventive war has been contemplated and launched not only in response to decline in relative power, but also in anticipation of such a decline. The destruction of the Danish fleet by the British in 1807 is one example. Although Denmark was neutral, Great Britain was afraid of a possible Franco–Danish naval alliance that would immensely increase Napoleon's naval power and thus put British national security in jeopardy. As a consequence, the Royal Navy launched a surprise attack at the port of Copenhagen, seized seventy-five ships, and removed the potential threat conclusively.[56]

Finally, the Soviet Union's relationship with the United States in the mid-1980s provides an example of a declining state facing a high external threat but being unable to counterbalance the source of that threat. Here, the Soviet system could not even keep functioning, let alone sustain an antagonism with the United States for world supremacy. The choice of appeasement developed almost naturally, with the Soviet leader Mikhail Gorbachev making enormous concessions to the strategic opponent of the Soviet Union merely to gain some time to pursue the reforms necessary to stabilize the crumbling Soviet state.[57]

THUCYDIDES ON STRATEGY

The above framework can of course be used to analyse what is arguably the most important issue of current international politics: the grand strategic choices stemming from the current rise of China, especially regarding China's strategic relationship with the United States.[58] China's rise has been meteoric since the late 1970s, defying those that doubted it.[59] China does have its share of problems (e.g. an ageing population and a real-estate bubble), but so does the United States (e.g. a spiralling federal debt and a decline in education).[60] All in all, one cannot be very wrong by postulating that, for the time being at least, China is a relatively rising power with an increasingly global reach, whereas the United States a relatively declining one.[61] As far as the perceptual aspect is concerned, it is indeed true that Washington was, for better or for worse, slow to come to regard Beijing as a threat.[62] Be that as it may, nowadays China is listed as strategic rival or competitor by the United States, NATO and the European Commission. The current containment policy of President Donald Trump, specifically targeting China, demonstrates that Washington perceives China as a highly threatening strategic opponent. The feelings are clearly mutual, since the Chinese President Xi Jinping is renowned for his concern with Chinese national security and has long ago promulgated a so-called 'comprehensive national security concept' that features balancing the United States.[63]

Here, we have two great powers—one rising and one declining—perceiving each other as highly threatening. Their concomitant behaviour conforms to what the framework would predict. To start with, China has grown perceptibly intransigent through the years. It has indeed gone a long way from a relatively mild stance vis-à-vis Japan regarding the Diaoyu/Senkaku Islands in the late 1990s, to the rough 'wolf warrior' diplomacy that Chinese diplomats employed against any perceived affront in 2019–21—and may employ again if need arises.[64] Chinese belligerence in the South China Sea and in relation to Taiwan demonstrate that China is determined to pursue its claims with little aptitude for compromise. In the same vein, the United States, after having adopted for years the notion that China was a 'strategic partner' (i.e. a state that poses a low threat) and consequently accommodating Beijing (for instance, their assistance to China's entering the World Trade Organization), have now fully come around to viewing China as a 'strategic adversary' (i.e. a state that poses a considerable threat). Consequently, the U.S. now tries to balance China (for instance, with military activities in East Asia and closer ties with a number of regional actors, including an alliance with Japan, Australia and India), or even wage economic war against it—a sort of preventive war, though not with military means.

If the above theoretical presentation drawn from Thucydides' analysis is correct, then it becomes possible to outline a theory that may serve as a predictive and explanatory tool regarding the determinants of grand strategic choices. The structural determinant—namely the static and dynamic balance of power between a state and its strategic opponent—needs to be combined with the magnitude of the threat posed by that strategic opponent, as perceived by the political leadership of the aforementioned state. This threat perception will influence the pattern of that state's expansion should its power be on the rise, and also influence the state's choice between buck-passing, balancing, appeasement or even preventive war should its power be declining.

This concludes the discussion of the determinants of grand strategy. Let us now deal with the concepts of the strategy of annihilation and exhaustion.

The Strategies of Annihilation and Exhaustion: Past, Present and Future

These two forms of strategic design and their employment during the Peloponnesian War have been analysed in detail in the preceding chapters. The more widespread of the two has been the strategy of annihilation. It has been repeatedly pointed out that this strategy aims at the destruction of the armed forces of the enemy through a decisive battle, that the most well-known practitioner of this strategy was Napoleon, and that its greatest theoretical exponent is Clausewitz, who combined it with the direct approach.

The grand strategy of Sparta during the Peloponnesian War conforms completely to the Napoleonic/Clausewitzian model. The Spartans were trying for years to bring about a decisive battle on land and, as soon as they acquired the necessary naval power, they followed a similar approach at sea. During the war, Sparta managed to achieve decisive victories both on land and at sea. On land, since the

Athenians did not come out of their walls to offer battle, the decisive victory was won against the Argives and their allies at Mantinea in 418 BCE, securing Spartan supremacy in the Peloponnese. At sea, the defeat of the Athenians at Aegospotami in 405 BCE gave Sparta the final victory in the Peloponnesian War. In other words, one can see in Spartan grand strategy the epitome of the strategy of annihilation, a strategy that was destined to dominate Western strategic thought for a long time.

The supremacy of the strategy of annihilation reached its zenith during the period from the end of the Napoleonic Wars until the end of the Second World War (1815–45). During that period, it was consciously employed for the first time by the Confederate General Robert E. Lee during the American Civil War (1861–5). Lee's great victories at the Second Bull Run (1862) and Chancellorsville (1863) created a severe crisis within the Union's high command. In the long run, however, the Union's material superiority proved enough to ensure victory in the war. It is very interesting, nevertheless, that the strategy of the Union's forces under the command of General Ulysses S. Grant was also a variation of the strategy of annihilation. Once again, the approach was direct, aiming at the destruction of the enemy's armed forces through attrition, making use of the vast superiority of the Union in manpower and materiel. In general, the combination of direct approach, attrition and material superiority has ever since constituted the way in which the armed forces of the United States approach war.[65]

In Europe, the strategy of annihilation was mastered by the Prussian (and later German) General Staff, under the leadership of Field-Marshal Helmuth von Moltke.[66] Under the political direction of Bismarck, the decisive victories of the Prussian army against the Austrians at Sadowa in 1866 and against the French at Sedan in 1870 led to dramatic changes to the contours of the political map of Europe, culminating in the creation of the German Empire. The campaigns of Moltke are classic examples of the Clausewitzian approach to war. To start with, war was used as a tool for the achievement of political ends, which were each time set by the political leadership; moreover, the conduct of the war itself was never allowed to jeopardize the achievement of those aims. Furthermore, Moltke consciously aimed at the destruction of the armed forces of the opponent, since it was correctly understood at that time that they constituted the centre of gravity of the war effort of both Austria and France.[67]

The strategy of annihilation was also used during the two world wars. However, the total mobilization of the belligerents made it impossible to win a war through victory in a single battle, no matter how great this victory was. In fact, it is no accident that the very concept of 'battle' was widened in scope during that period: instead of the isolated encounter of the Spartan and Napoleonic era, the new concept of battle covered extensive operations which went on for weeks or even months, such as the Battle of Verdun (1916) or the Battle of Britain (1940–1).[68] War began to extend beyond the armed forces of the combatants to include the whole material and moral potential of a country (i.e. total war).[69] Consequently, the cost of the use of military force started to increase exponentially while, conversely, a strategy of annihilation became a less attractive tool.

The advent of nuclear weapons completed this process. Since 1945, although the employment of war as an instrument of policy has not disappeared, it has been greatly restricted, especially among nuclear powers. In other words, it was no longer possible to regard a nuclear war as a viable means to achieve political aims,[70] since neither side could avoid devastation; with the current state of technology, this is also somewhat true for a protracted conventional war, especially among great powers.[71] Nevertheless, this does not infer that the phenomenon of war is about to disappear. A look at the post-Cold War international system shows that the use of force in both international and domestic relations remains a potent measure. On the other hand, it can be persuasively argued that the idea of a war between great powers, both at the nuclear and the conventional level, has become obsolete.[72]

Regardless, this has not led the great powers to abandon the pursuit of victory. Instead, it led to the revival of the strategy of exhaustion. As previously outlined, this strategy gives emphasis to a number of means beyond the traditional military ones, while relying to a large extent on causing economic damage to the opponent.[73] The strategy of exhaustion already had a glorious past. One may recall the victorious strategy of Pericles in the first phase of the Peloponnesian War (see Chapter Three). The Athenians declined to give battle on land, remaining safely behind their walls. At the same time, with the help of their naval power, they simultaneously quelled the revolts of their allies/subjects and launched progressively escalating naval reprisals against the Spartans. In addition, the political dexterity of Pericles took care of the domestic legitimacy of his grand strategy. The outcome was that the Spartans recognized that they could not defeat Athens and so abandoned their attempt to overthrow the Athenian Empire (leading to the Peace of Nicias).

Many centuries later, another great power, seventeenth-century England/Great Britain, adopted a grand strategy of exhaustion similar to that of Pericles; this was the so-called 'British way of warfare' (see Chapter One). More recently, one can see that the United States in the twentieth century, in order to deal with the Soviet Union during the Cold War, drew from past experience and resorted to a grand strategy of exhaustion. In fact, there are quite a few similarities between the United States' strategy during the Cold War and the grand strategy of exhaustion that Pericles suggested to the Athenians in order to deal with the Spartans.[74] In the case of the former, the gradual exhaustion of the Soviet Union was brought about by several factors: (a) containment of the Soviet power through a complex of alliances around the borders of the USSR; (b) economic and technological embargo through denial of Soviet access to Western economic resources and high technology; (c) undermining the domestic legitimacy of the Soviet political system through support to dissidents and encouragement of ethnic movements; (d) intensification of the technological arms race (e.g. 'Star Wars'), so as to exhaust the opponent financially; (e) rejection of appeasement, so as to prevent the Soviet Union from registering gains from possible American concessions, and to ensure that the American leadership of the West would not be endangered in the process; (f) investment in powerful armed forces and maintenance of high defence budgets for a long period, so as to preserve the balance of power (internal balancing); (g) maintenance of qualitative superiority through investment in high technology; (h) support of various opponents of the Soviet Union (e.g. China, Afghan guerrillas); and (i) undermining the international image of the Soviet Union and delegitimization of the Soviet model in the eyes of the international public opinion. The Soviet system eventually could not withstand combined American pressures, and the attempt to reform it (*perestroika*) brought about its total collapse.

The Cold War is not the only contemporary instance of the utilization of the strategy of exhaustion. A cursory examination of the strategy followed by the U.S. and its NATO allies in Bosnia in 1995 will suffice to prove this point. Here, economic warfare, diplomatic isolation, strengthening of the opponent's local adversaries, psychological pressure and other means of grand strategy were used to bring about the exhaustion of the opponent. Thus, the air strikes were but one component of that strategy. Prior to these strikes, the power of the Bosnian Serbs had been eroded by economic warfare and diplomatic isolation. In addition, the U.S. helped manipulate the local balance of power, both through arms supplies to Serbia's local antagonists (Croatia, Bosnian Muslims) and through engineering the alliance between Bosnian Muslims and Bosnian Croats. Last but not least, the U.S. also took good care to rally domestic support for its policies in Bosnia (domestic legitimacy). With these combined elements in operation, the exhaustion of the opponent was ensured. Subsequently, the application of limited military force of exemplary character was enough to coerce the Bosnian Serbs to submit to the terms imposed by the U.S. and NATO through the Dayton Agreement.

In the coming decades, the employment of the strategy of exhaustion is bound to become more popular. In fact, as the cost of the application of military force increases and the sensitivity of Western societies to casualties grows, the pursuit of victory will become possible to a large extent through the strategy of exhaustion. Technological trends (such as the revolution in military affairs, the third offset strategy, artificial intelligence) based on the ability to collect, transmit and intercept information, as well as to deliver firepower against any target anywhere,[75] will facilitate the military dimension of this strategy in the same way as the technological developments in ancient Greece (e.g. triremes) made naval raids an important pillar of the Periclean grand strategy.

A similar argument has been advanced by Edward Luttwak, who has argued in favour of a 'post-heroic' concept of war, laying stress on such means as economic embargoes, blockades and air strikes in an attempt to minimize casualties, even at the expense of a swift decision that involves potentially higher casualty rates.[76] Luttwak, however, mistakenly attributes this concept to the Romans; actually, the Periclean grand strategy is the ideal type of post-heroic warfare. For instance, an analogy may, *inter alia*, be drawn between the way in which the Athenians used their navy and the discussion that is nowadays taking place regarding the utilization of long-range weapons to manipulate the cost to the other side without oneself suffering casualties. Another analogy can be found between Pericles' refusal to face the Spartan infantry in battle and the reluctance of today's Western powers to be drawn in large-scale land operations, even against relatively weak powers. Both Pericles and current Western strategic planners care less about the 'glory of war' and more about the attainment of certain political ends with the smallest possible number of casualties.[77]

However, the increasing popularity of the strategy of exhaustion does not mean that the Clausewitzian approach to war, as exemplified by Spartan grand strategy in the Peloponnesian War, will be relegated to the history books. This is because, even with the adoption of the strategy of exhaustion, the direct approach will continue to be dominant, at least at the higher levels of strategy. In fact, we have already mentioned that even the Periclean grand strategy—the archetype of the strategy of exhaustion—achieved decisive results only when following a direct approach and after striking against Sparta itself with the operations of Pylos, Sphacteria and Cythera. Furthermore, the strategy of annihilation is not at all eradicated, especially between opponents of vastly unequal strength.

Evidence from four instances of military force deployment by the U.S. in recent times lends credence to the applicability of the themes of exhaustion versus annihilation, combined with a direct approach.[78] In the first case, after Iraq's invasion of Kuwait in August 1990, economic sanctions were placed on Iraq, the hope being that the economic damage inflicted would induce Saddam Hussein to see the error of his ways and withdraw Iraqi forces from the country. Since this pure strategy of exhaustion did not work, a substantial portion of annihilation was added to the mix. The core element of Iraqi power—namely the Iraqi armed forces—was subjected to a ruthless barrage through every means (military, economic, psychological, etc.) at the Allies' disposal. The air strikes took a heavy toll on the Iraqi armed forces, whereas the economic blockade and diplomatic isolation of their country ensured that losses in military hardware could not be replaced. In the meantime, the immense psychological pressure demoralized their personnel. Propaganda outlining the inevitability of defeat led to mass surrender of their forces. The killer blow was delivered by the large-scale land operations, which constitute another textbook case of destruction of the opponent's armed forces, precisely according to the precepts of Napoleon and Clausewitz. Incidentally, these operations provide an excellent example of direct approach at the strategic level of war (destruction of the centre of gravity of the enemy power) coupled with indirect approach at the operational level (the massive westerly movement that preceded the operations and took the Iraqi command and troops by surprise).[79]

The war in Kosovo is another case in point. In this case, the emphasis was not on the 'decisive battle' on land, but on the gradual physical emasculation of the Serbian war machine and the psychological dislocation of the Serbian political leadership, thereby compelling the latter to comply with the terms imposed by NATO. As was the case with Iraq, the arms embargo prevented the Serbs from replacing the losses sustained by the aerial bombardment, while the pressure was further increased by aid to the Kosovo Liberation Army (KLA) and economic warfare, which laid stress on an oil embargo. In the meantime, Yugoslavia remained internationally isolated, while the Western powers launched a huge propaganda campaign in an attempt to damage the international image of the Serbian leaders, comparing them to the Nazis. Initially, NATO air bombardments took more of an indirect approach, leaving many strategic facilities, such as television stations and power grids, untouched. However, since expectations of swift Serb capitulation proved wrong (see below), NATO gradually escalated the bombing and resorted to a direct approach, turning against the centre of gravity of the Serbian war effort, namely Serbian military power. The prospect of large-scale land operations was held in reserve, and the Serbian political leadership eventually gave way before this could become an actuality. The operations ended with the NATO allies completely achieving the strategic objective set out at the beginning of the campaign: Serbian forces withdrawing from Kosovo and being replaced by NATO ones.[80]

Annihilation elements dominated the strategic mix in the campaign in Afghanistan that followed the terrorist attacks in New York and Washington, DC on 11 September 2001. Due to the political circumstances surrounding that war, it was rather easy for the United States to achieve international legitimacy and completely isolate its opponent. The political–diplomatic measures deployed were also highly promising. The Northern Alliance, the ex-king of the country and various other tribal leaders were utilized in this respect. The military component of the American strategy resembled that of the Kosovo War (although at much greater intensity), with the important difference being that the Taliban and al-Qaeda forces were weaker than those of Serbia, while the Northern Alliance could be moulded into a far more formidable force than the KLA. Though the approach adopted by the U.S. armed forces was decidedly post-heroic,[81] it was also a direct one, striking at the enemy's centre of gravity (its armed forces). The fact that the Northern Alliance offensive compelled the Taliban to concentrate their armed forces assisted American air power tremendously; the U.S. Air Force kept striking at the enemy armed forces, actually retargeting areas struck only weeks or days before. The result was a rather speedy collapse of the Taliban regime.[82]

After the end of the Kuwait War in 1991, Iraq had been on the receiving end of a strategy of exhaustion that relentlessly sapped its strength. However, the political objectives of the American invasion of 2003—namely regime change and democratization—once again brought annihilation to the forefront. After an initial attempt at a decapitating strike against Saddam Hussein himself, the U.S. armed forces resorted to the familiar direct approach, striking at the centre of gravity of the enemy power (the Iraqi armed forces). Once again, this was combined with an indirect approach at operational level: while the Iraqis concentrated on defending certain fortified urban centres (e.g. Al-Nasiriyah), the Americans simply bypassed them and headed for Baghdad. In the meantime, even when land operations temporarily halted, the U.S. Air Force kept pounding the enemy armed forces, eventually paving the way for their swift destruction and the collapse of Saddam Hussein's regime.[83]

THUCYDIDES AND STRATEGY IN PERSPECTIVE

These cases demonstrated how the United States, the strongest military power since 1945, has approached war up to the present day. A central role is played by the exhaustion of the opponent through economic warfare (destruction of the opponent's base of production, economic embargo) and diplomatic isolation. In this way, the United States attempts to exploit the central position it currently occupies in the international economic and political system. Its position in the international division of labour is such that its decision to impose measures like economic embargoes and sanctions against opponents is reasonably expected to have dire economic consequences for the latter, at least in the long run. In addition, at the diplomatic level, the dominant international position of the U.S. enables it to draw a huge number of other countries by its side, thus condemning its opponent to diplomatic isolation, at least until recently (for example, the Global South has been largely indifferent to the Ukraine war and has certainly not rallied around the U.S. on that matter). As far as military strategy is concerned, the approach is direct, aiming at the destruction of the opponent's armed forces. Here as well, the United States tries to exploit its comparative advantages, namely superiority in firepower and supremacy at sea, as well as in the air, cyberspace and space.

Finally, great emphasis is placed on technological superiority, especially in the field of intelligence. This has two dimensions: first, the emphasis on technological superiority aims at minimizing casualties through the use of technologically advanced weapons systems that the opponent will be unable to strike at effectively (e.g. aircraft and cruise missiles);[84] secondly, the emphasis on technology for the collection, processing and transmission of intelligence in real time often constitutes the only way to counter opponents that do not possess substantial armed forces or a significant economic base (e.g. terrorist groups such as the Houthis), or who do possess such assets but perform large-scale concealment thereof.

Despite this, the opponents of the U.S. armed forces have not remained idle. On the contrary, they have been relatively quick to adjust to what the Americans have been up to. Incidentally, they have proven adept at using both annihilation and exhaustion whenever the circumstances warranted. To begin with, as previously mentioned, the Taliban realized the hard way that it was suicidal to try to stand up to American 'smart' firepower during the 2003 invasion. Instead, they opted for a military strategy of exhaustion, avoiding large engagements with U.S. forces. Granted, they would still try to inflict some casualties on the Americans, basically through improvised explosive devices, but the idea at first was to rebuild their own battered forces. The Taliban relied on their superior staying power, their uncanny ability to absorb casualties, and their stronger ties with the local population compared to the 'infidel' Americans or the corrupt Afghan government forces.[85] In the end, the U.S. forces, though militarily undefeated and having lost fewer than 2,500 dead in almost twenty years of operations, ignominiously abandoned Afghanistan (and much materiel) to the Taliban having achieved worse than nothing for their efforts.[86] Exhaustion had triumphed over firepower, technology—and money.

In the meantime, it had been the turn of the Russians to demonstrate that they also knew a thing or two about the strategy of exhaustion. Their fairly easy victory in 2008 when the Georgians suicidally attacked them was one such example of annihilation.[87] Following this, however, the Russians went after bigger fish. After the overthrow of the pro-Russian Yanukovych government in Ukraine in 2014 (which, incidentally, the Russians consider an instance of U.S. 'hybrid war'— that is, another application of the strategy of exhaustion), unidentified military forces took over Crimea without firing a shot, while simultaneously staging an armed insurrection at several provinces in Ukraine. Shortly afterwards, Russia annexed Crimea, and the insurrection established itself in the eastern provinces of Donetsk and Lugansk (though it was speedily crushed in the western city of Odessa). Clearly, even though a comprehensive 'Gerasimov doctrine' did not exist, the Russians were indeed employing a strategy utilizing a variety of means, including heavy doses of disinformation and propaganda, while remaining resolutely below the threshold of all-out war (i.e. a strategy of exhaustion).[88] The U.S. responded by ratcheting up sanctions on Russia. While these sanctions admittedly hurt Moscow,[89] they clearly were not enough to reverse Russia's actions— or in fact deter what was to come later.

Russia's large-scale invasion of Ukraine on 24 February 2022 signified Moscow's abandonment of exhaustion and its resort to annihilation. This was the natural corollary of the now-expanded Russian political objectives, namely seizure of large chunks of Ukraine and virtually complete political control over that country. After its initial mishaps (see below), Russia has intensified its effort and seems bent on beating Ukraine through annihilation and its close relative, attrition.[90] The U.S. response was (and is) bound to hinge on the aforementioned perceptual aspect of its bilateral relationship with Russia, irrespective of whether it regards Russia as posing a high or a low threat to them. The Biden administration was unequivocal in this respect: Russia poses a high threat to the U.S., thus meriting a powerful combination of exhaustion (severe sanctions) and annihilation (increasing arms supplies to Ukraine). The Trump administration, however, seems to be taking a different view and is probably changing course.

The return of great-power conflict—be it between the West and Russia, or China, or both—could conceivably bring the strategy of annihilation back to the forefront. The Ukraine war already witnesses more annihilation than exhaustion, something which is not a reassuring prospect in the nuclear era. On the other hand, it may be precisely the advent of the 'balance of terror' that will ensure the continued supremacy of the strategy of exhaustion, similar to what happened during the Cold War. The United States and China may well find themselves locked in a long-winded political, economic and ideological antagonism, possibly featuring proxy wars aimed at the strategic exhaustion of the opponent but thankfully avoiding an old-school war of annihilation between them (see also the postscript of the present book).

Once again, all this shows the continued relevance of Thucydides' strategic analysis. The preceding analysis of the grand strategies of Athens and Sparta made it clear that each of the two combatants tried to exploit their comparative advantages and simultaneously to neutralize the respective advantages of the opponent. The U.S. currently tries to do precisely the same thing. The grand strategy that the United States is expected to follow in the coming years is based on the exploitation of their comparative advantages (namely their central position in the international economic and political system; their superior firepower and technology; and their supremacy at sea, in the air and in space) and the neutralization of the respective advantages of its potential opponents (namely better knowledge of the terrain; possibly higher determination for continuation of the war; higher casualty tolerance). Furthermore, the fact that the American technological superiority has enabled the U.S. to operate in a military league of its own (at least on occasion) brings to mind the way in which the naval supremacy of Athens enabled it to enter a completely new mode of warfare, transcending the traditional mode which had been based on the infantry phalanx.

Underestimating the Enemy: From Alcibiades to the Present

As highlighted in the previous chapters, Thucydides thought that the turning point of the war was the Athenian expedition to Sicily in 415 BCE, undertaken at the instigation of Alcibiades.[91] Up to now, our analysis has but briefly touched upon this highly interesting phase of the Peloponnesian War (see Map 5). In our opinion, the Sicilian expedition was a strategic blunder of the first magnitude, whose consequences were made even worse by horrendous ineptitude at the tactical level. In the current section, we will concentrate on the strategic plan that brought the Athenians to Sicily, rather than dwelling much on the tactical aspects of that campaign.[92] Thucydides makes it clear that this plan was fundamentally flawed, since it was based on a considerable underestimation of the enemy the Athenians were to encounter in Sicily.[93]

Underestimating the enemy is something of a recurring theme in history. A frequent example is to estimate the enemy forces as numerically weaker than is actually the case. In the present analysis, we will examine a kind of enemy underestimation different from the one pertaining to 'bean-counting'. We are interested in instances where the enemy is presented as 'inferior' due to cultural, racial or other factors, but where this supposition lacks any objective foundation. Consequently, using as a starting point Thucydides' analysis of the Sicilian expedition, we will present other cases where the underestimation of the enemy led to strategic failure and will attempt to offer some insights as to the possible recurrence of this theme in the future.

We have already presented the war aims of the Athenians when they decided to undertake the Sicilian expedition, namely the conquest of Sicily (and possibly of Italy and other territories around the western Mediterranean littoral) with a view to acquiring overwhelming strength and subsequently establishing domination over mainland Greece and the rest of the Greek world. If one were to believe Alcibiades' speech to the Athenian *Ecclesia*, the first step in this process—the Sicilian expedition—should have been a mere pushover for the Athenians. According to him, the inhabitants of the Greek cities in Sicily, numerous though they were, did not feel they possessed a homeland and were constantly shifting their allegiance from city to city. In addition, the *hoplite* armies of those cities were not particularly strong:

> Nor should you rescind your resolution to sail to Sicily, on the ground that you would be going to attack a great power. The cities in Sicily are peopled by motley rabbles, and easily change their institutions and adopt new ones in their stead; and consequently the inhabitants, being without any feeling of patriotism, are not provided with arms for their persons, and have not regularly established themselves on the land; every man thinks that either by fair words or by party strife he can obtain something at the public expense, and then in the event of a catastrophe settle in some other country, and makes his preparations accordingly. From a mob like this you need not look for either unanimity in counsel or unity in action; but they will probably one by one come in as they get a fair offer, especially if they are torn by civil strife as we are told. Moreover, the Sicilians have not so many hoplites as they boast [...].[94]

This picture of the Greek city-states in Sicily sounds, of course, inherently unlikely. The Athenians ought to know what a Greek city was like, and therefore reject the view that their kindred cities in Sicily were inhabited by shapeless mobs, ready to abandon their allegiance to their city.[95] However, they obviously indulged in an exercise in collective wishful thinking.[96] But that was not all: Alcibiades claimed that the conquest of Sicily was quite likely and that the very undertaking of the expedition would have a humbling effect on the Peloponnesians:

> [L]et us make the expedition, and so humble the pride of the Peloponnesians by sailing off to Sicily, and letting them see how little we care for the peace that we are now enjoying. At the same

time we shall either become masters, as we very easily may, of the whole of Hellas through the accession of the Sicilian Hellenes, or in any case ruin the Syracusans, to the no small advantage of ourselves and our allies.[97]

This was wide off the mark, to say the least. As illustrated in the previous chapter, far from being humbled, the Spartans immediately understood that Athens had overextended and that they were themselves presented with a golden opportunity to win the war. The above passages should be sufficient to do away with the notion that Alcibiades was a great statesman, as some people still believe.[98] Besides, this notion completely collapses if one examines his claim that Athens was to 'very easily' conquer that group of overcrowded, badly governed and weakly armed cities that allegedly comprised Sicily.

In fact, such a state of affairs was simply untrue. Syracuse, a colony of Corinth and the chief opponent of Athens at Sicily, had for long been a powerful city. At the time of the Persian invasion of Greece, Gelon, tyrant of Syracuse, was master of a large part of Sicily and arguably the most powerful Greek ruler. Approached by envoys from Sparta and Athens for aid against the Persians, he promised a force of 200 triremes, 20,000 *hoplites*, 2,000 cavalry, an equal number of archers, slingers and light horsemen, plus corn for the entire Greek army. This force never reached Greece, either because of disputes over the overall command of the anti-Persian struggle or, more likely, because of the Carthaginian invasion of Sicily.[99] Be that as it may, both this episode and the fact that Gelon and the other Greeks of Sicily managed to defeat the Carthaginians speaks volumes of the power of Syracuse and the general condition of the Greek cities in Sicily.

What about the condition of these cities at the time of the Athenian expedition? Nicias was hardly a brilliant strategist and carries much of the blame for the eventual annihilation of the Athenian expeditionary force. Yet one must admit that, prior to the expedition, he gave his fellow citizens an accurate picture of the situation:

> From all that I hear we are going against cities that are great and not subject to one another, or in need of change, so as to wish to pass from enforced servitude to an easier condition, or be in the least likely to accept our rule in exchange for freedom; and, to take only the

Hellenic cities, they are very numerous for one island. Besides Naxos and Catana, which I expect to join us from their connection with Leontini,[100] there are seven others armed in every way just like our own power, particularly Selinus and Syracuse, the main objectives of our expedition. These are full of hoplites, archers, and dart throwers, have triremes in abundance and multitudes to man them; they also have money, partly in the hands of private persons, partly in the temples at Selinus, and at Syracuse tribute of first-fruits from some of the barbarians as well. But their chief advantage over us lies in the number of their horses, and in the fact that they grow their grain at home instead of importing it.[101]

Thus, Nicias presents a completely different picture from the one presented by Alcibiades. The Sicilian Greek cities are not only determined to retain their independence, they are rich and powerful, have a military and naval organization similar to the mainland Greek cities, and possess two great assets, namely superiority in cavalry and self-sufficiency in foodstuffs. Thucydides makes it clear that this picture was accurate. According to him, when the campaign started going downhill, the Athenians at the expeditionary force deeply regretted it:

These were the only cities that they had yet encountered, similar to their own in character, under democracies like themselves, which had ships and horses, and were of considerable magnitude. They had been unable to divide and bring them over by holding out the prospect of changes in their governments, or to crush them by their great superiority in force [...].[102]

The actual course of the campaign vindicated Nicias. The Athenians failed to secure allies in Sicily other than Naxos and Catana, plus the majority of the native Sicels.[103] The Syracusan military forces were admittedly not on a par with the battle-hardened troops from mainland Greece, a fact that resulted in initial victories for the Athenians. However, the Syracusans did not lack bravery, and it would not be long before they were brought up to standard.[104] In the meantime, however, the complete Syracusan superiority in cavalry created a host of problems for the Athenians.[105] The Athenians tried to exploit their initial successes by besieging Syracuse, but at that point, with the Syracusans about to sue for peace, the Spartans entered the fray by sending them aid under the brilliant general Gylippus.[106] Soon, the situation was reversed. Gylippus' troops occupied some important outposts, effectively turning the Athenians from besiegers to the besieged.[107] As if this were not enough, the Syracusans showed extreme ingenuity and developed a powerful navy.[108] Although initially worsted, the Syracusan navy created a sensation by defeating the hitherto undefeated Athenian navy three times in succession.[109] All of a sudden (and Nicias' superstitious procrastination is much to blame for this), the Athenians were trapped in Sicily.[110] An attempt to escape by land failed and resulted in the total annihilation of the expeditionary force. Those who did not perish were sold as slaves or ended up in the stone quarries.[111]

One might object to the above analysis by pointing out that the Athenians made quite a few mistakes in their conduct of the operations (e.g. they delayed their attack on Syracuse) and that, although they had undoubtedly underestimated the enemy, they were still able to come very close to victory. The answer to this objection is twofold. First, the Syracusans themselves made mistakes. Prior to the arrival of the Athenians at Sicily, the Syracusan statesman Hermocrates had come up with the ingenuous proposal that the Syracusan fleet should come out and meet the Athenians in Italy, either at Taras or the promontory of Iapygia (the south-eastern tip of Italy). This would make it considerably difficult for the Athenians to cross the Ionian Sea, since they would have to take pains to keep their force together for fear of being destroyed piecemeal and thus be compelled to advance very slowly.[112] As such, Hermocrates' plan was not adopted.

Second, and most important, the magnitude of the opposition in Sicily, not to mention the Peloponnesian aid, and the distances involved made it simply impossible for the Athenians to retain their conquests in Sicily even if they had managed to force the capitulation of Syracuse. An example of this was the Spartan triumph over Argos at Mantinea mentioned in the previous chapter. Even such a great victory against a nearby opponent, coupled with the help of powerful oligarchic elements inside Argos, was not enough to retain this city within the Spartan sphere of influence.[113] How then, one might ask, could Athens maintain control of such a distant and populous place like Sicily, especially in the face of the renewed Spartan challenge in

THUCYDIDES AND STRATEGY IN PERSPECTIVE

Greece proper? The speedy collapse of the Athenian designs in Sicily as soon as the Peloponnesian aid appeared should speak for itself. It is ironic that Nicias, for all his incompetence during the campaign, had captured the essence of the situation prior to it:

> [T]he Sicilians, even if conquered, are too far off and too numerous to be ruled without difficulty. Now it is folly to go against men who could not be kept under even if conquered, while failure would leave us in a very different position from that which we occupied before the enterprise.[114]

The above analysis should leave no doubt with regard to the evaluation of the Sicilian expedition as a strategic move. It was a huge blunder, resulting from frivolous attitude and an almost unbelievable underestimation of the enemy.[115] Thucydides' analysis highlights the dangers inherent in such underestimation.

Nevertheless, this is a lesson that has had to be re-learnt numerous times in the course of history. Ancient statesmen were not the only ones prone to underestimating the opponents of their states; similar instances abound in modern times as well.[116] A most striking example is that of the Russo-Japanese War (1904–5). Imperial Russia at the turn of the nineteenth century, although impressive on the map and possessing armies of awesome numerical strength, was hopelessly backward both socially and economically; moreover, its military establishment was plagued by numerous weaknesses, its system of government was corrupt and inefficient, and the whole country was infested by revolutionary groups ready to cause trouble.[117] Territorial expansion was considered a suitable way to escape from the various difficulties. In the Far East, however, Russian ambitions clashed with those of the Japanese. The differences were not necessarily irreconcilable: the Japanese were willing to cede Manchuria to the Russians provided they would secure Korea for themselves. However, the key Russian decision-makers thought otherwise. According to one of them, Russia needed 'a short victorious war to stem the tide of revolution'. Czar Nicholas himself was calling the Japanese 'short-tailed monkeys', while leading Russian generals were trying to estimate whether one Russian soldier equalled one-and-a-half or two Japanese ones.[118]

This underestimation of the enemy was even worse than the one committed by Alcibiades and was paid for dearly. Japan was fast becoming an industrialized country, was already an important naval power and, most importantly, enjoyed the considerable advantage of geographical proximity to the area of operations, in sharp contrast to the Russians, who had to transport supplies along the single-track Trans-Siberian Railway. The war began with a Japanese surprise attack on the Russian fleet at Port Arthur, continued with some ferocious land battles in which the Japanese won with heavy casualties for both sides, and culminated in a great Japanese naval victory at Tsushima Strait. Contrary to what was believed in St. Petersburg, the Japanese were no mere 'short-tailed monkeys'.[119]

Another famous example of miscalculating the enemy was the underestimation of the Soviet Union by Hitler (and some of the generals of the German High Command) prior to the German invasion in 1941 (Operation Barbarossa). By this, we do not refer so much to the underestimation of the numerical strength and the technological condition of the Red Army; these were quite natural effects of the extreme secrecy maintained by the Soviet system, which made it difficult for the Germans to obtain accurate intelligence.[120] What we are really talking about is the belief, stemming consciously (in the case of Hitler) or subconsciously (in the case of some leading German generals) from racist attitudes, whereby Russians were viewed as 'inferior' and thus no match for the German armies.

According to Hitler, Russia had been organized and developed by a Germanic elite, the native Slavs being 'subhuman' and thus unable to rule and develop their country. The Bolshevik revolution, however, had toppled that Germanic elite. Consequently, this led to internal rottenness and made the 'colossal empire in the East ripe for dissolution'. After the initial German victories, resistance was bound to collapse; as Hitler told Field-Marshal Gerd von Rundstedt: 'You have only to kick in the door and the whole rotten structure will come crashing down'. In his eyes, the hated Slavic 'subhumans' were incapable of withstanding the Aryan onslaught.[121] There is no evidence that Colonel-General Franz Halder, Chief of the General Staff of the German Army, consciously subscribed to such views. However, even this supposedly detached professional soldier regarded the

Russians as 'inferior'. This was the very word (*minderwertig*) with which he described the Russian soldier in his estimates prior to the launch of 'Barbarossa'.[122]

The course of the war in the East showed how utterly nonsensical these views were, and little further comment is needed in this regard. Two things should be pointed out. First, that there were plenty of officers within the German army who had fought the Russians in the First World War and thus could testify to the great fighting valour of the Russian soldier;[123] no excuses can be made for the underestimation of the enemy in this respect. Second, that the defective intelligence mentioned above is not to blame for Hitler's decision to invade the Soviet Union. Hitler later found it convenient to claim that had he known of the true Soviet strength, he would never have launched the invasion,[124] but this was merely an *ex post facto* rationalization. Hitler did not launch Operation Barbarossa because he had been misled by some intelligence estimates, but because of his belief in the racial inferiority of the Russians and his desire to create an empire in the East.[125]

There is a common thread running through these above examples: the enemy, for one reason or another, is wishfully regarded as 'not up to standard' and the results were invariably disastrous. The question that now arises is whether future political leaders will heed Thucydides' warning and be objective in their assessment of their enemies, or whether they will follow Alcibiades' path and engage in fanciful and ultimately unfortunate designs.

With the supposedly increased current awareness about different cultures and understanding thereof, underestimating the enemy in a manner similar to the one described above should be rare. However, we contend that there are two areas where, in the future, one is still likely to underestimate an opponent: the morale of an armed force and/or population, and their determination to continue a given struggle.

Recent experience seems to confirm this view. The disastrous Soviet intervention in Afghanistan is a clear case in point. The Soviet political leadership was highly complacent as regards that intervention. For instance, a resolution of the Central Committee of the Communist Party of the Soviet Union dated 31 December 1979 (four days after the intervention) declared nonchalantly that '[t]he situation in the country becomes normal'.[126] The Soviet leaders did not intend their troops to stay in Afghanistan for any length of time, and their main objective was to garrison the most important Afghan towns and the roads connecting them in the belief that this would be enough to secure the country.[127] In other words, they severely underestimated the scale and the ferocity of the opposition, as well as overestimating the resolve of their own Afghan allies in Kabul.

Israel's intervention in Lebanon (1982–5) also ended unsuccessfully, though less dramatically than the Soviet one in Afghanistan. This was not so much due to a failure in assessing enemy capabilities (although the Druze and certain elements of the Syrian armed forces did perform better than expected), but rather as a result of a persistent underestimation of enemy resolve (e.g. the resolve of Palestine Liberation Organization and Syrian forces to hang on to West Beirut), coupled with an arguable overestimation of the resolve of Israeli public opinion to continue the war, or even to embark upon it in the first place.[128]

Furthermore, the UN intervention in Somalia (1992–5) did not fail because the military capabilities of the various local warlords had been misjudged. Instead, it failed because it had not been correctly appraised that those warlords were more determined than the intervening powers to go on with the struggle.[129]

Finally, there is strong evidence that the Russian leadership seriously underestimated the Ukrainian resistance while planning the February 2022 invasion. While the relevant Russian decision-making process remains opaque, numerous sources insist that, in a manner reminiscent of Czar Nicholas vis-à-vis the Japanese, Vladimir Putin expected little or no Ukrainian resistance and was willing to believe only those who conformed to those views. The force structure of the Russian Army testifies to that: the invasion force split into too many axes of invasion, thus blatantly violating the principle of concentration of force and effort, and displaying a rather cavalier attitude to logistical issues.[130] In all fairness, after the initial miscalculation, the Russian leadership did see the error of its ways and became much more serious in their conduct of the war.[131] Still, regardless of how Russia fares in the end, this underestimation of the enemy has without doubt cost it considerably in terms of lives, resources, time and, most importantly, Russia's standing in the world.

The vice of underestimating an enemy will not be eradicated in the future. On the other hand, considering enemies as inferior simply because they happen to live far away or belong to a different culture should be quite a rare occurrence. Nevertheless, there will still be difficulties in accurately estimating important imponderables such as the morale and the determination of the enemy. In fact, it might even be argued that each side will tend to view itself as the more determined or the one with the higher morale.[132]

EPILOGUE

This book set out to highlight Thucydides' contribution to the study of strategy. From the analysis that followed, Thucydides' text emerged as a classic. To start with, it contains the first detailed presentation of a theory of grand strategy. Furthermore, it graphically illustrates how grand strategies are formulated and put to the test. In addition, it provides us with a superb analysis of a great number of central concepts of modern strategic theory.

To a great extent, contemporary analysts have made no significant contribution to Thucydides' treatment of these concepts. To paraphrase Gilpin, it is doubtful whether modern strategists know anything about strategy that was unknown to Thucydides. Without doubt, technology has been profoundly transformed since Thucydides' time. Nonetheless, 'there is a certain logic of hostility, a dilemma about security that goes with interstate politics in a self-help system. Alliances, balances of power, and choices in policy between war and appeasement have remained similar over the millennia'.[1] Thucydides was as cognizant of this logic as any present-day analyst.

However, Thucydides has been somewhat neglected as a strategist. In all probability, this is due to his tremendous success as a historian and international relations analyst. Still, this is unfair. It is true that perceptive scholars and policymakers have long ago appreciated Thucydides' qualities as a strategist and his continued relevance to the field.[2] Thankfully, this appreciation is growing, but there is still a lot to be done. We hope that the present book has contributed to this direction.

POSTSCRIPT[1]

THE FUTURE OF THE SINO–AMERICAN GEOPOLITICAL ANTAGONISM

A COMMENT ON THE THUCYDIDES' TRAP

It would not be an overstatement to assert that Thucydides' *History of the Peloponnesian War* has become one of the most cited primary sources in the history of the international relations discipline.[2] Since the early modern era, Thucydides has been a teacher to towering figures such as Hobbes, Lincoln, Marshall and even Lenin.[3] Yet a problem often arises: Thucydides has become an easy victim of confirmation bias—that is, the proclivity to discriminately focus on and recall information in a way that confirms one's own presumptions. Thus, modern scholars have often selectively interpreted Thucydides' work to model pressing strategic puzzles of their time.[4] For instance, America's Vietnam War debacle was seen as analogous to the Athenian catastrophe in Sicily. Imperial overextension theory soon arose, and eminent scholars argued that Thucydides' Book VI, which eloquently describes the debate in Athens that led to that disastrous expedition, constituted the culmination of Thucydides' work.[5] By the mid-1970s, American theorists who believed that Soviet influence had become overwhelming appealed to Thucydides to raise alarm that the United States was on track to lose the Cold War. They argued that Sparta, an oligarchic power akin to the Soviet Union, had defeated Athens, a democracy similar to the United States.[6]

THUCYDIDES ON STRATEGY

Thucydides' *History* has again become the epicentre of a strategic debate about the future of Sino–American relations in an era of hegemonic transition. The so-called 'Thucydides' trap', a term popularised by Graham Allison, has now come to define this debate. Thucydides' trap refers 'to the natural, inevitable discombobulation that occurs when a rising power threatens to displace a ruling power'.[7] Yet Thucydides' trap 'entraps' Thucydides' work into a facile analogising.[8] Allison uses the Peloponnesian War analogy to gauge the geopolitical antagonism between China and the United States. According to him, the Sino–American geopolitical antagonism makes a war between the two countries all the more possible due to what he calls 'loss of control', 'inadvertent escalation', and 'sleepwalking into conflict'.[9]

Allison is an influential scholar who has made substantial contributions to the theory of international relations.[10] Yet his effort to draw contemporary analogies through the selective referencing of a few lines of the *History of the Peloponnesian War*, a classic Greek text written in one of the most complex dialects of Ancient Greek,[11] misses Thucydides' 'essential richness in favor of false rigor'.[12] The result is a concept called the 'Thucydides' trap', in which Allison argues that on account of the structure of the interstate system, when one great power threatens to displace another, war is usually the result of inadvertent escalation. This assertion, however, distorts Thucydides' own logic, which not only examines the structure of the interstate system but also looks to sub-systemic factors, such as leadership, domestic structures and strategic culture, as shapers of strategic behaviour.

We have identified two serious misrepresentations of Thucydides' classical treatise in Allison's argumentation on inadvertent escalation and hegemonic transition. The Thucydides' trap is occasionally 'lost in translation' and thus misrepresents important nuances from Thucydides' *History of the Peloponnesian War*. In other cases, the concept is 'lost in history' and fails to take into account the Greek interstate system's dynamics during the *Pentecontaetia*, the fifty-year period between the end of the Persian Wars and the breakout of the Peloponnesian War.

Inadvertent escalation is front and centre in Allison's Thucydides' trap.[13] The alleged causal mechanism is easy to follow: both sides wish to avoid war, but they tragically cannot. Structure is destiny, and as power shifts from a hegemon to an aspiring hegemon, war tragically

POSTSCRIPT

all but ensues, even though both sides go to great lengths to avert it.[14] According to Allison, the basis for this utterly structural hypothesis is found in Thucydides' *History of the Peloponnesian War* I 23. Yet, in the translation Allison cites, this much-quoted extract has been inaccurately translated as 'It was the *rise* of Athens and the *fear* that this instilled in Sparta that made the war *inevitable*'.[15] We believe that Thomas Hobbes' first English translation of the *History of the Peloponnesian War* in 1629 better captures the insight of Thucydides.[16] In Hobbes' words: 'I conceive to be the growth of the Athenian power, which putting the Lacedaemonians [Spartans] into fear necessitated the war'. Hobbes' translation more closely reflects the spirit of Thucydides' original text by rendering the Greek term ἀνάγκη (*anankê*) as 'necessity' rather than Crawley's term 'inevitability'. Inevitability pertains to mechanical and deterministic outcomes where human agency is irrelevant, where leaders are passive figures unable to change the course of events.[17]

The inaccurate translation of the original text has enormous implications for any purely structural, modern Thucydidean analogy. To be sure, Allison attempts to circumvent the issue of structural inevitability by attributing a degree of hyperbole to Thucydides' original term (this should be attributed to the translator and not to Thucydides, however). Allison then drives the debate towards 'inadvertent escalation' similar to theories trying to explain the outbreak of the First World War.[18] To start with, historians at present tend to look askance upon that old explanation of the First World War as supposedly an inadvertent war; on the contrary, they emphasise the premeditated nature of that war.[19] Moreover, and more important for our argument, events in Thucydides' own history render the charge of inadvertent escalation unpersuasive as a cause of the Peloponnesian War. In fact, as we have seen in the main body of this book, during a critical moment for bilateral relations, Pericles, the Athenian statesman much admired by Thucydides, rejected Sparta's ultimatum to revoke the Athenian embargo against Megara (the so-called Megarian Decree), going instead to great lengths to persuade the Athenian demos not to cave in to the Spartan demands.

As we have shown in this book, Pericles' choice for war was based upon his theory of victory, which contended that a war of exhaustion would eventually prove to the Spartans that a continental power had no path to victory against a maritime power like Athens. Likewise, when the Spartans had the opportunity to avoid war and take their bilateral dispute with Athens to 'binding arbitration' (as the relevant clause in the Thirty Years' Peace treaty demanded), they also declined. Hence, the Peloponnesian War did not erupt due to inadvertent escalation. Rather, it was a 'war of premeditation'; in other words, a calculated outcome of a 'rational cost-benefit analysis and strategic agency between two adversaries with clashing policy objectives'.[20] As Mary Nichols has correctly argued, 'Thucydides leaves ample room in his account for human control of events leading to the war'.[21]

This essential insight in Thucydides' work is completely ignored in Allison's popularized Thucydides' trap formulation. For Allison, the Peloponnesian War springs from tragedy, not from strategic choice. As populism has lately become a fashionable research topic, Allison even argues that it was the populist 'street' which carried Pericles towards his confrontation with Sparta, as he 'bent to popular pressure and reluctantly drew up plans for war'.[22] Yet this characterization is totally antithetical to Thucydides' own view about Pericles' extraordinary leadership and 'unflappable intellectual resolve'.[23] In his eulogy about Periclean leadership, Thucydides argued that Pericles 'could contain the will of the people without limiting people's freedom'. He was not influenced by the demands of the people, but he shaped the demands: 'In short, what was nominally a democracy was becoming in his hands government by the first citizen'.[24] Here lies a key Thucydidean insight into the consequentiality of political leadership and its impact on strategy and war. Hence, unlike Allison, who argues that populism was a factor contributing to the Peloponnesian War, Thucydides clearly frames Pericles' decisive role in strategizing for the war: 'We must not fall behind them [our fathers], but must resist our enemies in any way and in every way, and attempt to hand down our power to our posterity unimpaired'.[25] As we have seen, Pericles was so competent that he even persuaded the Athenians to follow a post-heroic strategy and hide behind walls while the Spartans destroyed Athenian property unchecked—it was due to this achievement that Hans Delbrück lavished praise on Pericles.[26]

If a historical analogy is to be of educational value, it must accurately assess both the likeness and the incongruity between the historical epochs it analogises.[27] In the Thucydides' trap, a core tenet is that China is Athens and the United States is Sparta, and that while Athens was a rising power, it had not yet overtaken Sparta when the war broke out.[28] If the power shift has not yet occurred, then the 'ruling power' possesses a powerful incentive to preventively attack the rising power from a position of relative strength, thereby increasing its odds of winning the 'inevitable' war.[29] Thus, a theory of hegemonic transition can be simplified to a theory of preventive war—thoroughly theorized by modern realists—where a ruling power decapitates a rising power and 'strangles the baby in its cradle'.[30] However, according to Thucydides, the 'power shift' in favour of Athens had already occurred long before the outbreak of the war in 431 BCE. By the end of the First Peloponnesian War (460–45 BCE), if not earlier, 'rising' Athens had already overtaken 'ruling' Sparta. As we have already argued in Chapter Two of this book, the Thirty Years Peace essentially put an end to the Spartan pretensions of being the sole hegemon in Greece. In that treaty, Sparta had even acknowledged the very legitimacy of the Athenian empire.[31] Undoubtedly, after 445 BCE, Athens had surpassed Sparta as the dominant power in Greece and perhaps throughout the Mediterranean world. By then, Athens had already expelled the world's largest empire, Persia, from the Aegean Sea and Asia Minor, and had established its own naval empire, which spanned from the Aegean to the Black Sea, and was capable of dispatching expeditionary forces to fight wars in Sicily, Byzantium, Asia Minor, Cyprus and Egypt.[32]

Athens was projecting its force many hundreds of miles away from its territory, while introvert Sparta was limited to its neighbourhood, unable to undertake even a rudimentary naval expedition. In the Greek interstate system of the time, power transition had already been achieved in favour of the rising power—Athens. Yet today, power transition is still at an early stage, as China lags behind the United States in most indicators of composite national strength. Some analysts have even argued the Chinese power has already peaked and may never surpass that of the U.S.[33] Thus, the argument that Sino–American power dynamics are analogous to Athenian–Spartan power dynamics before the outbreak of the war is misleading.

The popularized Thucydides' trap employs only a single variable throughout its causal process and quintessential prediction: the variable of power differentials. Accordingly, it constitutes a highly structural interpretation of hegemonic war that gravely oversimplifies Thucydides' analysis on the causes of the Peloponnesian War. Thucydides instead went to great lengths to provide accurate details on the crucial arguments delivered during vigorous political debates in both Sparta and Athens. This emphasis on statesmanship indicated that Thucydides was not a structural determinist; rather, he well understood the impact of political leadership on strategic choice. Thucydides built his narrative around 'climactic moments' when statesmen had to make important collective decisions. So focused is Thucydides' attention to climactic moments of decision that spirited debates (*demegories*/δημηγορίες) 'occupy a far greater proportion of the space in Thucydides than in any other historical work from antiquity and perhaps any other time'.[34] In the words of Daniel Garst, 'Far from viewing historical figures as driven by forces outside their control, Thucydides sees them as the conscious initiators of events'.[35]

Thucydides emphasized the importance of leadership, eloquently describing the crucial impact of statesmanship on power differentials.[36] First, he elaborates upon the outstanding achievements of the Athenian statesman Themistocles who, against all odds, turned a small backwater agricultural city in Attica into a naval superpower that annihilated the all-mighty navy of the Persian Empire—the dominant superpower of the time in the Mediterranean interstate system.[37] In advancing Athens' power, Themistocles first clashed with landowners as he shifted the city's resources towards shipbuilding, meanwhile founding the port of Piraeus at a strategically defensible location.[38] He also reformed the Athenian political system by empowering the lowest class of citizens (*thetes*/θῆτες) to became rowers in the newly built oar-driven warships called triremes. At a critical strategic moment, Themistocles persuaded the Athenians to abandon their own homeland, board their ships and await the right opportunity to fight back against the Persians—a decision which was so daring and difficult to execute that it cannot easily fit into the rationalization of strategy. Second, Thucydides describes the great statesmanship of Pericles, who doubled down on the strategic innovation of Themistocles, Pericles' mentor, by strategically re-conceptualizing Athens as an island.[39] When the Peloponnesian War began, Pericles proposed a grand strategy of exhaustion that utilized Athens' naval supremacy and defensive walls. Finally, in contrast to these two admired statesmen, Thucydides is critical of the leadership of Alcibiades, attributing to him the ultimate defeat of Athens.[40] Right before the start of the war, Thucydides endorsed the actions of Archidamus, the Spartan king, who argued for prudent strategic restraint.[41]

Thucydides thus viewed agency and political leadership as key factors shaping decisions about war and peace, victory and defeat, and was a strong advocate of strategic prudence (*sophrosyne*/ σωφροσύνη). Prudence, in the work of Thucydides, is a leadership quality that involves rationality (e.g. matching means with strategic ends), self-restraint of human nature's worst tendencies (e.g. hubris), and foresight.[42]

For Thucydides, political leadership determines the strategic choices of a state and the way state applies its power, thereby affecting the threat posed to other states. For instance, Athens' particularly expansionist behaviour under the guidance of Alcibiades eventually led to the formation of a counter-threat coalition which included not only Sparta, but also Syracuse and Persia. It was this coalition that ultimately led to the Athenian defeat. In modern times, many scholars have argued that the relatively restrained way the United States has applied its power since 1991 (i.e. scrupulously avoiding any expansion of U.S. territory) explains why Europe and other U.S. allies have not attempted to balance against it.[43] Hence, the structural argument that 'power balances power' is conditional upon the threat intensity, which is ultimately determined by a state's strategic choices, which in turn are shaped by statesmanship and leadership.[44]

Antagonism between two great powers is a necessary but not sufficient condition for the outbreak of hegemonic war. When one side sees a path to victory at an acceptable cost, then war may indeed ensue. In Thucydides' history, the Syracusan leader Hermocrates made exactly this point, anticipating what nowadays is called expected utility theory. In his words:

> No one is forced to engage in it [war] by ignorance, or kept out of it by fear, if he fancies there is anything to be gained by it. To the former the gain appears greater than the danger, while the latter would rather stand the risk than put up with any immediate sacrifice.[45]

Today, the cost of war between two nuclear superpowers, with each capable of annihilating the other's society (otherwise known as mutually assured destruction), is such that no rational statesman would pursue an all-out confrontation.[46] Hence, given modern technology's sophistication and ever-expanding frontier, China and the United States will make every effort to avoid fighting a direct war that adopts a military strategy of annihilation. Yet this mutual deterrence does not preclude that the two behemoths will not fight proxy wars like the United States and the Soviet Union did during the Cold War. There may exist a grey zone where the two will try to contain or even roll back each other's initiatives. While a strategy of annihilation is most unlikely, a strategy of exhaustion is not. Additionally, the theory of nuclear deterrence is based on a relatively static technological frontier. Yet in the age of artificial intelligence and cascading technological disruptions, great powers are on alert to avoid technological surprises by which one side may enjoy a moment of strategic primacy and land a so-called splendid first strike.[47] The nature of such technological innovation is not amenable to bilateral arms control agreements (the ability for verification of artificial intelligence–software technology is difficult) between China and the United States. Therefore, it is expected that competition in the technological arena will remain fierce. It is in this domain that prudent statesmanship is needed to support Sino–American strategic stability within an environment of rapid technological change. Of course, no one can prophesise that leaders will always exercise prudence and opt for self-restraint under fierce strategic antagonism, but the cost of irrationality is prohibitively high.

When traditional methods cannot produce results, one must expect the use of unconventional strategies such as insurgencies, proxy wars, covert actions and subversion, all of which aim to create domestic instability. The most paradigmatic case of hybrid warfare recorded in Thucydides was the instigation of the helots' revolt by the Athenians.[48] As Sparta's peculiar socioeconomic order was fragile and the helots constituted a vast majority within the Spartan population, an upheaval would directly challenge Sparta's own socioeconomic existence.[49] Indeed, when an Athenian-instigated revolt did occur— in conjunction with the Pylos/Sphacteria expedition—it had such a fearful effect upon the Spartans that they immediately sued for peace.

POSTSCRIPT

Today, the Sino–American strategic antagonism may be shifting towards unconventional warfare, wherein each of the two antagonists tries to exploit the domestic vulnerabilities of the other.[50] If outright war is impossible to win due to mutually assured destruction, and if peace is impossible to establish due to an incompatibility of political objectives, then the antagonists may enter the grey zone of competition, where every interaction—trade, investment, infrastructure, supply chains, social media, lawfare—is weaponized.[51] This competition entails that rival hegemons are entering a protracted multi-theatre/multi-front race of exhaustion. This race has already started and has a lot of similarities with Cold War 1.0. At the end of this marathon, the more fragile polity will break down and the more resilient one will prevail.

To sum up, in order to unlock the strategic wisdom of Thucydides, his book must be studied holistically, rather than casually. Crucially, the notion that Athens and Sparta sleepwalked into war does not match events as Thucydides describes them. In particular, an examination of the *Pentecontaetia* reveals that Athenian power mattered gravely, as did the strategic choices made in Athens and Sparta through vigorous political debates. And it is in those debates that Thucydides emphasizes the consequentiality of strategic judgement and prudent leadership.[52] In light of this analysis, the future of the Sino–American hegemonic transition is not yet written and depends on the strategic choices made by leaders in Washington and Beijing.[53] Thucydides' ultimate purpose was to be didactic (*didactikos*/διδακτικός)[54]—that is, to cultivate prudent leaders versed in the art of statesmanship.

APPENDIX

STRATEGIC CONCEPTS IN THUCYDIDES' *HISTORY*

We conclude by presenting a number of strategic concepts as they appear in Thucydides' text. Naturally, Thucydides did not use contemporary strategic jargon. Nevertheless, one cannot help being impressed by the remarkable clarity and dexterity with which he uses a multitude of supposedly modern concepts. Two things should be mentioned. First, it will become apparent that certain extracts can fall under various headings, since they contain more than one concept. Secondly, that following selection does not claim to be exhaustive; indeed, given the richness of Thucydides' text, it seems hardly possible to produce an exhaustive list of the various strategic concepts covered therein. This limitation notwithstanding, we hope that contemporary scholars might find some use in what follows.

Alliances: 'A power which has never in the whole of her past history been willing to ally herself with any of her neighbors, is now found asking them to ally themselves with her. [...] What once seemed the wise precaution of refusing to involve ourselves in alliances with other powers, lest we should also involve ourselves in risks of their choosing, has now proved to be folly and weakness'. (I 32)

'Could there be a clearer guarantee of our good faith than is offered by the fact that the power which is at enmity with you, is also at enmity with us'. (I 35)

'Identity of interests is the surest of bonds whether between states or individuals'. (I 124)

THUCYDIDES ON STRATEGY

'Now the only sure basis of an alliance is for each party to be equally afraid of the other: he who would like to encroach is then deterred by the reflection that he will not have odds in his favor'. (III 11)

'The adverse attitude of the Spartans in the whole Plataean affair was mainly adopted to please the Thebans, who were thought to be useful in the war at that moment raging'. (III 68)

'For the future we do not enter into alliance, as we have been used to do, with people whom we must help in their need, and who can never help us in ours'. (VI 13)

Appeasement: 'I hope that you will none of you think that we shall be going to war for a trifle if we refuse to revoke the Megara decree [...]. Why, this trifle contains the whole seal and trial of your resolution. If you give way, you will instantly have to meet some greater demand, as having been frightened into obedience in the first instance; while a firm refusal will make them clearly understand that they must treat you as equals. [...] For all claims from an equal, urged upon a neighbor as commands, before any attempt at arbitration, be they great or be they small, have only one meaning, and that is slavery'. (I 140–1)

Arms control: 'Perceiving what they were going to do, the Spartans sent an embassy to Athens. They would have themselves preferred to see neither her nor any other city in possession of a wall [...]. They begged her not only to abstain from building walls for herself, but also to join them in throwing down the remaining walls of the cities outside the Peloponnesus. They did not express openly the suspicious intention with regard to the Athenians that lay behind this proposal but urged that by these means the barbarians, in the case of a third invasion, would not have any strong place, such as in this invasion he had in Thebes, for his base of operation; and that the Peloponnesus would suffice for all as a base both for retreat and offense'. (I 90)

Balance of power: 'The Athenians hearing this, sent Phaeax to see if they could not by some means so convince their allies there and the rest of the Sicilians of the ambitious designs of Syracuse, as to induce them to form a general coalition against her, and thus save The People of Leontini'. (V 4)

APPENDIX

'An alliance with Athens would no longer be open to her [Argos]. This was a resource which she had always counted upon, by reason of the existing tensions, if her treaty with Sparta were not maintained'. (V 40)

'To leave each of the contending parties in possession of one element, thus enabling the King when he found one party troublesome to call in the other'. (VIII 46)

'[Tissaphernes wished] to keep them evenly balanced by not throwing his weight into either scale'. (VIII 87)

Balancing, external: 'The means will be, first, the acquisition of allies, Hellenic or barbarian it matters not, so long as they are an accession to our strength naval or financial'. (I 82)

'They resolved to send embassies to the King and to such other of the barbarian powers as either party could look to for assistance, and tried to ally themselves with the uncommitted states at home'. (II 7)

Balancing, internal: 'The development of our home resources.' (I 82)

'The money required for these objects shall be provided by our contributions'. (I 121)

Bipolar international system: 'The preparations of both the combatants were in every department in the last state of perfection; and he [Thucydides] could see the rest of the Hellenic race taking sides in the quarrel; those who delayed doing so at once having it in contemplation'. (I 1)

'This coalition, after repulsing the barbarian, soon afterwards split into two sections [...]. At the head of the one stood Athens, at the head of the other Sparta, one the first naval, the other the first military power in Hellas'. (I 18)

Border disputes: 'The Athenians received another addition to their confederacy in the Megarians; who left the Spartan alliance, annoyed by a war about boundaries forced on them by Corinth'. (I 103)

'And entering the Tegean territory, began to divert into Mantinean land the water about which the Mantineans and Tegeans are always fighting, on account of the extensive damage it does to whichever of the two countries it flows into'. (V 65)

THUCYDIDES ON STRATEGY

Coercive diplomacy: 'For the only light in which you can view their [the Athenians'] land is that of a hostage in your hands, a hostage the more valuable the better it is cultivated'. (I 82)

'[Archidamus] it is said, expected that the Athenians would shrink from letting their land be wasted, and would make their submission while it was still uninjured'. (II 18)

'I shall do my best to compel you by laying waste your land'. (IV 87)

Defence planning: 'It is necessary to punish an enemy not only for what he does, but also beforehand for what he intends to do, if the first to relax precaution would not also be the first to suffer'. (VI 38)

Domino theory: 'But if Syracuse falls, all Sicily falls also, and Italy immediately afterwards; and the danger which I just now spoke of from that quarter will before long be upon you'. (VI 91)

Economics and strategy: 'The coast populations now began to apply themselves more closely to the acquisition of wealth, and their life became more settled; some even began to build themselves walls on the strength of their newly acquired riches. For the love of gain would reconcile the weaker to the dominion of the stronger, and the possession of capital enabled the more powerful to reduce the smaller cities to subjection'. (I 8)

'[Pelops] arriving from Asia with vast wealth among a needy population, acquired such power that, stranger though he was, the country was called after him'. (I 9)

'War is a matter not so much of arms as of money, which makes arms of use'. (I 83)

'Capital, it must be remembered, maintains a war more than forced contributions'. (I 141)

'Success in war depending principally upon conduct and capital'. (II 13)

'The generals accepted their [the besieged Potidaeans] proposals [...] [as Athens] had already spent two thousand talents upon the siege'. (II 70)

'A grand total of two hundred and fifty vessels employed on active service in a single summer. It was this, with Potidaea, that most exhausted her [Athens'] revenues'. (III 17)

APPENDIX

'The Athenians sent it [the fleet], upon the plea of their common descent [with the Leontini], but in reality to prevent the exportation of Sicilian corn to the Peloponnesus'. (III 86)

'They possess most gold and silver, by which war, like everything else, flourishes'. (VI 34)

'Whatever property there is in the country will most of it become yours, either by capture or surrender; and the Athenians will at once be deprived of their revenues from the silver mines at Laurium, of their present gains from their land and from the law courts, and above all of the revenue from their allies, which will be paid less regularly, as they lose their awe of Athens and see you addressing yourselves with vigor to this war'. (VI 91)

'Their expenditure being now not the same as at first, but having grown with the war grew, while their revenues decayed'. (VII 28)

Expected utility as an incentive for war: 'No one is forced to engage in it [war] by ignorance, or kept out of it by fear, if he fancies there is anything to be gained by it. To the former the gain appears greater than the danger, while the latter would rather stand the risk than put up with any immediate sacrifice'. (IV 59)

'The party attacked, whose own country is in danger, can scarcely discuss what is prudent with the calmness of men who are in full enjoyment of what they have, and are thinking of attacking a neighbor in order to get more'. (IV 92)

Fear and national security policy: 'The Spartans out of fear of you want war'. (I 33)

'Do not [...] drive the rest of us in despair to some other alliance'. (I 71)

'Fear being our principal motive, though honor and interest afterwards came in'. (I 75)

'If we did accept an empire that was offered to us, and refused to give it up under the pressure of three of the strongest motives, fear, honor and interest'. (I 76)

'They [the Amphipolitans] considered that Brasidas had been their preserver and courting as they did the alliance of Sparta for fear of Athens, in their present hostile relations with the latter'. (V 11)

THUCYDIDES ON STRATEGY

'Fear makes us hold our empire in Hellas, and fear makes us now come, with the help of our friends, to safely order matters in Sicily'. (VI 83)

Force-to-space ratio: 'As to his [the enemy's] numbers, these need not too much alarm you. Large as they may be he can only engage in small detachments, from the difficulty of landing'. (IV 10)

Friction, chance and unpredictability in war: 'Consider the vast influence of accident in war, before you are engaged in it. As it continues, it generally becomes an affair of chances, chances from which neither of us is exempt, and whose event we must risk in the dark'. (I 78)

'For war of all things proceeds least upon definite rules, but draws principally upon itself for contrivances to meet an emergency'. (I 122)

'The opportunities of war wait for no man'. (I 142)

'The course of war cannot be foreseen'. (II 11)

'[Sensible men] think that war, so far from staying within the limit to which a combatant may wish to confine it, will run the course that its chances prescribe'. (IV 18)

'Fortune, it was thought, might have humbled them [the Spartans], but the men themselves were the same as ever'. (V 75)

'We know that the fortune of war is sometimes more impartial than the disproportion of numbers might lead one to suppose'. (V 102)

Geography: 'Their [the Corcyreans'] geographical situation makes them independent of others'. (I 37)

'At the same time the island [Corcyra] seemed to lie conveniently on the coasting passage to Italy and Sicily'. (I 44)

'Potidaea [...] lies most conveniently for any action against the Thracian cities'. (I 68)

Horizontal escalation: 'The attacks of the Athenians upon the Peloponnesus, and in particular upon Laconia, might, it was hoped, be diverted most effectively by annoying them in return, and by sending an army to their allies'. (IV 80)

'Let us [the Syracusans] also send to Sparta and Corinth and ask them to come here and help us as soon as possible, and to keep alive the war in Hellas'. (VI 34)

APPENDIX

Hostile feelings—hostile intentions: 'If peace was ever desirable for both parties, it is surely so at the present moment, before anything irremediable befall us and force us to hate you eternally, personally as well as politically'. (IV 20)

Imperialism: 'That the Athenians should cherish this ambition and practice this policy is very excusable; and I do not blame those who wish to rule, but those who are too ready to serve'. (IV 61)

Legitimacy, domestic: 'A free and a famous city has through all time been ours. The quality which they condemn is really nothing but a wise moderation; thanks to its possession, we alone do not become insolent in success and give way less than others in misfortune'. (I 84)

'In short, I say that as a city we are the school of Hellas [...] Such is the Athens for which these men, in the assertion of their resolve not to lose her, nobly fought and died'. (II 41)

Legitimacy, international: 'Men's feelings inclined much more to the Spartans, especially as they proclaimed themselves the liberators of Hellas. No private or public effort that could help them in speech or action was omitted'. (II 8)

'In short, only show yourselves as liberators, and you may count upon having the advantage in the war'. (III 13)

'[The Athenians] being ambitious in real truth of conquering the whole [of Sicily], although they had also the specious design of aiding their kindred and other allies in the island'. (VI 6)

Logistics: 'The country offered no resources in itself, and even in summer they could not send round enough'. (IV 27)

'Dividing the whole fleet into three divisions, allotted one to each of their number, to avoid sailing all together and thus lacking sufficient water, or provisions at the stations where they might land'. (VI 42)

Loss-of-strength gradient: 'Few indeed have been the large armaments, either Hellenic or barbarian, that have gone far from home and been successful. They cannot be more numerous than the people of the country and their neighbors, whom fear unites; and if they fail for want of supplies in a foreign land, to those against whom their plans were laid they nonetheless leave renown, although they may themselves have been the main cause of their own discomfort'. (VI 33)

Military discipline: 'Regard discipline and vigilance as of the first importance'. (II 11)
   'And in action think order and silence all important'. (II 89)

Military initiative: 'The enemy's vessels being as many or more than our own, we are constantly anticipating an attack. Indeed they may be seen exercising, and it lies with them to take the initiative'. (VII 12)

Military necessity: 'Besides, anything done under the pressure of war and danger might reasonably claim indulgence even in the eye of the god'. (IV 98)

Military tactics: 'After this they joined battle, the Argives and their allies advancing with haste and fury, the Spartans slowly and to the music of many flute players—a standing institution in their army, that has nothing to do with religion, but is meant to make them advance evenly, stepping in time, without breaking their order, as large armies are apt to do in the moment of engaging'. (V 70)
   'All armies are alike in this: on going into action they get forced out rather on their right wing, and one and the other overlap with this their adversary's left; because fear makes each man do his best to shelter his unarmed side with the shield of the man next him on the right, thinking that the closer the shields are locked together the better will he be protected'. (V 71)

Military training: 'The long training of action was of more use for saving lives than any brief verbal exhortation, though ever so well delivered'. (V 69)

Misperceptions: 'Our resources are what they have always been, and our error has been an error of judgment, to which all are equally liable'. (IV 18)

Morale: 'Zeal is always at its height at the commencement of an undertaking'. (II 8)

APPENDIX

'For before what is sudden, unexpected, and least within calculation the spirit quails'. (II 61)

'Beaten men do not face a danger twice with the same determination'. (II 89)

'We may expect to find the Athenians as much on their guard as men generally are who have just taken a city [i.e. relaxed]'. (III 30)

'I hope that none of you in our present strait will think to show his wit by exactly calculating all the perils that encompass us, but that you will rather hasten to close with the enemy, without staying to weigh the odds, seeing in this your best chance of safety'. (IV 10)

'How impossible it is to drive back an enemy determined enough to stand his ground and not to be frightened away by the surf and the terrors of the ships sailing in'. (IV 10)

'He resolved not to disgust the army by keeping it in the same place, and broke up his camp and advanced'. (V 7)

'A fresh assailant has always more terrors for an enemy than the one he is immediately engaged with'. (V 9)

'Every armament was most terrible at first; if it allowed time to run on without showing itself, men's courage revived, and they saw it appear at last almost with indifference'. (VI 49)

'The unlooked-for spectacle of Syracusans daring to face the Athenian navy would cause a terror to the enemy, the advantages of which would far outweigh any loss that Athenian science might inflict upon their inexperience'. (VII 21)

'For the most part, where there is the greatest hope, there is also the greatest ardor for action'. (VII 67)

National character: '[The Athenians] were born into the world to take no rest themselves and to give none to others'. (I 70)

'Indeed, after the Spartans, the Chians are the only people that I have known who knew how to be wise in prosperity, and who ordered their city the more securely the greater it grew'. (VIII 24)

'But here, as on so many other occasions, the Spartans proved the most convenient people in the world for the Athenians to be at war with. The wide difference between the two characters, the slowness and want of energy of the Spartans as contrasted with the dash and enterprise of their opponents, proved of the greatest service, especially to a maritime empire like Athens. Indeed this was shown by the Syracusans, who were most like the Athenians in character, and also most successful in combatting them'. (VIII 96)

National interest: 'They should show, first, that it is expedient or at least safe to grant their request'. (I 32)

'No one can quarrel with a people for making, in matters of tremendous risk, the best provision that it can for its interest'. (I 75)

'Calculations of interest have made you take up the cry of justice—a consideration which no one ever yet brought forward to hinder his ambition when he had a chance of gaining anything by might'. (I 76)

'If, right or wrong, you determine to rule, you must carry out your principle and punish the Mytilenians as your interest requires'. (III 40)

'The question before us as sensible men is not their guilt, but our interests. [...] We are not in a court of justice, but in a political assembly; and the question is not justice, but how to make the Mytilenians useful to Athens'. (III 44)

'In their present hostile relations with the latter [Athens] they [the Amphipolitans] could no longer with the same advantage or satisfaction pay Hagnon his honors'. (V 11)

'Of all the men we know they [the Spartans] are most conspicuous in considering what is agreeable honorable, and what is expedient just'. (V 105)

'Expediency goes with security, while justice and honor cannot be followed without danger'. (V 107)

'If we are now here in Sicily, it is equally in the interest of our security, with which we perceive that your interest also coincides'. (VI 83)

'As for the assertion that it is beyond all reason that we should free the Sicilian, while we enslave the Chalcidian, the fact is that the latter is useful to us by being without arms and contributing money only; while the former, the Leontines and our other friends, cannot be too independent. Besides, for tyrants and imperial cities nothing is unreasonable if expedient, no one a kinsman unless sure; but friendship or enmity is everywhere a matter of time and circumstance'. (VI 84–5)

APPENDIX

Naval power: 'For your first endeavor should be to prevent, if possible, the existence of any naval power except your own; failing this, to secure the friendship of the strongest that does exist'. (I 35)

'Remember that there are but three considerable naval powers in Hellas, Athens, Corcyra, and Corinth, and that if you allow two of these three to become one, and Corinth to secure us for herself, you will have to hold the sea against the united fleets of Corcyra and the Peloponnesus. But if you receive us, you will have our ships to reinforce you in the struggle'. (I 36)

'Unless we can either beat them at sea, or deprive them of the revenues which feed their navy, we shall meet with little but disaster'. (I 81)

'Seamanship, just like anything else, is a matter requiring skill, and will not admit of being taken up occasionally as an occupation for times of leisure; on the contrary, it is so exacting as to leave leisure for nothing else'. (I 142)

'The rule of the sea is indeed a great matter'. (I 143)

'The visible field of action has two parts, land and sea. In the whole of one of these you are completely supreme, not merely as far as you use it at present, but also to what further extent you may think fit: in fine, your naval resources are such that your vessels may go where they please, without the King [of Persia] or any other nation on earth being able to stop them'. (II 62)

Neutrality: 'The Argives were in a most flourishing condition, having taken no part in the war against Athens, but having on the contrary profited largely by their neutrality'. (V 28)

Numerical superiority: 'Confidence might possibly be felt in our superiority in hoplites and population'. (I 81)

'We have many reasons to expect success—first, superiority in numbers and in military experience'. (I 121)

'No irritation [...] must provoke us to a battle with the numerical superiority of the Peloponnesians'. (I 143)

'As a rule, numbers and equipment give victory'. (II 87)

'Hostilities recommenced, victory remaining with The People, who had the advantage in numbers and position'. (III 74)

THUCYDIDES ON STRATEGY

'Since the Peloponnesian Dorians are our superiors in numbers and near neighbors, we Ionians looked out for the best means of escaping their domination'. (VI 82)

Overextension: 'You leave many enemies behind you here to go there [to Sicily] far away and bring more back with you'. (VI 10)

'But the Spartans derived most encouragement from the belief that Athens, with two wars on her hands, against themselves and against the Sicilians, would more easy to subdue'. (VII 18)

'But what most oppressed them was that they had two wars at once'. (VII 28)

Power: 'We have therefore no right [...] to content ourselves with an inspection of a city without considering its power'. (I 10)

'It has always been the law that the weaker should be subject to the stronger'. (I 76)

'The strong do what they can and the weak suffer what they must'. (V 89)

'The contest not being an equal one, with honor as the prize and shame as the penalty, but a question of self-preservation and of not resisting those who are far stronger than you are'. (V 101)

'By a necessary law of their nature they rule wherever they can'. (V 105)

'What an intending ally trusts to is not the goodwill of those who ask his aid, but a decided superiority of power for action'. (V 109)

'Those who do not yield to their equals, who keep terms with their superiors, and are moderate toward their inferiors, on the whole succeed best'. (V 111)

'The Spartans [...] had no right to give orders to us more than we to them, except that of being the strongest at that moment'. (VI 82)

Pre-emption: 'Men do not rest content with parrying the attacks of a superior, but often strike the first blow to prevent the attack being made'. (VI 18)

Prestige: 'The Spartans sent us to try to find some way of settling the affair of our men on the island, that shall be at once satisfactory to

APPENDIX

your interests, and as consistent with our dignity in our misfortune as circumstances permit'. (IV 17)

'Nothing that happened in the war surprised the Hellenes so much as this [the Spartan surrender at Sphacteria]. It was the general opinion that no force or famine could make the Spartans give up their arms, but that they would fight on as they could, and die with them in their hands'. (IV 40)

'At this time Sparta had sunk very low in public estimation because of her disasters'. (V 28)

'The imputations cast upon them [the Spartans] by the Hellenes at the time, whether of cowardice on account of the disaster in the island, or of mismanagement and slowness generally, were all wiped out by this single action [the Spartan victory at Mantinea]'. (V 75)

'The Hellenes, after expecting to see our city ruined by the war, concluded it to be even greater than it really is, by reason of the magnificence with which I represented it at the Olympic games'. (VI 16)

Preventive war: 'Finally, the growth of the Athenian power could no longer be ignored as their own [the Spartans'] confederacy became the object of its encroachments. They then felt that they could endure it no longer, but that the time had come for them to throw themselves heart and soul upon the hostile power, and break it, if they could, by commencing the present war'. (I 118)

'The Thessalians, who were sovereign in those parts and whose territory was menaced by its foundation, were afraid that it might prove a very powerful neighbor, and so they harassed and made war upon the new settlers continually until they at last wore them out in spite of their originally considerable numbers'. (III 93)

'The Spartans, hearing of the walls that were being built, marched against Argos [...]. They took and razed the walls which were being built'. (V 83)

'If the Syracusans were allowed to go unpunished for their depopulation of Leontini, to ruin the allies still left to Athens in Sicily, and to get the whole power of the island into their hands, there would be a danger of their one day coming with a large force as Dorians to the aid of their Dorian brethren, and as colonists, to the aid of the Peloponnesians who had sent them out, and joining these in pulling down the Athenian empire. The Athenians would, therefore, do well to unite with the allies still left to them, and to make a stand against the Syracusans'. (VI 6)

Principle of concentration of force: 'They were afraid that the Potidaeans and their allies might take advantage of their division to attack them, if they divided their force in two'. (I 64)

'They have a wide sea to cross with all their armament, which could with difficulty keep its order through so long a voyage, and would be easy for us to attack as it came on slowly and in small detachments'. (VI 34)

Principle of unity of command: 'They are incapacitated [...] by the want of the single council chamber requisite to prompt and vigorous action'. (I 141)

'The generals should be few and elected with full powers, and an oath should be taken to leave them entire discretion in their command'. (VI 72)

Security dilemma: 'And at last, when almost all hated us, [...] it appeared no longer safe to give up our empire'. (I 75)

'We assert that we are rulers in Hellas in order not to be subjects; liberators in Sicily that we may not be harmed by the Sicilians; that we are compelled to interfere in many things, because we have many things to guard against'. (VI 87)

Surprise: 'Thebes [...] foreseeing that war was at hand, wished to surprise her old enemy in time of peace, before hostilities had actually broken out'. (II 2)

'The Acarnanians from the ambuscade set upon them from behind, and broke them at the first attack, without their staying to resist; while the panic into which they fell caused the flight of most of their army'. (III 108)

'The enemy who, retaining always the ability to attack, would fall upon his troops unexpectedly wherever they pleased'. (IV 29)

'The landing having taken them by surprise, as they fancied the ships were only sailing as usual to their stations for the night'. (IV 32)

APPENDIX

'About six hundred of the [Athenians] had fallen and only seven of the enemy, owing to there having been no regular engagement, but the affair of accident and panic that I have described'. (V 11)

Terrain: 'If [...] he should force them to engage in the thicket, the smaller number who knew the country would, he thought, have the advantage over the larger who were ignorant of it, and thus his own army might be imperceptibly destroyed in spite of its numbers, as his men would not be able to see where to support each other'. (IV 29)

'The tactics of Demosthenes had divided them into companies of two hundred, more or less, and made them occupy the highest points in order to paralyze the enemy by surrounding him on every side'. (IV 32)

Unequal growth: 'I conceive to be the growth of the Athenian power, which putting the Lacedaemonians [Spartans] into fear necessitated the war'. (I 23) [Hobbes trans]

'The Spartans voted that the treaty had been broken, and that war must be declared, not so much because they were persuaded by the arguments of the allies, as because they feared the growth of the power of the Athenians, seeing most of Hellas already subject to them'. (I 88)

NOTES

PREFACE

1. The Peloponnesian War has been inextricably linked with Thucydides. However, since he did not finish his work—and thus anyone who wishes to have a complete picture of that war is forced to rely on other ancient historians as well, chiefly Xenophon (Xenophon, *Hellenica*)—an obvious injustice is made. Although duly acknowledging that the present book perpetuates this injustice, we also wish to cite two mitigating factors. First, that none of the other ancient historians dealing with the Peloponnesian War remotely approaches Thucydides' analytical depth (Xenophon gives a fairly reliable, 'factual' presentation, but nothing more). Second, the contribution of other ancient historians notwithstanding, the overwhelming majority of the material on which the present book is based comes from Thucydides. Hence, we feel that we are not too wrong to talk about 'Thucydides' analysis' even when dealing with events actually mentioned by somebody else.
2. Louis J. Halle, *The Elements of International Strategy* (Lanham, MD: University Press of America, 1984), p. 15.
3. See, among others, Bruce Russett, 'A Post-Thucydides, Post-Cold-War World', *Occasional Research Papers* (Athens: Institute of International Relations, Panteion University, 1992).
4. See, among others, John Mueller, *Quiet Cataclysm: Reflections on the Recent Transformation of World Politics* (New York: HarperCollins, 1995), and Edward Morse, *Modernization and Transformation of International Relations* (New York: Free Press, 1976).
5. Robert Gilpin, *War and Change in World Politics* (Cambridge: Cambridge University Press, 1981), p. 7.
6. Athanassios G. Platias and Constantinos Koliopoulos, 'Grand Strategies Clashing: Athenian and Spartan Strategies in Thucydides' "History of the Peloponnesian War"', *Comparative Strategy*, 21, 5 (October–December 2002), pp. 377–99.

1. GRAND STRATEGY: A FRAMEWORK FOR ANALYSIS

1. Michael I. Handel, *Masters of War: Classical Strategic Thought* (London: Frank Cass, 1992), p. 1; Sun Tzu, *The Art of War* (trans. Samuel B. Griffith) (Oxford: Oxford University Press, 1963); Carl von Clausewitz, *On War* (ed./trans. Michael Howard and Peter Paret) (Princeton, NJ: Princeton University Press, 1989).
2. Robert B. Strassler (ed.), *The Landmark Thucydides: A Comprehensive Guide to the Peloponnesian War* (New York: Free Press, 1996).
3. Robert Gilpin, *War and Change in World Politics* (Cambridge: Cambridge University Press, 1981), p. 227.
4. Colin Gray has declared that 'the strategist's toolkit' is Clausewitz' *On War*; Colin S. Gray, *Modern Strategy* (Oxford: Oxford University Press, 1999), ch. 3. We do not dispute this claim, but want to point out that Thucydides' *History* may legitimately aspire to at least equal status.
5. Gray, *Modern Strategy*, p. 1, emphasis in text.
6. Definition by the early nineteenth-century German war theorist Heinrich Dietrich von Bülow; see Peter Paret, 'Clausewitz', in Peter Paret (ed.), *Makers of Modern Strategy from Machiavelli to the Nuclear Age* (Princeton, NJ: Princeton University Press, 1986), p. 190.
7. Definition by the Swiss general and strategist Antoine Henry de Jomini (1779–1869); Henry de Jomini, *Summary of the Art of War* (ed. Brig. Gen. J.D. Hittle, abridged edn), reproduced in *Roots of Strategy, Book 2* (Harrisburg, PA: Stackpole Books, 1987), p. 460.
8. See B.H. Liddell Hart, *Strategy* (2nd rev. edn) (London: Meridian, 1991), p. 321.
9. See André Beaufre, *Introduction to Strategy* (London: Faber and Faber, 1965), p. 22.
10. Clausewitz, *On War*, bk. 1, p. 75.
11. For the 'horizontal dimension' of strategy, see Edward N. Luttwak, *Strategy: The Logic of War and Peace* (Cambridge, MA: The Belknap Press of Harvard University Press, 1987), p. 70.
12. For an analysis of the paradoxical logic of strategy, not free from overstatement, see Luttwak, *Strategy*.
13. Daniel J. Hughes (ed.), *Moltke on the Art of War: Selected Writings* (trans. Daniel J. Hughes and Harry Bell) (Novato, CA: Presidio, 1995), p. 45.
14. See Gunther E. Rothenberg, 'Moltke, Schlieffen, and the Doctrine of Strategic Envelopment', in Peter Paret (ed.), *Makers of Modern Strategy from Machiavelli to the Nuclear Age* (Princeton, NJ: Princeton University Press, 1986), pp. 296–325, as well as the famous analysis of Gerhard Ritter, *The Schlieffen Plan* (London: Wolff, 1958).
15. Bernard Brodie, *Strategy in the Missile Age* (Princeton, NJ: Princeton University

Press, 1959), p. 43. See also S.E. Finer, *The Man on Horseback* (Middlesex: Penguin Books, 1975).
16. Alfred Thayer Mahan, *The Influence of Sea Power Upon History, 1660–1783* (London: Sampson Low, Marston, 1892), p. 8.
17. See Jomini, *Summary of the Art of War*, reproduced in *Roots of Strategy, Book 2*, p. 460; Clausewitz, *On War*, bk. 2, p. 129; Helmuth von Moltke, *Moltkes Kriegslehren*, extract reproduced in Lawrence Freedman (ed.), *War* (Oxford: Oxford University Press, 1994), p. 221.
18. Colin S. Gray, *War, Peace, and Victory: Strategy and Statecraft for the Next Century* (New York: Simon and Schuster, 1990), p. 35.
19. See Luttwak, *Strategy*, p. 70.
20. Stalin ruled the Soviet Union from the beginning of the 1920s until the eve of the German invasion of 1941 by merely holding the party office of General Secretary, while Deng during the last years of his life was officially nothing more than Chairman of the Chinese Bridge Federation.
21. On this issue, see Bernard Brodie, *War and Politics* (London: Cassell, 1973).
22. Barton Whaley, *Stratagem: Deception and Surprise in War* (Cambridge, MA: MIT, 1969), p. 245.
23. See Edward N. Luttwak, *The Grand Strategy of the Roman Empire from the First Century A.D. to the Third* (Baltimore, MD: Johns Hopkins University Press, 1976); Edward N. Luttwak, *The Grand Strategy of the Soviet Union* (London: Weidenfeld and Nicolson, 1983); Luttwak, *Strategy*; Paul Kennedy, 'Grand Strategies in War and Peace: Toward a Broader Definition', in Paul Kennedy (ed.), *Grand Strategies in War and Peace* (New Haven, CT: Yale University Press, 1991), pp. 1–7. The French General André Beaufre uses the term 'total strategy'; see Beaufre, *Introduction to Strategy*.
24. See Gray, *War, Peace, and Victory*, pp. 38–41. In that text, Gray uses the term 'theory of war', but we believe that 'theory of victory' is a better term, as in fact used by Gray himself in 'Nuclear Strategy: The Case for a Theory of Victory', *International Security*, 4, 1 (Summer 1979), pp. 54–87.
25. Clausewitz, *On War*, bk. 8, pp. 627–8.
26. Lenin openly favoured both Russia's defeat in the war and a subsequent civil war that would enable him to establish the dictatorship of the proletariat. The German assistance to Lenin was not confined to helping him reach Russia in 1917, but also extended to granting financial support to the Bolsheviks. For these two points, see Dmitri Volkogonov, *Lenin: Life and Legacy* (London: HarperCollins, 1995), pp. 79–81, 109–28.
27. During the initial stages of Operation Barbarossa, the Germans were often welcomed as liberators by the Soviet population; see Heinz Guderian, *Panzer Leader* (New York: Da Capo, 1996), pp. 159, 193–4; J.F.C. Fuller, *The Conduct of War, 1789–1961* (London: Methuen, 1972), pp. 262–4. For the amazing results of the friendly policy towards the conquered population, followed—

on his own initiative—by the German Field-Marshal Ewald von Kleist, see Samuel W. Mitcham Jr., 'Kleist', in Correlli Barnett (ed.), *Hitler's Generals* (London: Weidenfeld and Nicolson, 1990), pp. 256–7.
28. There is no reason why the concepts of the operational and tactical level cannot be applied on the other components of grand strategy as well.
29. For an analysis of the concept of military strategy, see Barry Posen, *The Sources of Military Doctrine* (Ithaca, NY: Cornell University Press, 1984), ch. 1. It must be mentioned here that Posen uses the term 'military doctrine' to describe both military strategy and what we will later call 'operational doctrine'.
30. The spread of chemical (and to a lesser extent biological) weapons makes it preferable to talk about 'mass destruction forces' instead of 'nuclear forces', although the destructive capacity of chemical and biological weapons cannot be compared with that of nuclear ones.
31. Barry Posen distinguishes only the first three categories; see Posen, *The Sources of Military Doctrine*, p. 14. Robert J. Art distinguishes four purposes of force: defensive, deterrent, compellent, and swaggering (that is, the display of military force in order to enhance prestige); Robert J. Art, 'To What Ends Military Power', *International Security*, 4, 4 (Spring 1980), pp. 4–35.
32. For a further discussion of offensive and defensive military strategies, with special emphasis on the various forms of defence, see Athanassios Platias, 'High Politics in Small Countries' (PhD dissertation, Cornell University, 1986), pp. 31–58.
33. For a discussion, see ibid., pp. 32–4.
34. Alfred Vagts, *Defense and Diplomacy: The Soldier and the Conduct of Foreign Relations* (New York: King's Crown Press, 1956), ch. 8.
35. Thomas C. Schelling, *The Strategy of Conflict* (Cambridge, MA: Harvard University Press, 1960), part 4.
36. For a moral argument concerning the distinction between preventive and preemptive war, see Michael Walzer, *Just and Unjust Wars: A Moral Argument with Historical Illustrations* (2nd edn) (New York: BasicBooks, 1992), ch. 5.
37. The bibliography on deterrence is immense. For two classic analyses, see Glenn H. Snyder, *Deterrence and Defense* (Princeton, NJ: Princeton University Press, 1961), and Thomas C. Schelling, *Arms and Influence* (New Haven, CT: Yale University Press, 1966). See also Lawrence Freedman, *Deterrence* (Cambridge: Polity Press, 2004).
38. See the excellent analysis of Robert J. Art, 'The Influence of Foreign Policy on Seapower', *Sage Professional Papers in International Studies*, 2, 02–019 (Beverly Hills, CA and London: Sage Publications, 1973). See also Constantinos Koliopoulos, 'Understanding Strategic Surprise' (PhD dissertation, Lancaster University, 1996), ch. 7.
39. Art, 'To What Ends Military Power'.
40. André Beaufre prefers to view procurement as operational strategy in peace-

time; see Beaufre, *Introduction to Strategy*. For the importance of procurement strategies, see Ariel Levite and Athanassios Platias, 'Evaluating Small States' Dependence on Arms Imports: An Alternative Perspective', *Peace Studies Program Occasional Paper No. 16* (Ithaca, NY: Cornell University, 1983).

41. One should note that the lower levels of strategy appear solely in wartime. See the dissenting view of Beaufre, mentioned above.
42. The concept of the operational level entered Western strategic thought only in the 1980s. Characteristically, Constantine Fitzgibbon, the translator of the German General Heinz Guderian's book in English is somewhat at a loss when encountering this term (the book was translated in 1952). See Guderian, *Panzer Leader*, p. 22, fn. 1. Sir Basil Liddell Hart immediately after the Second World War made an unsuccessful attempt to bring back the usage of the pre-Napoleonic term 'grand tactics' which, in any case, was not as broad than the term 'operational level'. For a presentation of the pre-Napoleonic terminology, see Jomini, *Summary of the Art of War*, reproduced in *Roots of Strategy, Book 2*, p. 460, and Whaley, *Stratagem*, pp. 245–6.
43. German Field-Marshal Erich von Manstein makes it clear that, as far as Nazi Germany was concerned, the Crimean theatre was autonomous to such a degree, and that there was no interference even from the High Command itself; see Erich von Manstein, *Lost Victories* (Novato, CA: Presidio, 1994), pp. 204, 285.
44. Luttwak, *Strategy*, p. 92.
45. Luttwak, *Strategy*. The concept of operational method is closely connected with that of military doctrine. Military doctrine is a particular range of ideas that explains how an armed force will fight; see Gray, *War, Peace, and Victory*, p. 41. Obviously, the concept of military doctrine can be employed at all levels of military strategy, depending on the range of forces it covers. When a military doctrine governs all or most branches of the armed forces (e.g. the German Blitzkrieg in Operation Barbarossa), it then becomes part of military strategy. At the same time, there are smaller-range doctrines, which usually represent the way each service prefers to accomplish its mission. These can be called 'operational doctrines' or 'operational methods'. For instance, aerial bombardment can be conducted through the operational methods of deep interdiction, area bombing or precision bombing, and each of these operational methods can in turn be implemented through various tactical methods; see Luttwak, *Strategy*, p. 108. Of course, this is not the only contemporary use of the term 'military doctrine'; we have already encountered a different use by Barry Posen (see fn. 28). In Soviet strategic thought, the concept of military doctrine had a far broader meaning. For the Soviets, military doctrine had two dimensions: political-military and military-technical. The first specifically stated the requisite criteria for a Soviet decision to wage war, whereas the second concerned all aspects of military practice, from military strategy to tactics (as defined

above); see Todd Clark, 'Soviet Military Doctrine in the Gorbachev Years: Doctrinal Revolution and Counter-Revolution, 1985–1991', *Bailrigg Paper 24* (Lancaster: CDISS, Lancaster University, 1996), pp. 7–8.

46. Some analysts discern an even lower level, namely the technical one (military technology); see Luttwak, *Strategy*. We contend that technology would be better viewed as one of the structural factors influencing strategy, such as geography. For a treatise following this approach, see Martin van Creveld, *Technology and War* (New York: Free Press, 1989).
47. Immediately after that, he defined strategy as 'the use of engagements for the object of the war'; see Clausewitz, *On War*, bk. 2, p. 128. It has been argued that Clausewitz had also discerned what was later to be defined as operational level; see Wallace P. Franz, 'Two Letters on Strategy: Clausewitz' Contribution to the Operational Level of War', in Michael I. Handel (ed.), *Clausewitz and Modern Strategy* (London: Frank Cass, 1986), pp. 171–94.
48. Cf. the increased importance Clausewitz assigned to the availability of reserves at the tactical level, while at the same time claiming that reserves have no place in strategy, which must make use of all available forces; Clausewitz, *On War*, bk. 3, chs. 12–13.
49. This does not mean that senior commanders should not be brave, but only that personal bravery is not the primary thing to ask from them. French Field-Marshal Francois-Achille Bazaine, despite his unsurpassed bravery, proved disastrous as commander-in-chief of the French army during the Franco-Prussian War of 1870–1. In fact, there were instances where his very bravery was a disadvantage, since he insisted on being at the front line and thus was in no position to exercise overall command; see Michael Howard, *The Franco-Prussian War* (London: Routledge, 1988), p. 155.
50. For a comparative assessment of the effectiveness of the main belligerents in the Second World War at various levels of strategy, see Allan R. Millett and Williamson Murray (eds), *Military Effectiveness, Volume III: The Second World War* (Boston, MA: Unwin Hyman, 1988).
51. This was definitely realized a few years after the initial U.S. invasion; see Thomas E. Ricks, *Fiasco: The American Military Adventure in Iraq* (New York: Penguin Books, 2006), and Christopher J. Fettweis, 'On the Consequences of Failure in Iraq', *Survival*, 49, 4 (Winter 2007–8), pp. 83–98.
52. See Williamson Murray and Major General Robert H. Scales Jr., *The Iraq War* (Cambridge, MA: The Belknap Press of Harvard University Press, 2003).
53. Ben Barry, *Harsh Lessons: Iraq, Afghanistan and the Changing Character of War* (Abingdon: Routledge for The International Institute for Strategic Studies, 2017).
54. See John Erickson, *The Road to Stalingrad* (London: Weidenfeld and Nicolson, 1993), ch. 8.
55. The classic description of Xerxes' campaign can be found in Herodotus, VII–

IX. For the battles of Salamis and Plataea, see VIII 84–89 and IX 60–65. For a modern analysis, see J.F.C. Fuller, *The Decisive Battles of the Western World* (London: Eyre & Spottiswoode, 1954), ch. 1. For a less satisfactory analysis, attributing the Persian failure on the psychological need of every Persian king to achieve conquests, which in turn made them prone to committing the sin of overextension, see Barry S. Strauss and Josiah Ober, *The Anatomy of Error: Ancient Military Disasters and Their Lessons for Modern Strategists* (New York: St. Martin's Press, 1990), ch. 1. The psychological need for making conquests and the concomitant danger of overextension certainly existed, but if the Persians had not given battle at Salamis and had not committed that tactical blunder at Plataea, it is difficult to see how they would have lost the war. Many of the points highlighted in our analysis have been touched upon by the late Professor Olmstead, an eminent historian of the Persian Empire. However, he also made the completely unsubstantiated claim that even after Plataea, the Persians were still capable of 'throwing fresh troops upon the battle-weary allies and sweeping them rapidly to the southernmost tip of the Peloponnese'; A.T. Olmstead, *History of the Persian Empire* (Chicago, IL: The University of Chicago Press, 1948), p. 259. In fact, not only were the Persians unable to do anything of the sort but, as will be seen in the next chapter, immediately after Plataea, the Greeks were able to mount offensive operations against the Persians in Asia.

56. This section draws heavily on Posen, *The Sources of Military Doctrine*, p. 13.
57. For a more elaborate analysis of the concept of security, based on the distinction between strong and weak states, see Barry Buzan, *People, States and Fear* (2nd edn) (London: Harvester Wheatsheaf, 1991), ch. 2.
58. According to Paul Kennedy, the idea that grand strategy functions in peacetime as well as in wartime was Liddell Hart's (and, to a lesser degree, Edward Mead Earle's) own contribution to the study of the concept. In other words, this is a comparatively recent idea; see Paul Kennedy, 'Grand Strategies in War and Peace'.
59. Liddell Hart, *Strategy*, p. 322.
60. See also Michael Howard, 'The Forgotten Dimensions of Strategy', in Michael Howard, *The Causes of War* (London: Temple Smith, 1983), pp. 101–9.
61. Cf. Stephen M. Walt, *The Origins of Alliances* (Ithaca, NY: Cornell University Press, 1987), chs. 1, 2, 8.
62. See Henry Kissinger, *A World Restored: Metternich, Castlereagh and the Problems of Peace 1812–1822* (Boston, MA: Houghton Mifflin, 1973).
63. See David A. Baldwin, *Economic Statecraft* (Princeton, NJ: Princeton University Press, 1985); Paul Kennedy, *The Rise and Fall of the Great Powers: Economic Change and Military Conflict from 1500 to 2000* (New York: Random House, 1987).
64. The classic analysis on this subject is Alfred Thayer Mahan, *The Influence of Sea Power Upon the French Revolution and Empire, 1793–1812* (2 vols) (London: Sampson Low, Marston, 1893).

pp. [17–20] NOTES

65. For this concept, see Joseph S. Nye Jr., *Soft Power: The Means to Success in World Politics* (New York: PublicAffairs, 2004).
66. See Haralambos Papasotiriou, 'Byzantine Grand Strategy' (PhD dissertation, Stanford University, 1991), and Edward N. Luttwak, *The Grand Strategy of the Byzantine Empire* (Cambridge, MA & London: The Belknap Press of Harvard University Press, 2009).
67. Hans Delbrück, *History of the Art of War* (4 vols) (Lincoln, NE: University of Nebraska Press, 1975–85). See also Gordon A. Craig, 'Delbrück: The Military Historian', in Paret, *Makers of Modern Strategy*, pp. 326–53.
68. As Lawrence Freedman points out, wars are rarely confined to pitched battles that lead to a decisive victory of one combatant. However, this does not negate the utility of the ideal type of the strategy of annihilation as a tool of strategic planning and analysis. See Lawrence Freedman, 'The Changing Forms of Military Conflict', *Survival*, 40, 4 (Winter 1998–9), p. 40.
69. The term 'grand strategy of exhaustion' roughly coincides with what André Beaufre terms 'indirect strategy'; see Beaufre, *Introduction to Strategy*. Though he does distinguish between 'indirect strategy' and 'indirect approach', we feel that the confusion between these two terms cannot be altogether avoided, hence the term 'grand strategy of exhaustion' serves the analyst better.
70. The bibliography on Napoleon is immense. See among others Fuller, *The Conduct of War*, pp. 42–58; Peter Paret, 'Napoleon and the Revolution in War', in Paret, *Makers of Modern Strategy*, pp. 123–42; David G. Chandler, *The Military Maxims of Napoleon* (New York: Macmillan, 1997). For a critical view, see Correlli Barnett, *Bonaparte* (Ware: Wordsworth, 1997).
71. See B.H. Liddell Hart, *The British Way in Warfare* (London: Faber, 1932). For a critical presentation of the 'British way of warfare', see Colin Gray, 'History for Strategists', in Geoffrey Till (ed.), *Seapower: Theory and Practice* (Ilford: Frank Cass, 1994), pp. 23–5.
72. On Clausewitz, see Clausewitz, *On War*, and Michael Howard, *Clausewitz* (Oxford: Oxford University Press, 1983). For the association of Napoleon and Clausewitz with the strategy of annihilation, see Edward N. Luttwak, 'Toward Post-Heroic Warfare', *Foreign Affairs*, 74, 3 (May/June 1995), pp. 109–22, and Azar Gat, *The Development of Military Thought: The Nineteenth Century* (Oxford: Clarendon Press, 1992), pp. 1–45.
73. For the strategic thought of Liddell Hart, see Liddell Hart, *Strategy*, and Brian Bond, *Liddell Hart: A Study of his Military Thought* (London: Cassell, 1977).
74. For the early incarnations of the concept of indirect approach in Liddell Hart's strategic thought, as well as the fluidity of the concept, see John J. Mearsheimer, *Liddell Hart and the Weight of History* (Ithaca, NY: Cornell University Press 1988), pp. 89–93.
75. See, among others, Kennedy, 'Grand Strategies in War and Peace'; Papasotiriou, 'Byzantine Grand Strategy'.

NOTES pp. [21–24]

76. See the analysis in Papasotiriou, 'Byzantine Grand Strategy', pp. 34–7; see also Haralambos Papasotiriou, *Byzantine Grand Strategy, 6th–11th century* (Athens: Poiotita, 2000) (text in Greek), pp. 33–4.
77. See Platias, *High Politics in Small Countries*, ch. 2, and Michael I. Handel, *Weak States in the International System* (London: Frank Cass, 1981).
78. For a classic analysis, see Kennedy, *The Rise and Fall of the Great Powers*.
79. See Platias, *High Politics in Small Countries*, ch. 5; Ariel Levite, *Offense and Defense in Israeli Military Doctrine* (Boulder, CO: Westview, 1989).

2. ATHENS AND SPARTA: POWER STRUCTURES, EARLY CONFLICT AND THE CAUSES OF WAR

1. See Thucydides, I 89–117.
2. For these events, namely the crises of Corcyra and Potidaea, see Thucydides, I 24–68.
3. Thucydides, I 23.
4. In the same vein, the assassination of the Austrian Archduke Francis Ferdinand in 1914 obviously influenced the timing of the outbreak of the First World War. Still, it was a trivial thing compared to the deep structural causes of that war, the primary one being the rise of the power of Germany, the concomitant German attempt to change the status quo, and the ensuing threat perceptions by other European great powers. For two excellent structural analyses of the European interstate system prior to the outbreak of the First World War, see Paul Kennedy, 'The First World War and the International Power System', *International Security*, 9, 1 (1984), pp. 7–40, and Michael Mandelbaum, *The Fate of Nations* (Cambridge: Cambridge University Press, 1988), pp. 31–56.
5. For the concept of strategic culture, see Ken Booth, *Strategy and Ethnocentrism* (London: Croom Helm, 1979); Colin Gray, *Nuclear Strategy and National Style* (London: Hamilton Press, 1986); Yitzhak Klein, 'A Theory of Strategic Culture', *Comparative Strategy*, 10, 1 (January–March 1991), pp. 3–23; Thomas U. Berger, 'Norms, Identity and National Security in Germany and Japan', in Peter J. Katzenstein (ed.), *The Culture of National Security* (New York: Columbia University Press, 1996), pp. 317–56.
6. For an ancient description of the Athenian polity, see Aristotle, *Athenaion Politeia*. For modern accounts, see Anton Powell, *Athens and Sparta: Constructing Greek Political and Social History from 478 B.C.* (London: Routledge, 1988), and Donald Kagan, *Pericles of Athens and the Birth of Democracy* (London: Guild, 1990).
7. Herodotus was the first to point out the beneficial impact of the democratic regime as far as Athenian power was concerned; see Herodotus, V 78. See also Michael W. Doyle, *Empires* (Ithaca, NY: Cornell University Press, 1986), pp. 66–7.
8. For detailed analyses of the Spartan polity, see the majestic multivolume work of Paul A. Rahe, comprising (so far) the following books: *The Grand Strategy of*

p. [25]

Classical Sparta: The Persian Challenge (New Haven, CT & London: Yale University Press, 2015); *The Spartan Regime: Its Character, Origins, and Grand Strategy* (New Haven, CT & London: Yale University Press, 2016); *Sparta's First Attic War: The Grand Strategy of Classical Sparta, 478–446 B.C.* (New Haven, CT & London: Yale University Press, 2019); *Sparta's Second Attic War: The Grand Strategy of Classical Sparta, 446–418 B.C.* (New Haven, CT & London: Yale University Press, 2020); *Sparta's Sicilian Proxy War: The Grand Strategy of Classical Sparta, 418–413 B.C.* (New York & London: Encounter Books, 2023); and *Sparta's Third Attic War: The Grand Strategy of Classical Sparta, 413–404 B.C.* (New York & London: Encounter Books, 2024). For older works, see K.M.T. Chrimes, *Ancient Sparta: A Re-examination of the Evidence* (Manchester: Manchester University Press, 1949); Humphrey Michell, *Sparta* (Cambridge: Cambridge University Press, 1952); George L. Huxley, *Early Sparta* (London: Faber, 1962); A.H.M. Jones, *Sparta* (Oxford: Blackwell & Mott, 1967); W.G. Forrest, *A History of Sparta, 950–192 B.C.* (New York: Norton, 1968); G.E.M. de Ste. Croix, *The Origins of the Peloponnesian War* (London: Duckworth, 1972); M.I. Finley, 'Sparta', in M.I. Finley, *The Use and Abuse of History* (London: Penguin, 1990), pp. 161–77; Powell, *Athens and Sparta*. For the Spartan legal system, see D.M. MacDowell, *Spartan Law* (Edinburgh: Scottish Academic Press, 1986).

9. For the original Spartan text, the so-called *Rhetra*, which describes Spartan polity as it was supposedly created by the lawmaker Lycurgus, see Plutarch, *Lycurgus*, 6.1–2, 7–8. For the name of the Spartan citizen assembly which, contrary to what many people nowadays think, seems to have been *Ecclesia* and not *Apella*, see Ste. Croix, *The Origins of the Peloponnesian War*, pp. 346–7.

10. The exact procedure of the *ephors*' election is not known. See P.A. Rahe, 'The Selection of Ephors at Sparta', *Historia*, 29 (1980), pp. 385–401; P.J. Rhodes, 'The Selection of Ephors at Sparta', *Historia*, 30 (1981), pp. 498–502; H.D. Westlake, 'Reelection to the ephorate?' *Greek, Roman and Byzantine Studies*, 17 (1976), pp. 343–52.

11. In fact, things were not so simple. Austerity did not dominate Spartan life until the sixth century BCE. Moreover, the huge inequalities of wealth within Sparta were a source of continuous division. For a treatise that connects the onset of austerity with the rise of the power of the commoners in Sparta, see L.F. Fitzhardinge, *The Spartans* (London: Thames and Hudson, 1980). However, Fitzhardinge is completely wrong in claiming that the aristocratic families and the *Gerousia* lost their power in the process; the *Gerousia* and the nobles behind it were in firm control of the destinies of Sparta throughout the city's independent existence.

12. This was unanimously acknowledged in ancient Greece. See Herodotus, VII 104, VII 204, IX 62, IX 71; Thucydides, I 141, V 72, V 75; Xenophon, *Lacedaimonion Politeia*, 13. For the Spartan military organization, see Chrimes,

Ancient Sparta, pp. 356–96; Michell, *Sparta*, pp. 233–80 (pp. 274–80 deal with the Spartan navy); J.F. Lazenby, *The Spartan Army* (Warminster: Aris & Phillips, 1985).

13. Thucydides states that the ratio of slaves to freemen in Sparta was greater than in any other city; Thucydides, VIII 40. The ratio has been estimated between seven to one and ten to one; see, respectively, Paul Cartledge, *Sparta and Lakonia: A Regional History, 1300–362 B.C.* (London: Routledge & Kegan Paul, 1979), p. 175, and G.B. Grundy, quoted in Donald Kagan, *The Outbreak of the Peloponnesian War* (Ithaca, NY: Cornell University Press, 1969/1994), p. 26.
14. In fact, the *ephors* formally declared war against the helots each year upon entering office; Plutarch, *Lycurgus*, 28. Consequently, a Spartan could kill a helot without legally committing a homicide. In practice, however, although the Spartans could be extremely harsh on occasion, their treatment of the helots is believed to have been tolerably good. Furthermore, there was always a distinction between Laconian helots, who were normally loyal to Sparta, and Messenian helots, who were Sparta's greatest enemies; see Michell, *Sparta*, pp. 75–84.
15. See Thucydides, I 101, IV 41, IV 80.
16. Plutarch, *Lycurgus*, 24.
17. Thucydides, I 70. Unless otherwise noted, all quotations from Thucydides are from the Richard Crawley translation, published in 1874 and used in the valuable Strassler edition of Thucydides [Robert B. Strassler (ed.), *The Landmark Thucydides: A Comprehensive Guide to the Peloponnesian War* (New York: Free Press, 1996)]. In a few instances we have reverted to the first English translation of the Greek original by Thomas Hobbes (1629), despite its archaic style; see Richard Schlatter, *Hobbes's Thucydides* (New Brunswick, NJ: Rutgers University Press, 1975).
18. Thucydides makes much of the difference between Athenian and Spartan national character; see Thucydides, I 69, I 84, I 118, IV 55, V 54–5, VIII 24. See also Victor Davis Hanson, *A War Like No Other: How the Athenians and the Spartans Fought the Peloponnesian War* (New York: Random House, 2005), pp. 8–9, and W. Daniel Garst, 'Thucydides and the Domestic Sources of International Politics', in Lowell S. Gustafson (ed.), *Thucydides' Theory of International Relations: A Lasting Possession* (Baton Rouge, LA: Louisiana University Press, 2000), pp. 67–97.
19. Spartan foreign policy did fluctuate violently on occasion, but there was an amazing overall consistency in maintaining a high military capability and striving after hegemony first in the Peloponnese and then in the whole of Greece.
20. Thucydides, I 89–117. See also below.
21. This is a very interesting illustration of what is nowadays called a security dilemma, namely the situation that arises when the measures that increase the security of a state decrease the security of others. Thus, the Persian threat

p. [28]

prompted the Athenians to establish their empire ('fear being our principal motive'; Thucydides, I 75). The Athenian Empire provided security to Athens but soon proved to be a threat to Sparta and its allies. For an analysis of the security dilemma, see Robert Jervis, 'Cooperation Under the Security Dilemma', *World Politics*, 30, 2 (January 1978), pp. 167–214. For the Athenian Empire, see Russell Meiggs, *The Athenian Empire* (Oxford: Clarendon Press, 1972).

22. Thucydides, I 99. Similarly, Pericles stated that the strength of Athens derived from allied payments (Thucydides, II 13). The British East India Company used a similar scheme, forcing native Indian states to contribute money which it then used to raise sepoy troops, thus perpetuating both the financial drain of its opponents and its military supremacy in the Indian subcontinent; see Bruce P. Lenman, 'The Transition to European Military Ascendancy in India, 1600–1800', in John A. Lynn (ed.), *Tools of War: Instruments, Ideas and Institutions of Warfare, 1445–1871* (Urbana, IL & Chicago, IL: University of Illinois Press, 1990), pp. 100–30.

23. For the dynamics behind the growth of Athenian power, see Robert Gilpin, 'The Theory of Hegemonic War', in R.I. Rotberg and T.K. Rabb (eds), *The Origin and Prevention of Major Wars* (Cambridge: Cambridge University Press, 1988), pp. 21–3, and Doyle, *Empires*. Michael Doyle states that 'slave agriculture, imperial tribute and imperial mine produced monetary supremacy, which again produced commercial superiority, which in turn, through a stimulation of shipping, produced naval superiority, which in turn sustained the empire. And the empire generated the slaves, the tribute and the mines'; *Empires*, p. 63. This passage shows remarkably well the dynamic inherent in the elements of Athenian power. Still, one must point out that it overvalues the role of slave agriculture as a source of said power. Furthermore, naval superiority was the generator rather than the outcome of the acquisition of the empire and its concomitant wealth.

24. Thucydides, I 19. Some of Sparta's Peloponnesian allies, like Elis and Mantinea, were democracies and retained their preferred regime as long as they remained loyal to Sparta. Incidentally, this means that one should not exaggerate the importance of the supposedly antagonistic nature of the Spartan and Athenian socio-political systems; cf. Justin Rosenberg, *The Empire of Civil Society: A Critique of the Realist Theory of International Relations* (London: Verso, 1994). For the Peloponnesian League, see Kagan, *The Outbreak of the Peloponnesian War*, pp. 9–30, and Ste. Croix, *The Origins of the Peloponnesian War*, pp. 96–124, 333–42.

25. Kagan graphically states that the allies were bound together by distrust of Argos and the common interest of the preservation of the oligarchy; see Kagan, *The Outbreak of the Peloponnesian War*, p. 13.

26. This was precisely what the great Greek historian and statesman Polybius

argued a few centuries later. According to him, although Sparta's political organization was enough to ensure its dominant position in the Peloponnese, its limited economic power (a result of that very political organization) did not allow Sparta to extend its influence further. The message was clear: Sparta had to either change its political organization or confine itself to the Peloponnese. See Polybius, I 6. 49–50.

27. The rapid decline of the Spartan population during the fifth and fourth centuries BCE astonished the rest of the ancient Greeks; see Aristotle, *Politics* II 9, 1270a 33–34; cf. Xenophon, *Lacedaimonion Politeia*, 1. The subject has received detailed treatment from modern scholars; see among others Forrest, *A History of Sparta*, pp. 134–7; Ste. Croix, *The Origins of the Peloponnesian War*, pp. 331–2; Cartledge, *Sparta and Lakonia*, pp. 307–18. For a less satisfactory account that tries to minimize the importance of the decline, see Chrimes, *Ancient Sparta*, pp. 348–56.

28. Doyle, *Empires*, pp. 54–81.

29. In other words, this particular grand strategic design did not fit with Sparta's domestic political environment and thus failed the criterion of external fit.

30. For the idea of the creation of a Spartan Empire and the disastrous consequences this scheme brought about, see Forrest, *A History of Sparta*, pp. 123–6; Donald Kagan, *The Fall of the Athenian Empire* (Ithaca, NY: Cornell University Press, 1987), pp. 13, 27, 306, 328, 397–426; Barry S. Strauss and Josiah Ober, *The Anatomy of Error: Ancient Military Disasters and Their Lessons for Modern Strategists* (New York: St. Martin's Press, 1990); Doyle, *Empires*, p. 73. Strauss and Ober, drawing from Aristotle, claim that Sparta was in no position to conduct an imperialist policy because the strict military-oriented education of the Spartans made them overestimate the role of military power and consequently rendered them unable to conduct successful diplomacy and reach compromise; see Strauss and Ober, *The Anatomy of Error*, ch. 3. Despite Aristotle's authority, this claim must be rejected. Sparta had been successfully playing the diplomatic game for centuries and can hardly be called incapable of conducting diplomacy. Moreover, the Athenians (and later the Romans and so many others) did not acquire their empire through rhetorical and diplomatic skill, but basically through successful application of military power. Sparta's problem was not excessive emphasis on military power, but lack of adequate military power.

31. Thucydides, I 71.

32. Herodotus, IX 96–106.

33. Herodotus, IX 104; Thucydides, I 94.

34. For the reluctance of the Spartans to go on with the war, see Herodotus, IX 114. For Pausanias' conduct and the transfer of the leadership to Athens, see Thucydides, I 95–6.

35. Thucydides, I 90.

36. Thucydides, I 90–1. For an important critique of the concept of arms control,

see Colin S. Gray, *House of Cards: Why Arms Control Must Fail* (Ithaca, NY: Cornell University Press, 1992).

37. For Cimon's successes, see Thucydides, I 98–100, and Plutarch, *Cimon*. For a modern account of the Battle of Eurymedon, see Meiggs, *The Athenian Empire*, pp. 74–82, 454–5.
38. Thucydides, I 104.
39. Thucydides, I 103.
40. See Herodotus, IX 35; Isocrates, *Archidamus*, 99; Pausanias, *Laconica*, 11.7; Jones, *Sparta*, 61; Kagan, *The Outbreak of the Peloponnesian War*, pp. 54–5. It is a pity we do not know more about these battles and their surrounding circumstances.
41. Thucydides, I 101–3.
42. For the First Peloponnesian War, see Thucydides, I 105–8, I 111–15. For modern accounts, see Kagan, *The Outbreak of the Peloponnesian War*, pp. 77–130, and Ste. Croix, *The Origins of the Peloponnesian War*, pp. 187–200, 293–4.
43. See Thucydides, I 107–8.
44. If the Athenians had won and the Peloponnesian expeditionary force had been annihilated, then Tanagra would have been a turning strategic point.
45. Thucydides, I 108.
46. Ibid.
47. Thucydides, I 109–10.
48. See Meiggs, *The Athenian Empire*, pp. 109–28.
49. Thucydides, I 112. In the same year, Sparta concluded a Thirty Years' Peace with Argos; see Thucydides, V 14. The relationship between the Athenian–Spartan and the Argive–Spartan treaties is not known.
50. For the Cyprus campaign, see Thucydides, I 112. The historicity of the Peace of Callias has often been denied, especially since Thucydides does not mention it. However, there are compelling arguments for accepting that peace as genuine. For a summary of the relevant debate, see Meiggs, *The Athenian Empire*, pp. 129–51, 487–95.
51. See Meiggs, *The Athenian Empire*, pp. 129–51, 487–95, and Ste. Croix, *The Origins of the Peloponnesian War*, pp. 310–14.
52. It is unclear whether the Athenian fleet was similarly forbidden to sail east of those limits. Also, it is unlikely that the Persian king would have relinquished his right to exact tribute from the Greek cities, although he would be unable to exercise that right in practice; see Ste. Croix, *The Origins of the Peloponnesian War*, p. 313.
53. Thucydides, I 113–14.
54. If the revolts in Boeotia, Euboea and Megara and the Peloponnesian invasion were pre-planned to coincide with the expiration of the Five Years' Treaty, then the Spartan political leaders must be regarded as first-class strategists. If, on the other hand, the invasion was not part of a previously devised plan but

came as an immediate response to the opening of a 'window of opportunity' by the Megarian revolt, the Spartans must still receive credit for their rapid exploitation of that opportunity. For a more detailed treatment of the Spartan tendency to jump into windows of opportunity, see Powell, *Athens and Sparta*, pp. 118–28.
55. Thucydides, I 114.
56. Thucydides, II 21.
57. Thucydides, I 115; see also Ste. Croix, *The Origins of the Peloponnesian War*, pp. 293–4.
58. See Thucydides, I 24–55.
59. Thebes, when allied with the other Boeotians, was perhaps more powerful than Corinth, but it is unclear whether Thebes was a formal member of the Peloponnesian League at the time.
60. For these concepts, see A.F.K. Organski, 'The Power Transition', in James N. Rosenau (ed.), *International Politics and Foreign Policy: A Reader in Research and Theory* (New York: The Free Press of Glencoe, 1961), pp. 367–75; A.F.K. Organski and Jacek Kugler, *The War Ledger* (Chicago, IL: The University of Chicago Press, 1980); Robert Gilpin, *War and Change in World Politics* (Cambridge: Cambridge University Press, 1981). For a discussion of Thucydides' impact therein, see Despina A. Taxiarchi, 'The Impact of Thucydides in Post War Realist Thinking and Its Critique', *Thucydides: The Classical Theorist of International Relations, Études Helléniques/Hellenic Studies*, 6, 2 (Autumn 1998), pp. 132–9.
61. See the classic Charles Norris Cochrane, *Thucydides and the Science of History* (London: Oxford University Press, 1929), pp. 166–7; see also Gregory Crane, *Thucydides and the Ancient Simplicity: The Limits of Political Realism* (Berkeley, CA: University of California Press, 1998), ch. 2. For a most comprehensive analysis, see Jacqueline de Romilly, 'La vue d'en haut: Découverte des sciences de l'homme', in Jacqueline de Romilly (ed.), *La Construction de la vérité chez Thucydide* (Paris: Julliard, 1990), pp. 105–41.
62. Gilpin, *War and Change in World Politics*; Gilpin, 'The Theory of Hegemonic War'.
63. Organski and Kugler's *The War Ledger* was the first extensive study of hegemonic transition. For the definitional discussion of the concept in modern political science, see Jack S. Levy, 'Declining Power and the Preventive Motivation for War', *World Politics*, 40, 1 (October 1987), pp. 82–107. For a more recent discussion, see Stephen Van Evera, *Causes of War: Power and the Roots of Conflict* (Ithaca, NY & London, Cornell University Press, 1999), ch. 4. See also George Modelski, 'The Long Cycle of Global Politics and the Nation State', *Comparative Studies in Society and History*, 20, 2 (April 1978), pp. 214–35.
64. Gilpin, 'The Theory of Hegemonic War', p. 15.
65. Thucydides, I 23 [Hobbes translation]. This is an important instance where Thomas Hobbes renders accurately the original Greek and drives the point home.

66. Thucydides, I 70.
67. Ibid., I 118.
68. Diodorus, XI 50. It is accepted that Diodorus' chronology of this episode in the year 475–4 BCE is wrong; see Ste. Croix, *The Origins of the Peloponnesian War*, p. 171.
69. Thomas Hobbes, *Leviathan or the Matter, Forme and Power of a Commonwealth* (Oxford: Blackwell, 1946); Georg Wilhelm Friedrich Hegel, *Hegel's Philosophy of Right* (trans. T.M. Knox) (Oxford: Clarendon, 1952); Karl Marx, *Capital* (trans. Samuel Moore and Edward Aveling) (3 vols) (Chicago, IL: Charles H. Kerr, 1909–10).
70. Kenneth N. Waltz, *Man, the State, and War* (New York: Columbia University Press, 1959); Kenneth N. Waltz, *Theory of International Politics* (Reading, MA: Addison-Wesley, 1979); Gilpin, *War and Change in World Politics*.
71. It is interesting that two of the most prominent advocates of that school—Donald Kagan and Richard Ned Lebow—accept the validity of the classical Thucydidean explanation regarding the causes of the First Peloponnesian War; see Kagan, *The Outbreak of the Peloponnesian War*, pp. 77–130, and Richard Ned Lebow, 'Thucydides, Power Transition Theory and the Causes of War', in Richard Ned Lebow and Barry S. Strauss (eds), *Hegemonic Rivalry from Thucydides to the Nuclear Age* (Boulder, CO: Westview, 1991), pp. 125–65.
72. Richard Ned Lebow, *Between Peace and War: The Nature of International Crisis* (Baltimore, MD: Johns Hopkins University Press, 1987).
73. As John Mearsheimer puts it, 'France backed down, because it knew the United Kingdom would win the ensuing war, and because France did not want to pick a fight with the United Kingdom when it was more worried about the emerging German threat on its eastern border'; John J. Mearsheimer, *The Tragedy of Great Power Politics* (New York: W.W. Norton, 2001), p. 153.
74. See Bruce Bueno de Mesquita, *The War Trap* (New Haven, CT: Yale University Press, 1981).
75. Thucydides, IV 59.
76. Thucydides, II 8. Cf. Martin van Creveld, *The Transformation of War* (New York: Free Press, 1991), where he argues that the main cause of war is simply that men like war. Here, it must be pointed out that, though Thucydides does regard human nature as a cause of war, he never abandons the systemic 'big picture'.

3. PERICLEAN GRAND STRATEGY

1. A distant ancestor of this chapter is Athanassios Platias, 'Thucydides on Grand Strategy: Periclean Grand Strategy During the Peloponnesian War', *Thucydides: The Classical Theorist of International Relations, Études Helléniques/Hellenic Studies*, 6, 2 (Autumn 1998), pp. 53–103.

NOTES

2. See, for instance, J.F.C. Fuller, *The Decisive Battles of the Western World* (London: Eyre & Spottiswoode, 1954); Colin Gray, *The Leverage of Sea Power: The Strategic Advantage of Navies in War* (New York: Free Press, 1992); Chester G. Starr, *The Influence of Sea Power on Ancient History* (New York: Oxford University Press, 1995); Andrew Lambert, *Seapower States* (New Haven, CT: Yale University Press, 2018), pp. 1–79.
3. Among others, J.F.C. Fuller has stated that 'Pericles relied upon the strategy of exhaustion'; J.F.C. Fuller, *A Military History of the Western World, Vol. 1: From the Earliest Times to the Battle of Lepanto* (New York: Da Capo Press, 1954), p. 57. As it will be seen at a later point in this book, the Athenians were eventually to depart from the strategy devised by Pericles. For an analysis of the various strategies that the city of Athens adopted during the Peloponnesian War, see Donald Kagan, 'Athenian strategy in the Peloponnesian War', in Williamson Murray, MacGregor Knox and Alvin Bernstein (eds), *The Making of Strategy: Rulers, States, and War* (Cambridge: Cambridge University Press, 1994), pp. 24–55.
4. In fact, the term 'city-state system' is not totally accurate, since both city-states and bigger entities, such as the various kingdoms of Epirus and Macedonia, comprised ancient Greece. For an analysis of the politics in the Greek city-state system, see Raphael Sealey, *A History of the Greek City States, 700–338 B.C.* (Berkeley, CA: University of California Press, 1976).
5. See, for example, Peter J. Fliess, *Thucydides and the Politics of Bipolarity* (Baton Rouge, LA: Louisiana State University Press, 1966).
6. One might be tempted to find other additional poles of the system, such as the powerful Odrysian kingdom, situated in Thrace and described with admiration in Thucydides, II 95–101.
7. W.R. Connor, 'Polarization in Thucydides', in Richard Ned Lebow and Barry S. Strauss (eds), *Hegemonic Rivalry from Thucydides to the Nuclear Age* (Boulder, CO: Westview, 1991), pp. 54–7.
8. See the discussion in Carlo M. Santoro, 'Bipolarity and War: What Makes the Difference?' in Lebow and Strauss, *Hegemonic Rivalry from Thucydides to the Nuclear Age*, pp. 71–86. Thucydides' narrative suggests several historical parallels to the current reader. On the utility and pitfalls of historical comparisons, see Ernest R. May, *The Lessons of the Past: The Use and Misuse of History in American Foreign Policy* (New York: Oxford University Press, 1973); Richard E. Meastand and Ernest R. May, *Thinking in Time: The Uses of History for Decision Makers* (New York: Free Press, 1986). See also Michael Howard, *The Lessons of History* (New Haven, CT: Yale University Press, 1991), pp. 6–20.
9. Thucydides, I 23 [Hobbes translation].
10. Thucydides describes Pericles' account as follows: 'Apart from other sources of income, an average revenue of six hundred talents of silver was drawn from the tribute of the allies; and there were still six thousand talents of coined sil-

ver in the Acropolis, out of nine thousand seven hundred that had once been there, from which the money had been taken for the Propylaea, the other public buildings, and for Potidaea. This did not include the uncoined gold and silver in public and private offerings, the sacred vessels for the processions and games, the Medan spoils, and similar resources to the amount of five hundred talents. To this he added the treasures of the other temples. These were by no means inconsiderable, and might fairly be used. Nay, if they were ever absolutely driven to it, they might take even the gold ornaments of Athena herself; for the statue contained forty talents of pure gold and it was all removable [...]. Such was their financial position—surely a satisfactory one.' Thucydides, II 13.

11. This truth is captured by the statement of the Spartan king Archidamus that 'war is a matter not so much of arms as of money, which makes arms of use'; Thucydides, I 83.
12. Donald Kagan, *The Outbreak of the Peloponnesian War* (Ithaca, NY: Cornell University Press, 1969/1994), pp. 345–74. The same view is advanced in A.H.M. Jones, *Sparta* (Oxford: Blackwell & Mott, 1967), pp. 68–9. Richard Ned Lebow has taken a more moderate position, arguing that 'Athens had increased its power under Pericles and had largely recovered from the disasters of the 440s, but in 433 its power and reputation were still not what they had been in 450'; Richard Ned Lebow, 'Thucydides, Power Transition Theory and the Causes of War', in Lebow and Strauss, *Hegemonic Rivalry*, pp. 158–9.
13. Economic performance that determines a state's power and military success is always to be measured on a relative and not on an absolute basis. The crucial factor that seems to elude Kagan and his followers is to be doing better, even if only a little better, than one's rivals. In the long run, this asymmetry is reflected in the balance of power. This insight is utilized in, among others, Paul Kennedy, *The Rise and Fall of the Great Powers Economic Change and Military Conflict from 1500 to 2000* (New York: Random House, 1987), and John J. Mearsheimer, *The Tragedy of Great Power Politics* (New York: W.W. Norton, 2001), esp. ch. 3.
14. Thucydides, I 19. A similar case is that of the British Empire after the War of the American Independence (1775–83). Although the loss of the American colonies was a serious blow, British economic power kept growing at a fast pace, securing the global supremacy of Great Britain.
15. See, among others, Lisa Kallet-Marx, *Money, Expense and Naval Power in Thucydides' History 1–5.24* (Berkeley, CA: University of California Press, 1993).
16. See, among others, Robert Gilpin, *The Political Economy of International Relations* (Princeton, NJ: Princeton University Press, 1987); Edward Mead Earle, 'Adam Smith, Alexander Hamilton, Friedrich List: The Economic Foundations of Military Power', in Peter Paret (ed.), *Makers of Modern Strategy from Machiavelli to the Nuclear Age* (Princeton, NJ: Princeton University Press, 1986), pp. 217–61; Alfred Thayer Mahan, *The Influence of Sea Power Upon History, 1660–1783*

(London: Sampson Low, Marston, 1892); Alfred Thayer Mahan, *The Influence of Sea Power Upon the French Revolution and Empire, 1793–1812* (2 vols) (London: Sampson Low, Marston, 1893); E.H. Carr, *The 20 Years' Crisis, 1919–1939* (2nd edn) (London: Papermac, 1946/1995); Robert G. Gilpin, 'The Richness of the Tradition of Political Realism', in Robert O. Keohane (ed.), *Neorealism and its Critics* (New York: Columbia University Press, 1986), pp. 308–13. In light of this perceptive, realist analysis of the importance of economic factors, dating back to the days of Thucydides, it is amazing that political realism has been accused of having ignored the economic dimensions of international relations. See Gilpin, 'The Richness of the Tradition of Political Realism', pp. 308–13.

17. Thucydides, I 141–3.
18. Thucydides, I 144.
19. Ibid., I 80–1.
20. Jingoism was the sentiment of vulgar chauvinism that appeared in Great Britain at the turn of the nineteenth century in response to the challenges of Germany; see Paul Kennedy, *The Rise of the Anglo-German Antagonism 1860–1914* (London: Allen and Unwin, 1980).
21. Kagan, 'Athenian Strategy in the Peloponnesian War', p. 30.
22. Thucydides, I 141–2, II 13. For an analysis of the law of uneven growth, see Robert Gilpin, *War and Change in World Politics* (Cambridge: Cambridge University Press, 1981), and Robert Gilpin, 'The Theory of Hegemonic War', in R.I. Rotberg and T.K. Rabb (eds), *The Origin and Prevention of Major Wars* (Cambridge: Cambridge University Press, 1988), pp. 15–37.
23. Thucydides, I 139.
24. Bernard Brodie, *War and Politics* (London: Cassell, 1973), p. 1.
25. According to Doyne Dawson: 'The most original contribution of the Greeks to military thought was their self-conscious development of the concept of *raison d' état*: They perceived warfare as a rational and utilitarian instrument of politics'; Doyne Dawson, *The Origins of Western Warfare: Militarism and Morality in the Ancient World* (Boulder, CO: Westview, 1996), p. 79.
26. See Hans Delbrück, *History of the Art of War*, vol. 1 (Lincoln, NE: University of Nebraska Press, 1975), pp. 135–43.
27. B.H. Liddell Hart, *Strategy* (2nd rev. edn) (London: Meridian, 1991), p. 355.
28. According to tradition, the ancient Chinese Sun Tzu lived during the late sixth and the early fifth century BCE. However, it has been demonstrated that Sun Tzu was not a historical personage and that the text of their famous treatise *The Art of War* was written by various authors sometime in the fourth and even the third century BCE. In other words, the authors of the *Art of War* lived later than Thucydides or were at best younger contemporaries of his. For a summary of the literature regarding the identity of the author and the date of writing of *The Art of War*, see Sun Tzu, *The Art of War* (trans. Samuel B. Griffith) (Oxford:

Oxford University Press, 1963), pp. 1–12; Sun Tzu, *Art of War* (trans. Ralph D. Sawyer) (Boulder, CO: Westview, 1994), pp. 151–62; and *The Art of War: Sun Zu's Military Methods* (trans. V. H. Mair) (New York: Columbia University Press, 2007), pp. 1–23.

29. Sun Tzu, *The Art of War* (trans. Samuel B. Griffith), p. 13.
30. Thucydides, I 139. See also the extensive analysis in G.E.M. de Ste. Croix, *The Origins of the Peloponnesian War* (London: Duckworth, 1972), pp. 225–89, 381–93, 396–9. Ste. Croix argues—fairly convincingly in our opinion—that the Megarian Decree was a religious nuisance for individual Megarians rather than a full-scale economic embargo against Megara. The Megarians were deemed sacrilegious, hence they could not themselves appear at the ports of the Athenian Alliance and the agora of Athens. However, they could always appear at nearby places and transact their business through representatives.
31. Thucydides, I 140–1.
32. Ibid., I 144. For an interesting analysis of *xenelasia*, see Anton Powell, *Athens and Sparta: Constructing Greek Political and Social History from 478 B.C.* (London: Routledge, 1988), pp. 228–9.
33. Hitler said to his commander-in-chief shortly before the Polish campaign: 'Our enemies are little worms; I saw them at Munich'; Chester Wilmot, *The Struggle for Europe* (New York: Carol and Graf, 1952), p. 21. This statement demonstrates how decision-makers use past behaviour to predict future irresolution. For an analysis of this point, see Glenn H. Snyder and Paul Diesing, *Conflict Among Nations: Bargaining, Decision Making, and System Structure in International Crisis* (Princeton, NJ: Princeton University Press, 1977), p. 187. See also, Fred Charles Iklé, *How Nations Negotiate* (New York: Harper and Row, 1964), p. 82.
34. See Haralambos Papasotiriou, 'Byzantine Grand Strategy' (PhD dissertation, Stanford University, 1991). For other instances of successful use of appeasement, see Peter Karsten, 'Response to Threat Perception: Accommodation as a Special Case', in Klaus Knorr (ed.), *Historical Dimensions of National Security Problems* (Lawrence, KA: University Press of Kansas, 1976), pp. 120–63.
35. In all probability, it was for the same reasons that the U.S. rejected appeasement as a strategy towards the Soviet Union after the Second World War. See also the discussion in Chapter Five.
36. Thucydides, I 144, II 65.
37. Kennedy, *The Rise and Fall of the Great Powers*. The experience of the First Peloponnesian War, where Athens had clearly overextended (with the Egyptian campaign and Boeotian conquest) and had dearly paid for it, must have been all too vivid in Pericles' mind.
38. See Kenneth N. Waltz, *Theory of International Politics* (Reading, MA: Addison-Wesley, 1979), p. 168.
39. There is also a second dimension of external balancing, which is essentially to manipulate the international balance of power. A common ploy in this manip-

ulation is to follow the saying 'the enemy of my enemy is my friend'. The Athenians had repeatedly resorted to this ploy in their dealings with Argos. Unfortunately for Pericles, he lacked the alternative of a continental strategy in order to apply peripheral pressure on Sparta, since the Thirty Years' Treaty of 451 BCE between Argos and Sparta prohibited Argos from coming into play before 421 BCE. Following that, though, Athens could once again play the 'Argive card'. For the conflict between Sparta and Argos that erupted in the Peloponnese after the expiration of the Thirty Years' Treaty, and the Athenian role therein, see Thucydides, V 42–82, as well as the discussion in the next chapter. The Athenian relation with Argos is strongly reminiscent of U.S. relations with China during the Cold War.

40. See Thucydides, II 8, where he gives a detailed description of the allies of both Sparta and Athens, plus the status of the various Athenian allies, i.e. free or tributary states.
41. Thucydides, II 25.
42. Thucydides, II 9.
43. Thucydides, I 143.
44. Thucydides, II 24.
45. See Kallet-Marx, *Money, Expense and Naval Power*, pp. 110–11.
46. Thucydides, I 142–3.
47. For a similar approach adopted by Great Britain in the first part of the twentieth century, see Michael Howard, *Grand Strategy: Official History of the Second World War*, vol. 4 (London: HMSO, 1973), p. 1.
48. Josiah Ober, 'National Ideology and Strategic Defense of the Population, from Athens to Star Wars', in Lebow and Strauss, *Hegemonic Rivalry*, p. 254. One may discern here a similarity between the Athenian fortifications and the United States' Strategic Defence Initiative, which was intended to neutralize the Soviet strength. The similarity is even more striking if one considers that the Soviets reacted in the same way as the Spartans had done, i.e. coming up with arms control proposals.
49. Thucydides, I 143.
50. For a description of the qualities of the trireme, the standard warship in the Mediterranean at that time, see Chester G. Starr, 'The Athenian Century', in Robert Cowley (ed.), *Experience of War* (New York & London: Norton, 1992), p. 4.
51. Thucydides, II 62. The Athenians could indeed 'go where they please', but Pericles never claimed that they could seize and retain any overseas territory they wished. This fine point was lost to them when they undertook the Sicilian expedition.
52. For the classic analysis of the maritime grand strategy of Great Britain, see Mahan, *The Influence of Sea Power Upon History, 1660–1783*; Mahan, *The Influence of Sea Power Upon the French Revolution and Empire, 1793–1812*; and B.H. Liddell

Hart, *The British Way in Warfare* (London: Faber, 1932). For a modern scholar drawing the same comparison between Athens and Great Britain, see Starr, *The Influence of Sea Power on Ancient History*, pp. 40–1.

53. Paul Kennedy, *The Rise and Fall of British Naval Mastery* (London: Fontana, 1991), p. 11.
54. Donald Kagan puts the estimate at 2,000 talents a year—an enormous sum by Greek standards; see Kagan, *The Archidamian War* (Ithaca, NY: Cornell University Press, 1974/1990), pp. 36–40.
55. This term refers to the strategy adopted by Fabius, dictator of Rome, against Hannibal after the latter's victory at Lake Trasimene in 218 BCE. This strategy entailed avoidance of battle and the wearing down of the Carthaginian strength by 'military pin-pricks'; see Liddell Hart, *Strategy*, pp. 26–7. Liddell Hart correctly perceived that both the Periclean and the Fabian strategies were actually designs at the grand strategic level: 'The Periclean plan was a grand strategy with the aim of gradually draining the enemy's endurance in order to convince him that he could not gain a decision'; *Strategy*, p. 10.
56. Thucydides, I 143.
57. Ibid., I 141.
58. Thucydides, I 143.
59. See Thomas C. Schelling, *Arms and Influence* (New Haven, CT: Yale University Press, 1966), pp. 1–34. See also, Glenn H. Snyder, *Deterrence and Defense* (Princeton, NJ: Princeton University Press, 1961).
60. Cf. Victor Davis Hanson, *The Western Way of War* (New York: Alfred A. Knopf, 1989), p. 32.
61. For the long war assumption in Periclean strategy, see Thucydides, I 141. For the Spartans' view that the war would be completed successfully within a few years, see Thucydides, V 14.
62. Cf. Pericles' statement to his compatriots: 'And if I had thought that I could persuade you, I would have bid you go out and lay them waste with your own hands, and show the Peloponnesians that this at any rate will not make you submit'; Thucydides, I 143. The fact that he could not persuade them to actually do it should not be taken as an indication of the failure of his strategy, as some analysts have thought; cf. Donald Kagan, *On the Origins of War and the Preservation of Peace* (New York: Doubleday, 1995), p. 65. Pericles' statement was a rhetorical scheme, intended to show to the Athenians that the decision they had actually taken (namely, to abandon their land to the mercy of the enemy) was a necessary one.
63. Liddell Hart, *Strategy*, p. 355.
64. 'This overseas deployment marked a first for the Athenians: For the first time in history, their *hippeis* and mounts sailed on horse transports'; Leslie J. Worley, *Hippeis: The Cavalry of Ancient Greece* (Boulder, CO: Westview, 1994), pp. 87–8. This is an extremely interesting development, since the Athenian force—com-

prising navy, horse transports and mounted archers—essentially marks the origins of the combined arms operations. After the Athenian seizure of Cythera, an island located just south of Laconia, in 424 BCE, the Spartans were forced to raise a unit of 400 mounted archers; Thucydides, IV 55. See also Oliver Lyman Spaulding and Hoffman Nickerson, *Ancient and Medieval Warfare* (New York: Barnes and Noble Books, 1993), p. 57.

65. Thucydides, II 56.
66. This view is advanced by Donald Kagan; 'Athenian strategy in the Peloponnesian War', pp. 41–7.
67. Thucydides, I 142.
68. For an alternative view, see Donald Kagan; 'Athenian Strategy in the Peloponnesian War', pp. 46–7.
69. Cf. David A. Baldwin, *Economic Statecraft* (Princeton, NJ: Princeton University Press, 1985).
70. Thucydides, I 141–2, II 13. This might be conceived as a distant ancestor of the economic and technological denial that the West resorted to in order to isolate and weaken the Soviets during the Cold War.
71. The Melian Dialogue took place during the sixteenth year of the war (416 BCE) and is covered in Thucydides, V 84–113. To the question of the Melians: "'So you would not consent to our being neutral, friends instead of enemies, but allies of neither side.', the Athenians gave the characteristic reply: "No; for your hostility cannot so much hurt us as your friendship will be an argument to our subjects of our weakness, and your enmity of our power."'; Thucydides, V 94–5.
72. Thucydides, I 141–2.
73. Thucydides, V 16–17.
74. See Benjamin Schwarz, 'Strategic Interdependence: Learning to Behave like a Great Power', in Norman Levin (ed.), *Prisms and Policy: U.S. Security Strategy After the Cold War* (Santa Monica, CA: RAND, 1994), pp. 79–98. See also, Paul Bracken, 'Strategic Planning for National Security: Lessons from Business Experience', *RAND Note*, N-3005-DAG/USDP (February 1990), pp. 12–17.
75. Delbrück, *History of the Art of War*, vol. 1, p. 137.
76. Thucydides, II 21. The problem of the Periclean grand strategy was that it depended on loyalty to the city-state taking precedence over individual household and family loyalties; see Lin Foxhall, 'Farming and Fighting in Ancient Greece', in John Rich and Graham Shipley (eds), *War and Society in the Greek World* (London: Routledge, 1993), p. 142.
77. Thucydides, II 21, II 65.
78. See next chapter. Pericles died two years and six months after the start of the war; Thucydides, II 65. In 430 BCE, under the influence of the plague (see below), the Athenians flinched for a while and sent a peace embassy to Sparta. However, nothing came out of it, and Thucydides makes it clear that this was

merely a temporary whim of the Athenian *Ecclesia* (Thucydides, II 59, II 65); see also, the next chapter in this book.

79. Thucydides, II 35–46. A characteristic part of the speech reads as follows: 'In short, I say that as a city we are the school of Hellas; while I doubt if the world can produce a man, who where he has only himself to depend upon, is equal to so many emergencies, and graced by so happy a versatility as the Athenian. And that this is no mere boast thrown out for the occasion, but plain matter of fact, is proved by the power of the state acquired by these habits. For Athens alone of her contemporaries is found when tested to be greater than her reputation [...]. [T]he admiration of the present and succeeding ages will be ours [...]. Such is the Athens for which these men, in the assertion of their resolve not to lose her, nobly fought and died'; Thucydides, II 41. It is interesting to note that during the First World War, placards on London buses displayed extracts from Pericles' *Epitaph*, intended to remind the British public of the values for which they were fighting; see Paul Millett, 'Warfare, economy and democracy in classical Athens', in Rich and Shipley, *War and Society in the Greek World*, p. 179.

80. Thucydides, II 25. The Athenian capture of Pylos was even more helpful in this respect; see Thucydides, IV 3, IV 41. See also Josiah Ober, 'Classical Greek Times', in Michael Howard, George J. Andreopoulos and Mark R. Shulman (eds), *The Laws of War: Constraints on Warfare in the Western World* (New Haven, CT: Yale University Press, 1994), p. 22. From the above analysis, it can be surmised that a theory of victory against Sparta ought to contain two permanent elements, i.e. enlisting Argive alliance and fomenting a helot revolt. One must also point out that there is an interesting parallel between the assistance that Athens offered to the helots and the huge campaign of psychological operations that the West had launched toward the nations of Eastern Europe during the Cold War.

81. See Kenneth N. Waltz, *Man, the State, and War* (New York: Columbia University Press, 1959).

82. Thucydides, I 75.

83. Thucydides, II 63. However, it must be noted that there was another side of the coin as well. The subjects of the Athenian Empire stood to gain from the Athenian commercial activities, and the empire provided a number of collective goods, such as integration in a huge market, suppression of piracy, etc. Consequently, international legitimacy was not completely absent from the Athenian Empire; see Michael W. Doyle, *Empires* (Ithaca, NY: Cornell University Press, 1986), p. 57 and the sources cited therein. See also the next chapter.

84. Thucydides, II 8. See also the next chapter.

85. Kagan, 'Athenian strategy in the Peloponnesian War', p. 54.

86. Barry S. Strauss and Josiah Ober, *The Anatomy of Error: Ancient Military Disasters*

and Their Lessons for Modern Strategists (New York: St. Martin's Press, 1990), p. 47.
87. For the various repercussions of offensive strategies, see Stephen Van Evera, *Causes of War: Power and the Roots of Conflict* (Ithaca, NY & London: Cornell University Press, 1999).
88. Kallet-Marx, *Money, Expense and Naval Power*, p. 203.
89. See, among others, Steven Forde, *The Ambition to Rule: Alcibiades and the Politics of Imperialism in Thucydides* (Ithaca, NY: Cornell University Press, 1989).
90. See Alcibiades' account of the Athenians' war aims in Thucydides, VI 90, reproduced in the next chapter. See also the discussion in Chapter Five.
91. Thucydides, II 65.
92. Kagan, 'Athenian Strategy in the Peloponnesian War', p. 38.
93. Thucydides, II 47–54, III 87.
94. Arther Ferrill, *The Origins of War from the Stone Age to Alexander the Great* (London: Thames and Hudson, 1985), p. 127.
95. See Thucydides, IV 22.
96. Ferrill, *The Origins of War from the Stone Age to Alexander the Great*, p. 128.
97. For these two battles, see respectively Thucydides, IV 89–101 and V 6–11. For the Brasidas' expedition, see the next chapter.
98. As Starr has put it: 'the Spartans acquiesced in a peace treaty that led to massive discontent and defection of their allies, whose grounds of complaint against Athens were almost ignored in the treaty. Athens had done as well, or better, than could have been expected. The Aegean Empire was intact; in western waters its power had risen; the Peloponnesian League had been shaken'; Starr, *The Influence of Sea Power on Ancient History*, p. 43.
99. See, among others, Kagan, *The Archidamian War*; Strauss and Ober, *The Anatomy of Error*; Angelos Vlahos, *Commentary on Thucydides*, vol. I, bks I–IV (Athens: Estia, 1992) (text in Greek).
100. For a critical discussion of Pericles' decision, see Lebow, 'Thucydides, Power Transition Theory and the Causes of War', in Lebow and Strauss, *Hegemonic Rivalry*, pp. 147–56. Also, Barry S. Strauss, 'Of Balances, Bandwagons and Ancient Greeks', in Lebow and Strauss, *Hegemonic Rivalry*, pp. 203–4.
101. Baldwin, *Economic Statecraft*, p. 154.
102. Kagan, *On the Origins of War*, p. 64.
103. Thucydides, I 81.
104. For exponents of the 'feebleness' theory, see Vlahos, *Commentary on Thucydides*, pp. 401–5, as well as the sources cited in Kagan, *The Archidamian War*, pp. 28–9.
105. See Schelling, *Arms and Influence*.
106. Ibid.; see also, Stephen Cimbala, *Military Persuasion: Deterrence and Provocation in Crisis and War* (University Park, PA: Pennsylvania State University Press, 1994).

107. Thucydides, I 143.
108. This also explains why Pericles refrained from creating a fort on Spartan territory, a measure which was reserved for the future. It also shows the fallacy of Donald Kagan's statement that 'we may therefore disregard the construction of a fortress on the Peloponnese as part of the offensive element of the Periclean strategy'; *The Archidamian War*, p. 28.
109. See Alexander L. George, *Some Thoughts on Graduated Escalation*, RM-4844-IR (Santa Monica, CA: RAND Corporation, 1965).
110. Kagan, *The Archidamian War*, p. 41. For an excellent response to the critique of feebleness similar to that of the present book, see Delbrück, *History of the Art of War*, vol. 1, p. 140.
111. See Kagan, *On the Origins of War*, p. 65.
112. See W. Robert Connor, *Thucydides* (Princeton, NJ: Princeton University Press, 1984), p. 50.
113. See Bracken, 'Strategic Planning for National Security', pp. 14–15.
114. Thucydides, II 65.
115. Gray, *The Leverage of Sea Power*, p. 7.
116. Thucydides, I 144.

4. SPARTAN GRAND STRATEGY

1. For an analysis of the Spartan grand strategy during the initial phase of the war, see P.A. Brunt, 'Spartan Policy and Strategy in the Archidamian War', in P.A. Brunt, *Studies in Greek History and Thought* (Oxford: Clarendon, 1993), pp. 84–111.
2. Thucydides repeatedly makes this point; see Thucydides, I 67–8, I 71, I 86, I 118.
3. Thucydides, I 82. Archidamus' clear reference to an alliance with the Persians (foreigners) is an interesting predecessor of a number of cases where realpolitik brought irreconcilable enemies together. The alliance of France with the Ottomans against Spain during the Renaissance is the first such example in modern history, whereas the alliance of Catholic Cardinal Richelieu with the Protestant states of Europe against the Catholic Holy Roman Empire is another case in point. In the twentieth century, the Molotov–Ribbentrop Pact and Nixon's rapprochement with China constitute similar cases. For a comparison of the Spartan–Persian alliance with the modern diplomatic surprises mentioned above, see Barry S. Strauss and Josiah Ober, *The Anatomy of Error: Ancient Military Disasters and Their Lessons for Modern Strategists* (New York: St. Martin's Press, 1990), p. 75. For Richelieu's partnership with the Protestants, see J.H. Elliott, *Richelieu and Olivares* (Cambridge: Cambridge University Press, 1984/1991), pp. 113–42, and Henry Kissinger, *Diplomacy* (New York: Simon & Schuster, 1994), ch. 3. For the concept of diplomatic surprise and an analysis of some

modern instances of diplomatic surprise, see Michael I. Handel, *The Diplomacy of Surprise: Hitler, Nixon, Sadat* (Cambridge, MA: Harvard Center for International Studies, 1981), and Constantinos Koliopoulos, 'Understanding Strategic Surprise' (PhD dissertation, Lancaster University, 1996), pp. 208–16.
4. Thucydides, I 86.
5. Cf. Thucydides, IV 18, IV 21, IV 85, V 14. An impossible theory has been put forward by Gregory Crane, namely that Sthenelaidas stressed 'the fundamental bonds that bind human beings together', grasping that 'Sparta's personalized relationships with its allies are its strength'; see Gregory Crane, *Thucydides and the Ancient Simplicity: The Limits of Political Realism* (Berkeley, CA: University of California Press, 1998), pp. 212–21. Interstate alliances are not built on moral bonds, and this was perhaps far from the case with the Peloponnesian League. Alliances are vehicles through which the states try to enhance their security. As already pointed out, for Sparta the Peloponnesian League was a means of extending its influence and increasing its military strength, whereas for the allies it was a means of warding off external threats and, as far as the ruling classes were concerned, perpetuating oligarchic rule at home. If the League could not fulfil this purpose, the parties would be inclined to leave it, moral bonds among them notwithstanding. Actually, although Sparta did go to war and suffered some major defeats in the process, its allies had no scruples about defecting the League en masse after the Peace of Nicias showed that Sparta was not strong enough to guarantee their security. Thus, Sthenelaidas did not appeal to moral bonds, but simply misjudged the balance of power.
6. Thucydides, IV 85, V 14. Thucydides states that nobody in Greece expected that Athens would hold its position for more than three years if the Spartans invaded Attica; Thucydides, VII 28. In view of this, the statement of Barry Strauss and Josiah Ober that 'at the start of the Peloponnesian War in 431 [BCE], few people expected Athens to suffer a crushing defeat' (Strauss and Ober, *The Anatomy of Error*, pp. 47–8) is incomprehensible.
7. For analyses of the balance of power between Athens and Sparta after Sicily, see Thucydides, VIII 1, VIII 48, VIII 53. For a presentation of Spartan relations with the Persians, see David M. Lewis, *Sparta and Persia* (Leiden: E.J. Brill, 1977).
8. Thucydides, VIII 53. Tissaphernes was the powerful Persian satrap of Sardis in Asia Minor.
9. Donald Kagan holds a different view regarding the origins of the Peloponnesian War (the recurring issue of underlying versus proximate causes of war). Having doubted the growth of the Athenian power prior to the war (see previous chapter), the American historian claims that the Spartans were reluctant to start a war with Athens, but were dragged into it by their allies and their own bellicose *ephors*. See Donald Kagan, *The Outbreak of the Peloponnesian War* (Ithaca, NY: Cornell University Press, 1969/1994), esp. pp. 286–316. Actually, there is no evidence whatsoever to support the view that Spartan citizens wanted peace in

p. [74]

contrast to their *ephors* who wanted war. In addition, Kagan claims that the *ephors* must have initially been supporters of peace but changed their minds after the incidents of Corcyra and Potidaea (Kagan, *The Outbreak of the Peloponnesian War*, p. 307, fn. 46). If this was the case, one may well enquire why it was only the *ephors* that changed their minds while the majority of the Spartans continued to favour peace. This does not make sense and consequently renders Kagan's argument groundless. For analyses that, like the present one, endorse the Thucydidean view that Sparta began the war willingly in order to check Athenian power, see G.E.M. de Ste. Croix, *The Origins of the Peloponnesian War* (London: Duckworth, 1972), and Anton Powell, *Athens and Sparta: Constructing Greek Political and Social History from 478 B.C.* (London: Routledge, 1988), pp. 118–128. For an analysis of the debate in the Spartan Assembly regarding the issue of war against Athens, see A.W. Gomme, *A Historical Commentary on Thucydides*, vol. 1 (Oxford: Clarendon, 1998) (reprint), pp. 252–6.

10. A number of scholars have claimed that from the end of the Persian Wars there existed a group in Sparta which they have called the 'peace party' or the 'doves', in contrast to the 'war party' or the 'hawks'. The only evidence one can find for this is that in two sessions of the Assembly separated by about half a century (477 and 432 BCE, respectively), one part favoured war with Athens while the other one disagreed. The effort to explain the whole of Spartan security policy in the meantime as a struggle between these two parties is based on pure conjecture. It is highly interesting, however, that the exponents of this theory have depicted Archidamus as the leader of the 'peace party' (Brunt, 'Spartan Policy and Strategy in the Archidamian War', p. 111; A.H.M. Jones, *Sparta* [Oxford: Blackwell & Mott, 1967], pp. 63–71; Kagan, *The Outbreak of the Peloponnesian War*, pp. 87, 300–4) or the 'doves' (Ste. Croix, *The Origins of the Peloponnesian War*, pp. 142–3). However, his speech at the Spartan Assembly should leave no doubt that he was not at all averse to the idea of a war with Athens in principle. If coercive diplomacy failed, Archidamus was ready to go to war on completion of the relevant preparations. In this war, he believed that Sparta ought to follow a grand strategy of annihilation. A.H.M. Jones attempts to get round Archidamus' clear advocacy of an eventual war by claiming that the Spartan king 'evidently realized that it was hopeless to urge peace, and he therefore pressed for delay'; Jones, *Sparta*, p. 67. This is an unacceptable distortion of what Archidamus said in the Assembly. For a treatise that points out that there exists no evidence for considering Archidamus a 'dove', see Lewis, *Sparta and Persia*, pp. 46–8.

11. Sparta's Corinthian allies must have shared this belief as well; see the strategy they outlined in their speech in Thucydides, I 120–2. Although that strategy was basically sound and included many of the elements of the grand strategy Sparta actually followed (e.g. naval balancing, creation of a fort in Attica), the balance

of power was so adverse to the Peloponnesians that this strategy could not be implemented. Most importantly, the strategy outlined by the Corinthians lacked the crucial dimension of external balancing through an alliance with the Persians. The successful balancing of the Athenian naval power through Persian help was the decisive factor which gave victory to Sparta.

12. The same point is made by Brunt; 'Spartan Policy and Strategy in the Archidamian War', p. 88.
13. See Alcibiades' speech at Sparta in Thucydides, VI 90. Some scholars do not accept Alcibiades' account at face value, in the supposition that he was exaggerating so as to alarm the Spartans; cf. Donald Kagan, *The Peace of Nicias and the Sicilian Expedition* (Ithaca, NY: Cornell University Press, 1981/1992), pp. 254–7. Still, the Athenians had obviously embarked upon the conquest of Sicily. This by itself constituted pursuit of unlimited objectives. For an enthusiastic approval of Alcibiades' grand scheme as genuine and viable, see Jacqueline de Romilly, *Alcibiades* (Greek trans., 2nd edn) (Athens: Asty, 1995), pp. 103–4.
14. Thucydides, I 82; see also II 18–20. For the classic analysis of coercion in international relations, see Thomas Schelling, *Arms and Influence* (New Haven, CT: Yale University Press, 1966). For a general theory of coercive diplomacy, see Alexander L. George, David K. Hall and William E. Simons, *The Limits of Coercive Diplomacy* (Boston, MA: Little, Brown, 1971), and Alexander George, *Forceful Persuasion: Coercive Diplomacy as Alternative to War* (Washington, DC: United States Institute of Peace, 1991).
15. Thucydides, I 114–15. See also Raphael Sealey, *A History of the Greek City States, 700–338 B.C.* (Berkeley, CA: University of California Press, 1976), p. 321.
16. See Schelling, *Arms and Influence*. Also, James Alt, Randall Calvert and Brian Humes, 'Reputation and Hegemonic Stability: A Game Theoretical Analysis', *American Political Science Review*, 92 (June 1988), pp. 445–66; John D. Orne, *Deterrence, Reputation and the Prevention of Cold-War Cycles* (London: Macmillan, 1992). For an interesting discussion of this topic, see Daryl G. Press, *Calculating Credibility: How Leaders Assess Military Threats* (Ithaca, NY & London: Cornell University Press, 2005), pp. 8–41.
17. For an analysis of this point, see John J. Mearsheimer, *The Tragedy of Great Power Politics* (New York: W.W. Norton, 2001), pp. 162–4. See also Chapters Three and Five of the present book.
18. See Kagan, *The Outbreak of the Peloponnesian War*, pp. 123–6, as well as the discussion in Chapter Two of the present book.
19. Humphrey Michell points out that the Spartan monetary and financial system was 'primitive and absurd' and that the fiscal methods were 'impossible'; Humphrey Michell, *Sparta* (Cambridge: Cambridge University Press, 1952), p. 334. However, he also states that although the Peloponnesian League lacked a system of war finance and was based on an ad hoc arrangement, that arrange-

pp. [79–81]

ment nevertheless 'worked all right'; Michell, *Sparta*, p. 313. We argue that it did not; the League was desperately short of money, as became evident by their acute dependence on Persian funds.

20. This had been the constant nightmare of British policymakers in the last three centuries, and their motivation for preserving the balance of power in Europe. See Paul Kennedy, *The Rise and Fall of British Naval Mastery* (London: Fontana, 1991).
21. Thucydides, II 7.
22. Cf. Thucydides, VI 34.
23. Thucydides, IV 50. The Persian satrap Pissuthnes had been backing anti-Athenian elements in the east Aegean tributaries of the Athenian Empire since 440 BCE; see Thucydides, I 115, III 34. It has been pointed out that 'whether external support for internal political strife is aggression is one of the hardest diplomatic problems in all periods down to our own day' and thus it is not clear whether Pissuthnes' undoubtedly hostile actions constituted a technical breach of the Peace of Callias; Lewis, *Sparta and Persia*, p. 61.
24. For this treaty between Athens and Persia, also known as the Treaty of Epilycus (from the name of an Athenian negotiator), see A.T. Olmstead, *History of the Persian Empire* (Chicago, IL: The University of Chicago Press, 1948), p. 357; Russell Meiggs, *The Athenian Empire* (Oxford: Clarendon Press, 1972), pp. 134–5, 330; Ste. Croix, *The Origins of the Peloponnesian War*, p. 310; Lewis, *Sparta and Persia*, pp. 76–7; Donald Kagan, *The Fall of the Athenian Empire* (Ithaca, NY: Cornell University Press, 1987), pp. 19–22.
25. Thucydides, IV 75.
26. Plutarch has made the startling claim that, since the military training relaxed during wartime, the Spartans viewed war as a respite! See Plutarch, *Lycurgus*, 22.
27. See Thucydides, I 121. However, the Peloponnesian citizen armies could not easily campaign during the harvest period; cf. Thucydides, III 15.
28. See also Lin Foxhall, 'Farming and Fighting in Ancient Greece', in John Rich and Graham Shipley (eds), *War and Society in the Greek World* (London: Routledge, 1993), pp. 142–3.
29. Thucydides, I 58, I 97.
30. Thucydides, III 16.
31. Ibid., III 26–33.
32. For Brasidas' campaign, see Thucydides, IV 70, IV 78–88, IV 102–17, IV 120–34, V 2–3, V 6–13. This campaign has many similarities with the 'southern strategy' proposed to Hitler by Admiral Raeder, namely a massive German move to North Africa with a view to dismantling the British Empire in the Middle East. One might be tempted to pursue this analogy further still by pointing out the similarities between Brasidas and another daring commander, Erwin Rommel. However, there are at least two important differences. First,

Brasidas had to exercise considerable diplomatic skill apart from operational dexterity. Secondly, Brasidas' campaign conformed to a grand strategic design, whereas Rommel's exploits did not, for Hitler had decided to concentrate against the Soviet Union instead of the British Empire. For critical views of Rommel's conduct, see Martin van Creveld, *Supplying War* (Cambridge: Cambridge University Press, 1976), pp. 181–201, and Edward N. Luttwak, *Strategy: The Logic of War and Peace* (Cambridge, MA: The Belknap Press of Harvard University Press, 1987), pp. 210–21. For an analysis of Brasidas' campaign, see Simon Hornblower, *A Commentary on Thucydides*, vol. 2 (Oxford: Clarendon, 1996), pp. 38–61.

33. See Thucydides, III 100, III 114.
34. Thucydides, VII 27–8.
35. As recorded in Thucydides, VI 91. For a modern treatise that adopts this view, see Romilly, *Alcibiades*, pp. 140–3.
36. Angelos Vlahos, *Commentary on Thucydides*, vol. I, bks I–IV (Athens: Estia, 1992), pp. 401–8 (text in Greek). Cf. also the comment of A.H.M. Jones that 'neither side [Sparta and Athens] showed much intelligence and initiative in their operations'; Jones, *Sparta*, p. 70. It must be obvious that we are in total disagreement with these views.
37. Thucydides, I 122, V 17. Alcibiades might have played a role in the selection of Decelea as the locus for the establishment of the fort. However, even this may not have been the case, since the Spartans had from time immemorial been well acquainted with Decelea. According to Herodotus, because of an incident dating from the days of the Trojan War, the Spartans had always held the inhabitants of Decelea in high esteem and granted them special honours. Moreover, Herodotus goes on to say that the Spartans spared the lands of the Deceleans in the Peloponnesian War; Herodotus, IX 73. In other words, the Spartans did not need Alcibiades to inform them about the merits of that place.
38. For the problems associated with the creation of a permanent fort in Athens, see also Donald Kagan, *The Archidamian War* (Ithaca, NY: Cornell University Press, 1974/1990), pp. 350–1.
39. Thucydides, VI 93, VII 1–7. Some scholars have attributed this Spartan action to Alcibiades; see Romilly, *Alcibiades*, pp. 138–40. In fact, the same measure had been suggested to the Spartans by the Corinthian and Syracusan ambassadors (Thucydides, VI 88) and it is difficult to believe that Alcibiades' words carried greater weight with the Spartans. Moreover, the aid that was finally sent was much smaller than the one urged by Alcibiades. In general, one should not overestimate the contribution of Alcibiades to Spartan grand strategy. The Athenian exile always remained a controversial figure in the eyes of the Spartans, and his influence was therefore limited. See also Kagan, *The Peace of Nicias and the Sicilian Expedition*, pp. 257–9.
40. Cf. Thucydides, VII 18, VII 28. The doctrine of 'two-and-a-half wars' had been

suggested as the core military strategy of the United States during the Cold War. According to this, the U.S. ought to be prepared to simultaneously conduct a major war in Europe, another one in Asia, and retain some additional military capability for dealing with regional conflicts in the Western Hemisphere. This doctrine was never implemented. For an analysis of this doctrine in the post-Cold War security environment, see Paul K. Davis and Richard L. Kuger, 'New Principles for Force Sizing', in Zalmay M. Khalilzad and David Ochmanek (eds), *Strategy and Force Planning for the 21st Century* (Santa Monica, CA: RAND Corporation, 1997), pp. 95–140.
41. Thucydides, VIII 2.
42. Thucydides, VIII 3, VIII 26.
43. See Thucydides, VIII 46, VIII 87. Tissaphernes followed the strategy of '*divide et impera*' by providing inadequate help to the Spartans, with a view to exhausting both belligerents. Pharnabazus, on the other hand, helped the Spartans as much as he could, but the resources at his disposal were limited compared with those of Tissaphernes; see Xenophon, *Hellenica* A I 25; Lewis, *Sparta and Persia*, pp. 51–3, 86, 127; Donald Kagan, *The Fall of the Athenian Empire*, pp. 34, 247.
44. Xenophon, *Hellenica*, A IV 1–4, A V 1–7; Plutarch, *Lysander*, 4.
45. In the beginning of 406 BCE, a personal feud between Cyrus and the Spartan admiral Callicratidas led to the cessation of Persian payments. However, the two men quickly came to terms, and the payments were resumed; Xenophon, *Hellenica*, A VI 6–7, A VI 10–11, A VI 18; Plutarch, *Lysander*, 6. For Cyrus' tremendous financial help to the Spartans after their defeat at Arginusae the same year, see Xenophon, *Hellenica*, B I 11–14; Plutarch, *Lysander*, 9.
46. Thucydides, VIII 1.
47. Ibid., VIII 48–56; Xenophon, *Hellenica*, A IV 5–7. On the other hand, in 413–12 BCE, the Athenians also supported the Persian Amorges—an illegitimate son of Pissuthnes—who had staged a revolt against the king in south-west Asia Minor; see Thucydides, VIII 54. This was hardly conducive to earning King Darius' sympathy, but may have been an act of despair on Athens' part; see Kagan, *The Fall of the Athenian Empire*, pp. 31–2.
48. Thucydides, II 7, IV 50.
49. Herodotus, III 46–56, V 63–5, V 92; Thucydides, I 122, VI 53; Plutarch, *Moralia*, 859d. See also W.G. Forrest, *A History of Sparta, 950–192 B.C.* (New York: Norton, 1968), pp. 79–83.
50. Thucydides, II 8. See also III 13, III 31. On the other hand, it has already been demonstrated that Sparta did not receive much help of substance until after the Athenian disaster in Sicily; Sparta's soft power was just that—soft.
51. Thucydides, IV 81; see also IV 85–9, IV 106–8.
52. See also Foxhall, 'Farming and Fighting in Ancient Greece', in Rich and Shipley, *War and Society in the Greek World*, p. 143.
53. Thucydides, II 20, emphasis added. However, the Acharnians continued to be

ardent advocates of the continuation of the war even after the devastation of their land; see Kagan, *The Archidamian War*, pp. 51–2.
54. Thucydides, II 59.
55. The Athenians did offer battle outside their walls in 410 BCE. Interestingly enough, the Peloponnesians declined; Xenophon, *Hellenica*, A I 33–4.
56. Thucydides, V 16–17.
57. See Thucydides, III 70–86. The existence in most cities of a democratic faction that was looking to Athens for support was a factor that increased the international legitimacy of the Athenian grand strategy.
58. The regime and the customs of Sparta enjoyed high legitimacy among the Spartan citizens, at least until the middle of the fourth century BCE. Thucydides was one of the many Ancient Greek writers who praised the Spartan polity; see Thucydides, I 18, VIII 24. For praise of the Spartan customs and national character from Archidamus, who countered the accusations of the Corinthians presented in Chapter Two, see Thucydides, I 84. See also Xenophon, *Lacedaimonion Politeia*, and Plutarch, *Lycurgus*. However, it must be pointed out that Xenophon's, and especially Plutarch's, accounts present a highly idealized picture of Sparta.
59. For the oligarchic coup and subsequent developments, see Thucydides, VIII 47–98. For the negotiations of the oligarchs with the Spartans and the alleged conspiracy, see Thucydides, VIII 70–1, VIII 86, VIII 90–6. This oligarchic 'fifth column' can be regarded as a predecessor of the fascist fifth column that was reputedly in action during the siege of Madrid by Franco's troops in 1939.
60. Thucydides, II 65.
61. P.A. Brunt claims that the Spartans had to adopt a strategy of attrition; Brunt, 'Spartan Policy and Strategy in the Archidamian War', p. 94. However, only the cost-raising aspects of Spartan grand strategy can really be given this name. Annihilation was what the Spartans were chiefly aiming at. Even the annual devastation of Attica was primarily aimed at bringing about a decisive land battle. See above, as well as Victor Davis Hanson, *Warfare and Agriculture in Classical Greece* (Berkeley, CA: University of California Press, 1998) (rev. edn), pp. 131–73.
62. As far as most of the Spartans in 431 BCE were concerned, their nation was still stronger than Athens, and could and did afford to launch a preventive war. For the issue of moral justification of preventive war, see Michael Walzer, *Just and Unjust Wars: A Moral Argument with Historical Illustrations* (2nd edn) (New York: Basic Books, 1992), pp. 74–80. Two U.S. presidents, Franklin Roosevelt and John F. Kennedy, had rejected possible American strikes against Japan (prior to Pearl Harbor) and the Soviet missiles in Cuba, respectively, as incompatible with the United States' moral standing; see, respectively, Gordon Prange quoted in Ariel Levite, *Intelligence and Strategic Surprises* (New York: Columbia University Press, 1987), p. 154, and Robert Kennedy, *Thirteen Days:*

A Memoir of the Cuban Missile Crisis (New York: Norton, 1971), pp. 9, 15–17, 27.
63. Interestingly enough, moral qualms started troubling the Spartans *after* preventive war had failed to deliver the goods; see Thucydides, VII 18.
64. That the Spartans had been thinking the war would be decided swiftly by their invasions of Attica, and thus had not felt the need to take these measures, is obvious in Brasidas' speech cited in Thucydides, IV 85.
65. See the analysis in the previous chapter.
66. Sir Basil Liddell Hart has stated that 'the scales were definitely turned against Athens' by the time of Brasidas' expedition; B.H. Liddell Hart, *Strategy* (2nd rev. edn) (London: Meridian, 1991), p. 13. We consider this to be wrong: Athens could still obtain an advantageous peace after Brasidas' expedition.
67. Thucydides, V 28.
68. Thucydides, V 75. For Sparta's strategy against the resurgent Argos, culminating in the Battle of Mantinea, see Thucydides, V 57–76.
69. See the now classic analysis of Victor Davis Hanson, *The Western Way of War* (New York: Alfred A. Knopf, 1989).
70. This was the chief objection raised against such battles by two of the greatest eighteenth-century generals, namely Marshal Maurice de Saxe and King Frederick the Great. See their treatises reproduced in Thomas R. Phillips (ed.), *Roots of Strategy: A Collection of Military Classics* (London: John Lane the Bodley Head, 1943), chs. 3–4.
71. Cf. the discussion of the Battle of Plataea in Chapter One.
72. For the decisive effects of a timely Athenian and Elean intervention in Mantinea, see Kagan, *The Peace of Nicias and the Sicilian Expedition*, p. 134. Of course, other things could have happened as well: the Spartans could have achieved a crushing victory over the Argives some months earlier (Thucydides, V 59–60), or their Corinthian and Boeotian allies could in turn have timely intervened in Mantinea. All this clearly shows that Alcibiades was right when boasting that, with his policy (Athens' alliance with Argos), he forced the Spartans to 'risk their all on the issue of one day's fighting at Mantinea' (Thucydides, VI 16). This was something that happened to the Spartans from time to time. For two earlier instances when they were forced to risk (and win) their hegemony in the Peloponnese with decisive battles in Tegea and Dipaieis during the 470s and 460s BCE, see Chapter Two.
73. Thucydides, VII 18.
74. Gradually, the Spartans adopted the view that they should succeed the Athenians in creating an empire of their own in Greece. As was mentioned in Chapter Two, this undertaking was contrary to the Spartan political organization and led to catastrophe.
75. Thucydides, VIII 84. G.E.M. de Ste. Croix speculates that the Spartans perhaps had prepared a subtle diplomatic trap for the Persians: as soon as the war

ended, the Spartans, based on the wording of their treaty with the Persians, would claim that they had agreed to hand over to the Persians only the country surrounding the Greek cities of Asia Minor, but not the cities themselves; see Ste. Croix, *The Origins of the Peloponnesian War*, pp. 313–14. David Lewis, on the other hand, believes that the Spartans managed to find a successful solution to the problem: a formula must have reached, probably in 408–7 BCE (the so-called Treaty of Boiotios) where the Greek cities would remain autonomous and merely pay tribute to the Persians; Lewis, *Sparta and Persia*, ch. 5. Although such an arrangement would not be a 'sell-out' of the Asia Minor Greeks, it would not be liberation either.

76. For these battles, see Xenophon, *Hellenica*, A I 16–18, A VI 28–35.
77. Thucydides, VIII 1.
78. Xenophon, *Hellenica*, A VI 31.
79. See respectively Diodorus, XIII 52–3 and Aristotle, *Athenaion Politeia*, 34. 1.
80. For ancient accounts of this battle, see Xenophon, *Hellenica*, B I 22–30, Diodorus, XIII 105–6, and Plutarch, *Lysander*, 10–11. Diodorus' account seems to be the most accurate one; cf. Christopher Ehrhardt, 'Xenophon and Diodorus on Aegospotami', *Phoenix*, 24, 3 (1970), pp. 225–8. For an excellent modern analysis collating various ancient sources, see Donald Kagan, *The Fall of the Athenian Empire*, pp. 386–93.
81. See Xenophon, *Hellenica*, B II 19–23. It would be wrong to attribute the Spartan decision to sentiment, as David Lewis does; Lewis, *Sparta and Persia*, p. 112. Sentiment did not prevent the Spartans in 427 BCE from wiping from the face of the earth that most brave city, Plataea, which had been far more politically innocuous than Athens. For the Plataean affair, see Thucydides, III 52–68.

5. THUCYDIDES AND STRATEGY IN PERSPECTIVE

1. Thucydides, II 65.
2. See, for instance, John J. Mearsheimer, *The Tragedy of Great Power Politics* (New York: W.W. Norton, 2001), p. 58, and Athanasios Platias and Constantinos Koliopoulos, *The Art of Strategy: 50 Maxims for War, Politics, Business, and Everyday Life* (London: Hurst, 2025), ch. 2.
3. See André Corvisier and John Childs, 'Planning/Plans', in André Corvisier (ed.), *A Dictionary of Military History* (London: Blackwell, 1994), p. 654, and Doyne Dawson, *The Origins of Western Warfare* (Boulder, CO: Westview, 1996).
4. Hans Delbrück, *History of the Art of War*, vol. 1 (Lincoln, NE: University of Nebraska Press, 1975), p. 137. For different assessments of Pericles and his grand strategy, see the discussion in Chapter Three.
5. A.H.M. Jones calls him 'a patriotic, able and courageous king'; A.H.M. Jones, *Sparta* (Oxford: Blackwell & Mott, 1967), p. 71. W.G. Forrest, on the other hand, merely says that Archidamus conducted the invasions of Attica 'without

pp. [98–100]   NOTES

alacrity but without obvious incompetence'; W.G. Forrest, *A History of Sparta, 950–192 B.C.* (New York: Norton, 1968), p. 112.
6. See B.H. Liddell Hart, *Strategy* (2nd rev. edn) (London: Meridian, 1991).
7. See, for instance, John J. Mearsheimer, *Liddell Hart and the Weight of History* (Ithaca, NY: Cornell University Press 1988).
8. Liddell Hart, *Strategy*, p. 13.
9. For the battle of Aegospotami, see the sources cited in Chapter Four, n. 357.
10. For a similar approach, see Stephen Van Evera, *Causes of War: Power and the Roots of Conflict* (Ithaca, NY & London: Cornell University Press, 1999).
11. See the relevant extracts in the Appendix. Modern realist scholars have used these factors in order to explain the strategic behaviour of states with regard to alignment; see Stephen M. Walt, *The Origins of Alliances* (Ithaca, NY: Cornell University Press, 1987), and Athanassios Platias, 'High Politics in Small Countries' (PhD dissertation, Cornell University, 1986), pp. 82–97.
12. An early exposition of the impact that both the existing balance and the trends in the distribution of power have on states' grand strategies can be found in Kautilya, *Arthasastra* (trans. R. Shamasastry, 2nd edn) (Mysore: Wesleyan Mission Press, 1923), pp. 312–20. For an excellent treatise on the impact of the trends in the distribution of power, see A.F.K. Organski and Jacek Kugler, *The War Ledger* (Chicago, IL: The University of Chicago Press, 1980).
13. Conceivably, there is also a third possibility: that the balance of power between a state and its strategic opponent may not alter significantly in the long run. This possibility has independent significance only when the two opponents are roughly equal in power in the first place (otherwise, we have a clear case of stronger versus weaker state, with both of them acting accordingly). However, we know of no such instance in history; for better or for worse, two strategic opponents are unlikely to remain equal in power for very long.
14. See, among others, Joseph De Rivera, *The Psychological Dimension of Foreign Policy* (Columbus, OH: Charles E. Merrill, 1968); Robert Jervis, 'Hypotheses on Misperception', *World Politics*, 20, 2 (1968), pp. 454–79; Robert Jervis, *Perception and Misperception in International Politics* (Princeton, NJ: Princeton University Press, 1976).
15. Bernard Brodie, *Strategy in the Missile Age* (Princeton, NJ: Princeton University Press, 1959), p. 378. The technological and geographical environment may at times accentuate this capability-oriented perception of threat. Thus, whenever technology and/or geography are believed to favour the adoption of offensive military strategies, the political leadership of a state will tend to focus on the offensive capabilities of their state's strategic opponent and the concomitant 'window of vulnerability' these capabilities open. See George Quester, *Offense and Defense in the International System* (New York: Wiley, 1977), and Stephen Van Evera, 'The Cult of the Offensive and the Origins of the First World War', *International Security*, 9, 1 (Summer 1984), pp. 58–107.

16. See two excellent works, namely Raymond L. Garthoff, 'On Estimating and Imputing Intentions', *International Security*, 2, 3 (Winter 1977–8), pp. 22–32, and Sebastian Rosato, *Intentions in Great Power Politics: Uncertainty and the Roots of Conflict* (New Haven, CT & London: Yale University Press, 2021).
17. See H.H. Scullard, *A History of the Roman World, 753 to 146 B.C.* (4th edn) (London & New York: Routledge, 1980/1995), pp. 308–17.
18. On threat perception, see Klaus Knorr, 'Threat Perception', in Klaus Knorr (ed.), *Historical Dimensions of National Security Problems* (Lawrence, KA: Kansas University Press, 1976), pp. 78–119, and Raymond Cohen, 'Threat Perception in International Crisis', *Political Science Quarterly*, 93, 1 (1978), pp. 93–107. For detailed analyses of the role of threat perception in matters of strategic surprise, see Ariel Levite, *Intelligence and Strategic Surprises* (New York: Columbia University Press, 1987), and Constantinos Koliopoulos, 'Understanding Strategic Surprise' (PhD dissertation, Lancaster University, 1996).
19. See Jervis, 'Hypotheses on Misperception'. It has been pointed out that, even after such changes of threat perception, it is not easy to reverse extremist policies (i.e. overly competitive or overly cooperative) that had been previously adopted in accordance with the threat perception prevalent at the time; see Charles A. Kupchan, *The Vulnerability of Empire* (Ithaca, NY: Cornell University Press, 1994).
20. For definitions of 'great' and 'small' powers, see Platias, *High Politics in Small Countries*, pp. 483–92, and Mearsheimer, *The Tragedy of Great Power Politics*, p. 5.
21. See Robert Gilpin, *War and Change in World Politics* (Cambridge: Cambridge University Press, 1981). For the different forms of imperialism—namely military, economic and cultural—see Hans J. Morgenthau, *Politics Among Nations* (5th edn) (New York: Alfred A. Knopf, 1985). For the belief that there are no status quo states in the international system, save the occasional hegemon, see Mearsheimer, *The Tragedy of Great Power Politics*.
22. Of course, throughout history, states have continued their quest for expansion long after reaching the point of diminishing returns. For a treatise pointing out that the roots of overextension are often to be found in the domestic structures of states, see Jack Snyder, *Myths of Empire: Domestic Politics and International Ambition* (Ithaca, NY: Cornell University Press, 1991).
23. John Mearsheimer depicts four strategies for a state that is (or would like to be) on the rise: war (use of force), blackmail (threat of force), bait and bleed (weaken one's rivals by provoking a long and costly war between them), and bloodletting (taking measures to ensure that any war in which an adversary is involved is protracted and deadly); Mearsheimer, *The Tragedy of Great Power Politics*, pp. 138–9, 147–55. Thus, it transpires that 'war' and 'blackmail' are means to expansion, whereas 'bait and bleed' and 'bloodletting' are normally preludes to expansion.

24. Mearsheimer, *The Tragedy of Great Power Politics*, pp. 139, 157–62.
25. Haralambos Papasotiriou, 'Byzantine Grand Strategy' (PhD dissertation, Stanford University, 1991), p. 9; Mearsheimer, *The Tragedy of Great Power Politics*, pp. 162–4. One can point out a difference between tactical and strategic appeasement: tactical appeasement refers to concessions that are made as a temporary measure in order to gain time for a more assertive response later on; strategic appeasement, on the other hand, is a longer-term course. Here we will deal with strategic appeasement only.
26. Morgenthau, *Politics Among Nations*.
27. For the issue of interstate cooperation, see Joseph M. Grieco, *Cooperation Among Nations* (Ithaca, NY: Cornell University Press, 1990), pp. 40–9; Joseph M. Grieco, 'Anarchy and the Limits of Cooperation', in David Baldwin (ed.), *Neorealism and Neoliberalism: The Contemporary Debate* (New York: Columbia University Press, 1993), pp. 116–40; Arthur A. Stein, *Why Nations Cooperate* (Ithaca, NY & London: Cornell University Press, 1990).
28. See Thucydides, V 84–113.
29. Herodotus, VIII 115.
30. See Barry S. Strauss and Josiah Ober, *The Anatomy of Error: Ancient Military Disasters and Their Lessons for Modern Strategists* (New York: St. Martin's Press, 1990), ch. 1.
31. Thucydides, I 98–100.
32. Thucydides, I 105–8, I 111–15.
33. Ibid., I 113–15.
34. Ibid., I 139–41, I 144.
35. Thucydides, IV 3–5, IV 8–23, IV 26–38.
36. Thucydides, IV 89–101, V 6–20.
37. Thucydides, V 27–33.
38. Ibid., V 57–76.
39. Thucydides, VI–VII.
40. Actually, one cannot be sure whether the Persian political leadership perceived Athens as posing a high or a low threat. We assume the latter, since the western coast of Asia Minor, and the Greek world in general, was but a peripheral concern for the Persian Empire until the advent of Alexander the Great; cf. A.T. Olmstead, *History of the Persian Empire* (Chicago, IL: The University of Chicago Press, 1948). On the other hand, the Persian court may have regarded the loss of that area to the Athenian intruders as a heavy blow to its prestige, the Athenian support to the rebel Amorges adding insult to injury. Hence, the Persian political leadership could possibly perceive Athens as highly threatening, and the recovery of the western Asia Minor coast as a very important matter indeed; cf. David M. Lewis, *Sparta and Persia* (Leiden: E.J. Brill, 1977), pp. 25–6.
41. Thucydides, VIII 17–18, 36–7, 55–8.

42. Ibid., VIII 1.
43. Ibid., VIII 48–56.
44. Correlli Barnett attributes this change to a 'moral revolution' in Great Britain that supposedly began in the late eighteenth century and was completed in the first half of the nineteenth; see Correlli Barnett, *The Collapse of British Power* (Phoenix Mill: Allan Sutton, 1984). Barnett's analysis is highly impressive. However, he himself acknowledges the role initially played by the elimination of the high threats of previous eras; see Barnett, *The Collapse of British Power*, pp. 20–1.
45. For the international theoretical implications of Russia's intransigent expansion, see Athanasios Platias and Vasilis Trigkas, 'Ukraine and the Academy: One War, Many Theories', *China Quarterly of International Strategic Studies*, 9, 1 (2024), pp. 1–28.
46. Mearsheimer, *The Tragedy of Great Power Politics*, ch. 7.
47. The French, for their part, proved benevolent hegemons, going as far as to cede French territory in the United States to Spain so that the latter could make good its territorial losses to Great Britain; see Martin Wight, *Power Politics* (eds Hedley Bull and Carsten Holbraad) (London: Leicester University Press, 1978), pp. 127–30.
48. See John Gooch, 'The Weary Titan: Strategy and Policy in Great Britain, 1890–1918', in Williamson Murray, MacGregor Knox and Alvin Bernstein (eds), *The Making of Strategy: Rulers, States, and War* (Cambridge: Cambridge University Press, 1994), pp. 289–90; also, Mearsheimer, *The Tragedy of Great Power Politics*, pp. 238–52.
49. Correlli Barnett makes much of the previously mentioned belief in Anglo-American racial brotherhood and is highly critical of the British decision to appease the United States; see Barnett, *The Collapse of British Power*, pp. 255–63. Paul Kennedy and John Gooch, on the other hand, point out that Great Britain had to face a difficult strategic situation and had to make some hard choices. Concentrating on Germany was easily the lesser evil; see Paul Kennedy, *The Realities Behind Diplomacy: Background Influences on British External Policy, 1865–1980* (London: Fontana, 1981), pp. 107–8, 118–20, and Gooch, 'The Weary Titan', pp. 289–90. For the classic exposition of the British balancing logic, see Eyre Crowe, 'Memorandum on the Present State of British Relations with France and Germany', 1 January 1907, in G.P. Gooch and Harold Temperley (eds), *British Documents on the Origins of the War, Vol. III: The Testing of the Entente, 1904–6* (London: HMSO, 1928), pp. 398–420.
50. The United States was, strictly speaking, not an ally of the Entente Powers in the First World War, but an 'associated power'. Still, American power obviously augmented French power.
51. Similar arguments can be made with regard to Great Britain's balancing behaviour prior to the First World War.

52. According to Correlli Barnett, there was no way out of the predicament, and British independence was bound to be lost, since Great Britain had become totally dependent on American industry and technology in order to wage war, and would simply go bankrupt in the process; see Barnett, *The Collapse of British Power*, pp. 12–15.
53. For the famous comment of Churchill that 'if Hitler invaded Hell, I would make at least a favourable reference to the Devil in the House of Commons', see Winston S. Churchill, *The Second World War, vol. III: The Grand Alliance* (London: Guild, 1985), p. 331.
54. British grand strategy was successful in the sense that it preserved the survival and the independence of Great Britain. On the other hand, it has been criticized for failing to take care of the preservation of the balance of power in Europe, thus resulting in an all-powerful Soviet Union. For a critique of the British and American grand strategies on these grounds, see J.F.C. Fuller, *The Conduct of War, 1789–1961* (London: Methuen, 1972), ch. 13.
55. For the strategic relationship between Austria and Prussia at that time, see Dennis Showalter, *The Wars of Frederick the Great* (London: Longman, 1996).
56. This incident created a long-lived impression; see Jonathan Steinberg, 'The Copenhagen Complex', *Journal of Contemporary History*, 1, 3 (1966), pp. 23–46.
57. Although Gorbachev's attempt to save his state met with failure, this most probably shows that the Soviet Union was beyond salvation. It should not be construed to prove that appeasement was the wrong course of action.
58. For more details, see the postscript in this book.
59. For an article that argued forcefully that 'the Middle Kingdom is a middle power', see Gerald Segal, 'Does China Matter?' *Foreign Affairs*, 78, 5 (September/October 1999), pp. 24–36. However, Segal definitely overstated his case.
60. See, respectively, Jude Blanchette and Ryan Hass, 'Know Your Rival, Know Yourself', *Foreign Affairs*, 104, 1 (January/February 2025), pp. 88–101, and Amy Zegart, 'The Crumbling Foundations of American Strength', *Foreign Affairs*, 103, 5 (September/October 2024), pp. 136–47.
61. See Jeremy Garlick, *Advantage China: Agent of Change in an Era of Global Disruption* (London: Bloomsbury Academic, 2023).
62. Robert D. Blackwill and Richard Fontaine, *Lost Decade: The U.S. Pivot to Asia and the Rise of Chinese Power* (New York: Oxford University Press, 2024).
63. Sheena Chestnut Greitens, 'Xi's Security Obsession', *Foreign Affairs*, 28 July 2023, https://www.foreignaffairs.com/united-states/xis-security-obsession.
64. See, respectively, Erica Strecker Downs and Philip C. Saunders, 'Legitimacy and the Limits of Nationalism: China and the Diaoyu Islands', *International Security*, 23, 3 (Winter 1998/99), pp. 114–46, and Tyler Jost, 'Have China's Wolf Warriors Gone Extinct?' *Foreign Affairs*, 27 June 2024, https://www.foreignaffairs.com/china/have-chinas-wolf-warriors-gone-extinct.

65. For the American Civil War, see among others, Fuller, *The Conduct of War*, pp. 95–112, and Russell F. Weigley, 'Military Strategy and Civilian Leadership', in Knorr, *Historical Dimensions of National Security Problems*, pp. 38–77. The classical analysis on how the United States traditionally approach war is detailed in Russell F. Weigley, *The American Way of War: A History of United States Military Strategy and Policy* (New York: Macmillan, 1973).
66. For the Prussian/German General Staff, see Walter Goerlitz, *History of the German General Staff, 1657–1945* (New York: Praeger, 1959), and T.N. Dupuy, *A Genius for War: The German Army and General Staff, 1807–1945* (Falls Church, VA: NOVA, 1984).
67. For the Austro-Prussian War, see Geoffrey Wawro, *The Austro-Prussian War: Austria's War with Prussia and Italy in 1866* (Cambridge: Cambridge University Press, 1996). For the Franco-Prussian War, see Michael Howard, *The Franco-Prussian War* (London: Routledge, 1988). The relationship between the Prussian political and military leaderships was not untroubled. For the rivalry between Bismarck and Moltke, see Howard, *The Franco-Prussian War*, esp. pp. 350–9.
68. Liddell Hart proclaimed the term 'battle' obsolete and argued that the key idea is the 'strategic operation'; Liddell Hart, *Strategy*, p. 352. This has now become conventional wisdom.
69. For this development, see Fuller, *The Conduct of War*. For the transformation of the 'war of annihilation' to 'total war', as seen through the eyes of one of its leading practitioners, see Erich Ludendorff, *The Nation at War* (London: Hutchinson, 1938).
70. It goes without saying that the manipulation of the threat to resort to nuclear war is used as an instrument of policy (i.e. nuclear deterrence, compellence).
71. In theory, however, it is still possible to achieve a swift and decisive victory in a conventional war and therefore avoid the huge damage associated with a protracted conventional war; see John J. Mearsheimer, *Conventional Deterrence* (Ithaca, NY: Cornell University Press, 1983), pp. 1–66.
72. For the durability of war as a phenomenon and its likely survival both at present and in the future, see Martin van Creveld, *The Transformation of War* (New York: Free Press, 1991). For an analysis suggesting that war between great powers is obsolete, without however claiming that war in general tends to disappear, see Michael Mandelbaum, 'Is Major War Obsolete?' *Survival*, 40, 4 (Winter 1998–9), pp. 20–38.
73. See Hans Delbrück, *History of the Art of War* (4 vols) (Lincoln, NE: University of Nebraska Press, 1975–85). We have seen that the Spartans caused economic damage to Athens by devastating Attica. These actions, however, were not aimed primarily at this kind of damage, but were chiefly a means of forcing the Athenians to give battle outside their walls. Actually, the extent of crop devastation was relatively limited; see Victor Davis Hanson, *Warfare and Agriculture in Classical Greece* (rev. edn) (Berkeley, CA: University of California Press, 1998), pp. 131–73.

74. See Athanassios Platias, 'Post-Heroic Warfare: Lessons from the Periclean Grand Strategy', paper delivered at the 'International Conference on War in a Changing World', Jaffee Center for Strategic Studies, Tel Aviv University, 5–7 November 1996. For the American strategy during the Cold War, see among others John Lewis Gaddis, *Strategies of Containment* (New York: Oxford University Press, 1982), and John Lewis Gaddis, *The Long Peace* (New York: Oxford University Press, 1987). See also Diane Kunz, *Butter and Guns: America's Cold War Economic Diplomacy* (New York: Free Press, 1997).

75. For a state-of-the-art analysis, see Mick Ryan, *War Transformed: The Future of Twenty-First-Century Great Power Competition and Conflict* (Annapolis, MD: Naval Institute Press, 2022). For healthy correctives of the fairly widespread current obsession with military technology, see Colin S. Gray, *Weapons Don't Make War: Policy, Strategy, and Military Technology* (Lawrence, KA: University Press of Kansas, 1993), and Colin S. Gray, *Strategy for Chaos: Revolutions in Military Affairs and the Evidence of History* (London: Frank Cass, 2002).

76. Edward N. Luttwak, 'Toward Post-Heroic Warfare', *Foreign Affairs*, 74, 3 (May/June 1995), pp. 109–22.

77. It must be pointed out that some analysts have disputed the view that public opinion in Western countries is as sensitive to war casualties as conventional wisdom has it; see Bruce W. Jentleson, 'Normative Dilemmas and Political Myths: The Contemporary Political Context of the Use of Military Force', paper presented at 'Employing Air and Space Power at the Turn of the Millennium: Lessons and Implications', Fisher Institute for Air and Space Strategic Studies, Tel Aviv, December 1999. However, even if Jentleson is correct, it is undeniable that the agenda of perceived interests warranting military action involving heavy casualties has shrunk considerably since the end of the Second World War.

78. What follows is confined to the conventional military strategic aspects of these conflicts and does not delve on their broader strategic and political contexts.

79. For the Kuwait War, see among others Norman Friedman, *Desert Victory: The War for Kuwait* (Annapolis, MD: Naval Institute Press, 1991); Joseph S. Nye Jr. and Roger K. Smith (eds), *After the Storm: Lessons from the Gulf War* (Lanham, MD: Madison Books, 1992); Lawrence Freedman and Ephraim Karsh, *The Gulf Conflict, 1990–1991: Diplomacy and War in the New World Order* (Princeton, NJ: Princeton University Press, 1993). The land operations of the Allies are a remarkable instance of a crushing blow against enemy armed forces with minimal friendly casualties (147 dead).

80. Achievement of the strategic objective is the acid test of strategic effectiveness, and there is no doubt that NATO forces passed it with flying colours. On the other hand, the operational results of the campaign were less clear-cut. The power structure of the Serbian political leadership did sustain tremendous damage. In contrast, Serbian armed forces managed, for a substantial part of the

campaign, to avoid extensive destruction. Having quickly defeated the KLA, they could afford to remain concealed and dispersed, thus limiting the damage suffered from aerial bombardment. This situation changed in the later stages of the campaign, when the re-emergence of the KLA forced the concentration of the Serbian forces, thus making them targetable by the NATO bombing. It seems that this development played a crucial role in the Serbian leadership's decision to come to terms. For strategic analyses of the Kosovo War, see Benjamin Lambeth, *NATO's Air War for Kosovo: A Strategic and Operational Assessment* (Santa Monica, CA: RAND Corporation, 2001), and Harry Papasotiriou, 'The Kosovo War: Kosovar Insurrection, Serbian Retribution and NATO Intervention', *Journal of Strategic Studies*, 25, 1 (March 2002), pp. 39–62.

81. The first American casualty caused by the enemy took place in January 2002, about three months after the beginning of hostilities; there were earlier casualties through friendly fire.
82. For an analysis on the war on terror via Thucydides' text, see Victor Davis Hanson, 'A Voice from the Past: General Thucydides Speaks about the War', in Victor Davis Hanson (ed.), *An Autumn of War: What America Learned from September 11 and the War on Terrorism* (New York: Anchor Books, 2002). For prescient analyses by a veteran strategic analyst, see Michael Howard, 'A Long War?' *Survival*, 48, 4 (Winter 2006–07), pp. 7–14, and Michael Howard, 'Are we at war?' *Survival*, 50, 4 (August–September 2008), pp. 247–56.
83. It has been reported that the elite Iraqi armoured divisions lost almost 90 per cent of their tanks due to aerial bombardment. For an analysis, see Williamson Murray and Major General Robert H. Scales Jr., *The Iraq War* (Cambridge, MA: The Belknap Press of Harvard University Press, 2003).
84. The increased concern for minimizing casualties is a new element in the 'American way of war'. From Grant's era until the Vietnam War, American strategy was never much concerned with casualties.
85. See Carter Malkasian, *The American War in Afghanistan: A History* (New York: Oxford University Press, 2021), and Vanda Felbab-Brown, 'Why the Taliban Won: And What Washington Can Do About It Now', *Foreign Affairs*, 17 August 2021, https://www.foreignaffairs.com/print/node/1127675.
86. When the Americans first entered Afghanistan, their allies controlled about 10 per cent of the country. When the Americans left, their allies controlled merely a single valley, and after a while, they were not heard from again.
87. For whatever reason, Georgia started the shooting; see the report of the EU fact-finding mission ('Independent International Fact-Finding Mission on the Conflict in Georgia', September 2009, https://www.echr.coe.int/Documents/HUDOC_38263_08_Annexes_ENG.pdf). For political and strategic analyses of the war, see Ronald D. Asmus, *A Little War That Shook the World: Georgia, Russia, and the Future of the West* (New York: Palgrave Macmillan, 2010), and

Ruslan Pukhov (ed.), *The Tanks of August* (Moscow: Centre for Analysis of Strategies and Technologies, 2010).

88. For the non-existence of a 'Gerasimov doctrine,' see Mark Galeotti, 'I'm Sorry for Creating the "Gerasimov Doctrine"', *Foreign Policy*, 5 March 2018, https://foreignpolicy.com/2018/03/05/im-sorry-for-creating-the-gerasimov-doctrine/#, and Mark Galeotti, '"The Gerasimov Doctrine"', *Berlin Policy Journal*, 28 April 2020, https://berlinpolicyjournal.com/the-gerasimov-doctrine/. For the actual Russian hybrid warfare in its various aspects, see Mason Clark, *Russian Hybrid Warfare* (Washington, DC: Institute for the Study of War, 2020).

89. Anton Siluanov, then First Deputy Prime Minister of Russia and Russian Minister of Finance, admitted as much in June 2019 in Moscow, during the 4th International Forum 'Primakov Readings'.

90. For a brilliant analysis of the role of attrition in warfare throughout history, see Cathal J. Nolan, *The Allure of Battle: A History of How Wars Have Been Won and Lost* (New York: Oxford University Press, 2017).

91. Thucydides, II 65.

92. For detailed accounts, see Donald Kagan, *The Peace of Nicias and the Sicilian Expedition* (Ithaca, NY: Cornell University Press, 1981/1992), and Paul A. Rahe, *Sparta's Sicilian Proxy War: The Grand Strategy of Classical Sparta, 418–413 B.C.* (New York & London: Encounter Books, 2023).

93. Thucydides repeatedly makes this point; see Thucydides, VI 1, VI 20, VII 55. However, one cannot help pointing out that the great historian has contradicted himself in this respect by stating that the Sicilian expedition 'failed not so much through a miscalculation of the power of those against whom it was sent, as through a fault in the senders in not taking the best measures afterwards to assist those who had gone out'; Thucydides, II 65. This was obviously not the case, since Thucydides himself points out that the Athenians lavished a vast amount of resources both on the initial expedition and the subsequent reinforcements; see Thucydides, VI 31, VI 43–4, VII 16, VII 42.

94. Thucydides, VI 17.

95. The classic analysis of the religious and civic institutions of ancient Greece and Rome is Numa Denis Fustel de Coulanges, *The Ancient City: A Study on the Religion, Laws, and Institutions of Greece and Rome* (trans. Willard Small) (Garden City, NY: Doubleday Anchor Books, n.d.). The French original was published in 1864 and the English translation dates from 1873.

96. Cf. Thucydides, VI 1.

97. Ibid., VI 18.

98. Even Thucydides himself seems to have found it difficult to escape from Alcibiades' spell. Thus, although in Thucydides, II 65 he criticises Alcibiades for deviating from the Periclean grand strategy, it is in the very same section that (contradicting himself, as we mentioned above) he states that the Sicilian expedition was not an error of judgement with regard to the opposition to be

NOTES pp. [130–133]

expected. Thucydides has additionally praised Alcibiades by stating that 'in his public life his conduct of the war was as good as could be desired'; Thucydides, VI 15. We have already pointed out that Alcibiades indeed deserves credit for forging Athens' alliance with Argos; see Chapter Four, n. 72.

99. See Herodotus, VII 153–67.
100. The expulsion of the inhabitants of the city of Leontini from their homeland by the Syracusans was one of the reasons put forward for the Athenian intervention.
101. Thucydides, VI 20.
102. Thucydides, VII 55.
103. Ibid., VII 57–8.
104. For the initial qualitative disparity between Syracusan and Athenian troops, see Thucydides, VI 69, VI 72, VII 3. For the first Syracusan victory on land, see Thucydides, VII 6.
105. The Syracusan cavalry, which Alcibiades had not condescended to mention at all in his speech at the *Ecclesia*, was a major factor in the war in Sicily. It was continually harassing the Athenians (Thucydides, VI 52, VI 64, VII 5), which prevented them from pursuing the defeated Syracusan infantry (Thucydides, VI 70–1) and played a central role in the first Syracusan victory on land (Thucydides, VII 6).
106. Thucydides, VI 93, VII 1–7. Characteristically, Nicias failed to take any precautions against Gylippus' arrival until it was too late; Thucydides, VI 104, VII 1.
107. Thucydides, VII 23.
108. For the ingenuity of the Syracusans, see Thucydides, VII 36, VII 65.
109. For the initial Athenian defeat of the Syracusan navy, see Thucydides, VII 23. For the three Syracusan naval victories, see Thucydides, VII 41, VII 52, VII 69–71.
110. After the first Syracusan victory at sea, the Athenians were about to depart, but Nicias postponed the departure because of an eclipse of the moon; see Thucydides, VII 50.
111. Thucydides' narrative of the retreat and the final destruction of the Athenian force is not for the faint-hearted; see Thucydides, VII 72–87.
112. See Thucydides, VI 33–4.
113. See Thucydides, V 76–83.
114. Thucydides, VI 11.
115. Liddell Hart seems at a loss on how to evaluate the Sicilian expedition. Although quick to dissociate it from a 'proper' indirect approach, he would obviously prefer to see it succeeding: 'As a grand strategy of indirect approach it had the defect of striking, not at the enemy's actual partners, but rather at his business associates. Thereby, instead of distracting the enemy's forces, it drew fresh forces into opposition. Nevertheless, the moral and economic

results of success might well have changed the whole balance of the war if there had not been an almost unparalleled chain of blunders in execution. [...] The best-founded hopes of a recovery [from the alleged turning of the scales against Athens by Brasidas' expedition] came from Alcibiades' indirect approach—on the plane of grand strategy—to Sparta's economic root in Sicily'; Liddell Hart, *Strategy*, pp. 12–13.

116. For a brief sketch of a number of cases, see Van Evera, *Causes of War*, pp. 16–34.
117. See Paul Kennedy, *The Rise and Fall of the Great Powers Economic Change and Military Conflict from 1500 to 2000* (New York: Random House, 1987), pp. 232–41.
118. See Richard Ned Lebow, *Between Peace and War: The Nature of International Crisis* (Baltimore, MD: Johns Hopkins University Press, 1987), pp. 245–9, and Bruce W. Menning, *Bayonets Before Bullets: The Imperial Russian Army, 1861–1914* (Bloomington, IN: Indiana University Press, 1992), ch. 5.
119. For the diplomatic aspects of the war, see A.J.P. Taylor, *The Struggle for Mastery in Europe, 1848–1918* (Oxford: Oxford University Press, 1971), pp. 417–20, 422–7, 432–3. For the Japanese strategic surprise, see Patrick M. Morgan, 'Examples of Strategic Surprise in the Far East', in Klaus Knorr and Patrick M. Morgan (eds), *Strategic Military Surprise: Incentives and Opportunities* (New Brunswick, NJ: Transaction Books, 1983), pp. 43–76. For further references, see Paul Dukes, *A History of Russia: Medieval, Modern, Contemporary* (2nd edn) (Houndmills: Macmillan, 1990), p. 188, and Mearsheimer, *The Tragedy of Great Power Politics*, p. 466.
120. For the German intelligence estimates of the Red Army and German intelligence on the Soviet Union in general, see Heinz Guderian, *Panzer Leader* (New York: Da Capo, 1996), p. 143; B.H. Liddell Hart, *The Other Side of the Hill* (London: Papermac, 1993), pp. 257–62; William L. Shirer, *The Rise and Fall of the Third Reich* (London: Mandarin, 1991), pp. 797–9, 822; Kenneth Strong, *Men of Intelligence* (London: Ginger-Cassell, 1970), pp. 88–95; Michael I. Handel, *War, Strategy and Intelligence* (London: Frank Cass, 1989), p. 326.
121. See Adolf Hitler, *Mein Kampf*, quoted in Fuller, *The Conduct of War*, pp. 231–2; Albert Speer, *Inside the Third Reich* (London: Phoenix, 1995), p. 250; Alan Clark, *Barbarossa* (London: Phoenix, 1996), p. 43; John Erickson, *The Road to Stalingrad* (London: Weidenfeld, 1993), p. 232; John G. Stoessinger, *Why Nations Go to War* (2nd edn) (New York: St. Martin's Press, 1978), ch. 2; Alan Bullock, *Hitler and Stalin: Parallel Lives* (London: Fontana, 1993), pp. 748–51. It is indicative of Hitler's irrationality that prior to the launch of Operation Barbarossa he had also expressed the opposite view, namely that the inhabitants of European Russia and Siberia were in the long run biologically superior to the Germans; see Speer, *Inside the Third Reich*, pp. 150, 265.

122. Erickson, *The Road to Stalingrad*, pp. 46–7.
123. See Günther Blumentritt, 'Moscow', in William Richardson and Seymour Freidin (eds), *The Fatal Decisions* (London: Michael Joseph, 1956), pp. 37–9. The soldierlike narrative of General Blumentritt makes a strong impression.
124. See Strong, *Men of Intelligence*, p. 94.
125. For a similar argument, see Albert Seaton, *The Russo-German War 1941–45* (London: Arthur Barker, 1971), p. 49.
126. Reproduced in John Cooley, *Unholy Wars: Afghanistan, America and International Terrorism* (3rd edn) (London & Sterling, VA: Pluto Press, 2002), pp. 245–9.
127. Robert S. Litwak, 'The Soviet Union in Afghanistan', in Ariel E. Levite, Bruce W. Jentleson and Larry Berman (eds), *Foreign Military Intervention: The Dynamics of Protracted Conflict* (New York: Columbia University Press, 1992), pp. 65–94.
128. See Shai Feldman, 'Israel's Involvement in Lebanon: 1975–1985', in Levite, Jentleson and Berman (eds), Foreign Military Intervention, pp. 129–61.
129. As was pointed out in Chapter One, instability and conflict might be perpetuated in Iraq as well. However, we contend that this does not have much to do with American underestimation of enemy capability and the Iraqi will to resist the invasion, though the Iraqi armed forces did offer tougher resistance than anticipated. Conflict in Iraq would have erupted even if Saddam Hussein had surrendered without a fight. One might plausibly argue that the Americans misjudged the impact of regime change in Iraq, but this is something different from underestimating an enemy.
130. Bonnie Berkowitz and Artur Galocha, 'Why the Russian military is bogged down by logistics in Ukraine', The Washington Post, 30 March 2022, https://www.washingtonpost.com/world/2022/03/30/russia-military-logistics-supply-chain/; Edward Luttwak, 'Why Putin's invasion failed', UnHerd, 11 April 2022, https://unherd.com/2022/04/why-putins-invasion-failed/?=refinnar; Max Seddon, Christopher Miller and Felicia Schwartz, 'How Putin blundered into Ukraine—then doubled down', Financial Times, 23 February 2023, https://www.ft.com/content/80002564-33e8-48fb-b734-44810afb7a49.
131. See Mick Ryan, The War for Ukraine: Strategy and Adaptation Under Fire (Annapolis, MD: Naval Institute Press, 2024).
132. Cf. Charles A. Kupchan, 'Getting In: The Initial Stage of Military Intervention', in Levite, Jentleson and Berman (eds), Foreign Military Intervention, pp. 256–9; see also Van Evera, Causes of War, pp. 25–8.

EPILOGUE

1. Joseph S. Nye, *Understanding International Conflicts: An Introduction to Theory and History* (New York: HarperCollins, 1993), p. 1.

2. Consider the insertion of Thucydides' *History* in the syllabus of the U.S. Naval War College by Admiral Stansfield Turner in August 1972. 'For many students, that was an unknown book about an apparently irrelevant war by an author with an unpronounceable name. Yet to Turner it was the essence of his approach, "the best example of how you could use historical case studies to teach contemporary or strategic problems"'; Harry Summers, *On Strategy II: A Critical Analysis of the Gulf War* (New York: Dell, 1992), pp. 78–9. Professor Karl Walling has brought to our attention that this tradition is still alive at the U.S. Naval War College.

POSTSCRIPT: THE FUTURE OF THE SINO–AMERICAN GEOPOLITICAL ANTAGONISM: A COMMENT ON THE THUCYDIDES' TRAP

1. This draws from Athanassios Platias and Vasilis Trigkas, 'Unravelling the Thucydides' Trap: Inadvertent Escalation or War of Choice?' *The Chinese Journal of International Politics*, 14, 2 (Summer 2021), pp. 219–55.
2. For the influence of Thucydides on the modern international relations academia, the literature is vast; but for a good synopsis, see Edward Keene, 'The Reception of Thucydides in the History of International Relations', in Christine Lee and Neville Morley (eds), *A Handbook to the Reception of Thucydides* (Malden, MA: Wiley Blackwell, 2015); Robert Gilpin, 'The Theory of Hegemonic War', *The Journal of Interdisciplinary History*, 18, 4 (Spring 1988), pp. 591–613; Lowell S. Gustafson, *Thucydides' Theory of International Relations* (Baton Rouge, LA: Louisiana University Press, 2000).
3. Laurie M. Johnson, *Thucydides, Hobbes, and the Interpretation of Realism* (Ithaca, NY & London: Northern Illinois University Press, 1993); Garry Wills, *Lincoln at Gettysburg: The Words That Remade America* (New York: Simon & Schuster, 2012); Gregory Crane, *Thucydides and the Ancient Simplicity: The Limits of Political Realism* (Berkeley, CA: University of California Press, 1998). As Crane put it, 'even George Marshall explicitly pointed out the resemblance between the emerging Cold War and the tensions between Athens and Sparta'. Thucydides' thought has not only influenced American conservative thinkers from Strauss to Kagan, but also cosmopolitan communists, even Lenin himself, see: Louis Althusser, *Lenin and Philosophy and Other Essays* (New York: Monthly Review Press, 2001); Leo Strauss, *The City and Man* (Chicago: Chicago University Press, 1964).
4. For an analysis of this point, see Andrew R. Novo and Jay M. Parker, *Restoring Thucydides: Testing Familiar Lessons and Deriving New Ones* (Amherst, NY: Cambria Press, 2020), pp. 12–15, 172, and Keene, 'The Reception of Thucydides in the History of International Relations', pp. 17–19.
5. Stansfield Turner, *Address to the Chicago Council* (Navy League of the United States, 1973), p. 3; John Lewis Gaddis, *The Long Peace: Inquiries into the History of the Cold War* (Oxford: Oxford University Press, 1989), p. 221.

NOTES   pp. [141–143]

6. As U.S. diplomat Alan Misenheimer has put it, 'Scholars have discerned Thucydidean paradigms in dozens of large and small wars throughout history including the Vietnam War, Cold War, Two World Wars, American Civil War, and even a mid-19th century conflict between rival kingdoms in Fiji'; Alan G. Misenheimer, 'Thucydides, Benghazi and Honor', *Joint Force Quarterly*, 70. 3 (2013), p. 67. See also Donald Kagan, *The Peloponnesian War* (New York: Viking Press, 2003), p. XXV–XXVII, and J.E. Lendon, *Song of Wrath: The Peloponnesian War Begins* (New York: Basic Books, 2010), p. 25.
7. Graham Allison, *Destined for War: Can America and China Escape Thucydides's Trap?* (Boston, MA—New York: Mariner Books, Houghton Mifflin Harcourt, 2018), p. xvi.
8. For a critique along these grounds, see Jonathan Kirshner, 'Handle Him with Care: The Importance of Getting Thucydides Right', *Security Studies*, 28, 1 (January–March 2019), pp. 1–24; Jonathan Kirshner, 'Offensive Realism, Thucydides Traps, and the Tragedy of Unforced Errors: Classical Realism and US–China Relations', *China International Strategy Review*, 1 (2019), pp. 51–63; Novo and Parker, *Restoring Thucydides*.
9. Allison, *Destined for War*, pp. 160–84.
10. Graham Allison, *Essence of Decision: Explaining the Cuban Missile Crisis* (Boston, MA: Little, Brown and Company, 1971).
11. The Greek prose in Thucydides is much more complex than even the Homeric language, which preceded Thucydides by about four centuries and poses great challenges for translators. For a discussion on the complexity of Thucydidean language, see G.E.M. de Ste. Croix, *The Origins of the Peloponnesian War* (London: Duckworth Company Limited, 1972), pp. 54–5.
12. Novo and Parker, *Restoring Thucydides*, p. 174.
13. Allison may be right to stress the danger of inadvertent escalation during a Sino–American crisis. Yet, the point here is not that inadvertent escalation is not a serious complication that China and the United States should strive to manage during a crisis, but rather that inadvertent escalation was not a cause of the Peloponnesian War. Hence the causal mechanism present in Allison's theorization over the Thucydides' trap is not present in Thucydides' work.
14. The genealogy of the belief that the Peloponnesian War was an outcome of miscalculations and inadvertent escalation goes back to Donald Kagan's interpretation, which has become the orthodoxy in U.S. academia. Allison seems to be drawing heavily from Kagan at this point; see Donald Kagan, *The Outbreak of the Peloponnesian War* (Ithaca, NY: Cornell University Press, 1969), p. 354.
15. Allison, *Destined for War*, p. vii (Allison's emphasis).
16. Richard Schlatter, *Hobbes's Thucydides* (New Brunswick, NJ: Rutgers University Press, 1975).
17. This realization is not new; it has long been stressed by historians and international relations theorists alike. See Martin Ostwald, *Ananke in Thucydides*

(Atlanta, GA: Scholars Press, 1988); Hunter R. Rawlings, *A Semantic Study of Prophasis to 400 BC* (Wiesbaden: Hermes Einzelschriften, 1975); Ste. Croix, *The Origins of the Peloponnesian War*; Geoffrey Blainey, *The Causes of War* (New York: Macmillan, 1988); S.N. Jaffe, *Thucydides on the Outbreak of War: Character and Contest* (Oxford: Oxford University Press, 2017), p. 5. Interestingly, in Chapter 2 of his work cited here, Ste. Croix has presented all the extracts in Thucydides' work where the term *ananke* is found and proved that its meaning as 'inevitability' always relates to context. In some cases, Thucydides uses the term to highlight inevitability, whereas in others to highlight choice. In Thucydides, I 23, the context makes it evident that it is about choice. Moreover, as Connor has noted, *ananke* 'does not convey a philosophically deterministic meaning'; Walter R. Connor, *Thucydides* (Princeton, NJ: Princeton University Press, 1984), pp. 31–2. For a comprehensive review of the non-deterministic argument, see: Eric Robinson, 'Thucydides on the Causes and Outbreak of the Peloponnesian War', in Sara Forsdyke, Edith Foster and Ryan Balot (eds), *The Oxford Handbook of Thucydides* (Oxford: Oxford University Press, 2017), p. 115.

18. See Barbara W. Tuchman, *The Guns of August* (New York: MacMillan, 1962).
19. See Keir A. Lieber, 'The New History of World War I and What It Means for International Relations Theory', *International Security*, 32, 2 (Fall 2007), pp. 155–91.
20. Platias and Trigkas, 'Unravelling the Thucydides' Trap: Inadvertent Escalation or War of Choice?'
21. Mary P. Nichols, *Thucydides and the Pursuit of Freedom* (Ithaca, NY: Cornell University Press, 2015), p. 31.
22. Allison, *Destined for War*, p. 37.
23. Thucydides, II 65 [Hobbes trans.]. Actually, in the crucial question of the Athenian economic embargo against Megara that the Spartans wanted revoked, Pericles went against popular opinion and fought ferocious rhetorical battles in the Athenian *Ecclesia* to persuade the people not to cave in. He was even ridiculed for this behaviour by the comic poet Aristophanes.
24. Thucydides, II 65. See also Thucydides, I 139.
25. Thucydides, I 144.
26. See Hans Delbrück, *History of the Art of War*, vol. 1 (Lincoln, NE: University of Nebraska Press, 1975), p. 137.
27. For a comment on the historical differences and similarities between the interstate system of fifth-century BCE Greece and the current system, see: Paul A. Rahe, 'Sparta Ascendant, Athens Rising', in David L. Berkey (ed.), *Disruptive Strategies: The Military Campaigns of Ascendant Powers and Their Rivals* (Stanford, CA: Hoover Institution Press, 2021), pp. 34–5.
28. To be sure, in his book's appendix, Allison addresses what he frames as straw men arguments against his thesis, one of which is related to 'tipping points,

NOTES

tripwires or turning points'. He argues that it is irrelevant if a rising power has surpassed a ruling power, and states that war can break out at any point during the transition or after the transition has been completed. Yet an accurate analysis of the Peloponnesian War—if it is to be didactic—has to examine when the war occurred and why.

29. The modern literature on preventive war is vast. Some key works include Dale C. Copeland, *The Origins of Major War* (Ithaca, NY: Cornell University Press, 2000); Stephen Van Evera, *Causes of War: Power and the Roots of Conflict* (Ithaca, NY: Cornell University Press, 2001), pp. 129–31; and Dong Sun Lee, *Power Shifts, Strategy and War: Declining States and International Conflict* (New York: Routledge, 2007). A comprehensive synopsis is Jack S. Levy, 'Declining Power and the Preventive Motivation for War', *World Politics*, 40, 1 (October 1987), pp. 82–107. On U.S. preventive strategy against China, see John J. Mearsheimer, 'Gathering Storm: China's Challenge to US power in Asia', *The Chinese Journal of International Politics*, 3, 4 (Winter 2010), pp. 381–96.

30. For an interesting analysis on timing and prevention as applied to Sino–American relations, see David M. Edelstein, 'Time and the Rise of China', *Chinese Journal of International Politics*, 13, 3 (Autumn 2020), pp. 387–417.

31. As J.E. Lendon put it, 'It was an equal treaty'. Lendon, *Song of Wrath*, p. 98.

32. Lisa Kallet-Marx, *Money, Expense, and Naval Power in Thucydides' History 1–5.24* (Berkeley, CA: University of California Press, 1993), pp. 37–108.

33. Hal Brands and Michael Beckley, *Danger Zone: The Coming Conflict with China* (New York: W.W. Norton & Company, 2022), pp. 25–52.

34. The focus of Thucydides on political debates and the way many of those debates were stretched over days of discussions, with the winning proposition of one day being overturned the next day, is yet another argument against inevitability. For a comprehensive analysis on that point, see M. Cogan, *The Human Thing: The Speeches and Principles of Thucydides' History* (Chicago: University of Chicago Press, 1990).

35. Daniel Garst, 'Thucydides and Neorealism', *International Studies Quarterly*, 33, 1 (March 1989), p. 6; Mary P. Nichols, 'Leaders and Leadership in Thucydides' History', in Forsdyke, Foster and Balot (eds), *The Oxford Handbook of Thucydides*, pp. 459–74.

36. For a theoretical undertaking on the consequentiality of leadership in international affairs and its impact on power differentials that draws from the Chinese classics, see Xuetong Yan, *Leadership and the Rise of Great Powers* (Princeton, NJ: Princeton University Press, 2019). See also Robert Jervis, 'Do Leaders Matter and How We Would Know?' *Security Studies*, 22, 2 (April–June 2013), pp. 153–79.

37. By 480 BCE, Persia was the largest empire on earth. During that period, China was divided and transitioning from the Spring and Autumn to the Warring States era. On the strategic magnificence of Themistocles, see Robert

J. Lenardon, *The Saga of Themistocles* (London: Thames and Hudson, 1978), and Athanasios Platias and Vasilis Trigkas, 'Themistocles: Leadership and Grand Strategy', in Emmanuil Economou, Nicholas Kyriazis and Athanasios Platias (eds), *Democracy and Salamis: 2500 Years After the Battle that Saved Greece and the Western World* (Cham: Springer, 2022), pp. 99–129.

38. Thucydides, I 93. See also Robert Garland, *The Piraeus* (London: Bristol Classical Press, 2001), pp. 14–22.
39. John R. Hale, *Lords of the Sea: The Epic Story of Athenian Navy and the Birth of Democracy* (New York: Penguin, 2009); Andrew Lambert, *Seapower States: Maritime Culture, Continental Empires and the Conflict That Made the Modern World* (New Haven, CT: Yale University Press, 2018).
40. See also Lisa Kallet, *Money and Corrosion of Power in Thucydides: The Sicilian Expedition and Its Aftermath* (Los Angeles: University of California Press, 2001), pp. 147–51.
41. Thucydides, I 80–6.
42. Athanasios Platias and Vasilis Trigkas, 'Classical Realism and the Rise of Sino-American Antagonism: A Review Essay', *Political Science Quarterly*, 139, 1 (Spring 2024), pp. 79–93. See also, Athanasios Platias and Vasilis Trigkas, 'Strategic Universality in the Axial Age: The Doctrine of Prudence in Political Leadership', *Strategic Analysis*, 46, 2 (June 2022), pp. 157–70.
43. John Lewis Gaddis, *Strategies of Containment* (Oxford: Oxford University Press, 2005), p. 389; Stephen G. Brooks and William C. Wohlforth, *World Out of Balance* (Princeton, NJ: Princeton University Press, 2008).
44. Note that even Kenneth Waltz, the father of structural realism, ultimately acknowledges this by referring to Bismarck's strategy and its success in preventing the formation of a balancing coalition against Germany; Kenneth Waltz, 'A Response to My Critics', in Robert Keohane (ed.), *Neorealism and Its Critics* (New York: Columbia University Press, 1986), p. 343. See also Daniel L. Byman and Kenneth M. Pollack, 'Let Us Now Praise Great Men: Bringing the Statesman Back In', *International Security*, 25, 4 (Spring 2001), pp. 107–46. For an interesting exposition on statesmanship, see Mark A. Menaldo, *Leadership and Transformative Ambition in International Relations* (Northampton, MA: Edward Elgar Publishing, 2013). See also Yan, *Leadership and the Rise of Great Powers*.
45. Thucydides, IV 59.
46. The classic work on the subject is Robert Jervis, *The Meaning of the Nuclear Revolution: Statecraft and the Prospect of Armageddon* (Ithaca, NY: Cornell University Press, 1989). See also, Hans J. Morgenthau, 'The Four Paradoxes of Nuclear Strategy', *American Political Science Review*, 58, 1 (March 1964), pp. 23–35; Robert Jervis, *The Illogic of American Nuclear Strategy* (Ithaca, NY: Cornell University Press, 1984); Kenneth N. Waltz, 'Nuclear Myths and Political Realities', *American Political Science Review*, 84, 3 (September 1990), pp. 731–45.

47. On the relationship between first-strike advantages, pre-emption and accidents, see Thomas C. Schelling and Morton H. Halperin, *Strategy and Arms Control* (New York: The Twentieth Century Fund, 1961), pp. 14–16. On the impact of modern technology on the Sino–American nuclear balance, see Fiona S. Cunningham and M. Taylor Fravel, 'Dangerous Confidence? Chinese Views on Nuclear Escalation', *International Security*, 44, 2 (Fall 2019), pp. 61–109; Keir A. Lieber and Daryl G. Press, 'The New Era of Counterforce: Technological Change and the Future of Nuclear Deterrence', *International Security*, 41, 4 (Spring 2017), pp. 9–49; Michael C. Horowitz, 'When Speed Kills: Lethal autonomous weapon systems, deterrence and stability', *Journal of Strategic Studies*, 42, 6 (August 2019), pp. 764–88; Andrew Futter, *Hacking the Bomb: Cyberthreats and Nuclear Weapons* (Washington, DC: Georgetown University Press, 2018); Ryan Fedasiuk, 'Chinese Perspectives on AI and Future Military Capabilities', *Center for Security and Emerging Technology* (Washington, DC: Georgetown University, 2020).
48. Thucydides, I 42, II 25, IV 3–15.
49. Thucydides, IV 55.
50. See Timothy R. Heath, Weilong Kong and Alexis Dale-Huang, *U.S.-China Rivalry in a Neomedieval World: Security in an Age of Weakening States* (Santa Monica, CA: RAND Corporation, 2023), p. 167.
51. Hal Brands, 'The Lost Art of Long-Term Competition', *The Washington Quarterly*, 41, 4 (Winter 2019), pp. 31–51.
52. As Jonathan Kirshner rightfully argues, this Thucydidean categorical emphasis on prudent leadership has been the diachronic constant of the classical realist heritage; see Kirshner, 'Offensive Realism, Thucydides Traps, and the Tragedy of Unforced Errors'.
53. Jonathan Kirshner, *An Unwritten Future: Realism and Uncertainty in World Politics* (Princeton, NJ & Oxford: Princeton University Press, 2022).
54. Thucydides, I 22. See also Lisa Kallet, 'Thucydides' Workshop of History and Utility Outside the Text', in Antonios Rengakos and Antonis Tsakmakis (eds), *Brill's Companion to Thucydides* (Leiden: Brill, 2006), pp. 337–68.

SELECT BIBLIOGRAPHY

Allison, Graham, *Destined for War: Can America and China Escape Thucydides's Trap?* (Boston, MA—New York: Mariner Books, Houghton Mifflin Harcourt, 2018).
Art, Robert J., 'To What Ends Military Power', *International Security*, 4, 4 (Spring 1980), pp. 4–35.
Baldwin, David A., *Economic Statecraft* (Princeton, NJ: Princeton University Press, 1985).
Barnett, Correlli, *The Collapse of British Power* (Phoenix Mill: Allan Sutton, 1984).
Beaufre, André, *Introduction to Strategy* (London: Faber and Faber, 1965).
Bond, Brian, *Liddell Hart: A Study of his Military Thought* (London: Cassell, 1977).
Booth, Ken, *Strategy and Ethnocentricism* (London: Croom Helm, 1979).
Bracken, Paul, 'Strategic Planning for National Security: Lessons from Business Experience', *RAND Note*, N-3005-DAG/USDP (February 1990).
Brodie, Bernard, *War and Politics* (London: Cassell, 1973).
Brunt, P.A., 'Spartan Policy and Strategy in the Archidamian War', in P.A. Brunt, *Studies in Greek History and Thought* (Oxford: Clarendon, 1993), pp. 84–111.
Cartledge, Paul, *Sparta and Lakonia: A Regional History, 1300–362 B.C.* (London: Routledge & Kegan Paul, 1979).
Chandler, David G., *The Military Maxims of Napoleon* (New York: Macmillan, 1997).
Chrimes, K.M.T., *Ancient Sparta: A Re-examination of the Evidence* (Manchester: Manchester University Press, 1949).
Cimbala, Stephen, *Military Persuasion: Deterrence and Provocation in Crisis and War* (University Park, PA: Pennsylvania State University Press, 1994).
Clausewitz, Carl von, *On War* (ed./trans. Michael Howard and Peter Paret) (Princeton, NJ: Princeton University Press, 1989).
Cohen, Raymond, 'Threat Perception in International Crisis', *Political Science Quarterly*, 93, 1 (1978), pp. 93–107.
Connor, W. Robert, *Thucydides* (Princeton, NJ: Princeton University Press, 1984).
Craig, Gordon A., 'Delbrück: The Military Historian', in Peter Paret (ed.), *Makers*

SELECT BIBLIOGRAPHY

of Modern Strategy from Machiavelli to the Nuclear Age (Princeton, NJ: Princeton University Press, 1986), pp. 326–53.

Crane, Gregory, *Thucydides and the Ancient Simplicity: The Limits of Political Realism* (Berkeley, CA: University of California Press, 1998).

Dawson, Doyne, *The Origins of Western Warfare: Militarism and Morality in the Ancient World* (Boulder, CO: Westview, 1996).

Delbrück, Hans, *History of the Art of War* (4 vols) (Lincoln, NE: University of Nebraska Press, 1975–85).

Doyle, Michael W., *Empires* (Ithaca, NY: Cornell University Press, 1986).

Fliess, Peter J., *Thucydides and the Politics of Bipolarity* (Baton Rouge, LA: Louisiana State University Press, 1966).

Forde, Steven, *The Ambition to Rule: Alcibiades and the Politics of Imperialism in Thucydides* (Ithaca, NY: Cornell University Press, 1989).

Forrest, W.G., *A History of Sparta, 950–192 B.C.* (New York: Norton, 1968).

Forsdyke, Sara, Edith Foster and Ryan Balot (eds), *The Oxford Handbook of Thucydides* (Oxford: Oxford University Press, 2017).

Freedman, Lawrence, *Deterrence* (Cambridge: Polity Press, 2004).

Fuller, J.F.C., *The Decisive Battles of the Western World* (London: Eyre & Spottiswoode, 1954).

Garst, W. Daniel, 'Thucydides and the Domestic Sources of International Politics', in Lowell S. Gustafson (ed.), *Thucydides' Theory of International Relations: A Lasting Possession* (Baton Rouge, LA: Louisiana University Press, 2000), pp. 67–97.

George, Alexander L., *Forceful Persuasion: Coercive Diplomacy as Alternative to War* (Washington, DC: United States Institute of Peace, 1991).

———, *Some Thoughts on Graduated Escalation*, RM-4844-IR (Santa Monica, CA: RAND Corporation, 1965).

George, Alexander L., David K. Hall and William E. Simons, *The Limits of Coercive Diplomacy* (Boston, MA: Little, Brown, 1971).

Gilpin, Robert G., 'The Richness of the Tradition of Political Realism', in Robert O. Keohane (ed.), *Neorealism and its Critics* (New York: Columbia University Press, 1986), pp. 308–13.

———, 'The Theory of Hegemonic War', in R.I. Rotberg and T.K. Rabb (eds), *The Origin and Prevention of Major Wars* (Cambridge: Cambridge University Press, 1988), pp. 15–37.

———, *War and Change in World Politics* (Cambridge: Cambridge University Press, 1981).

Gomme, A.W., *A Historical Commentary on Thucydides* (5 vols) (Oxford: Clarendon, 1998) (reprint).

Gray, Colin S., *The Leverage of Sea Power: The Strategic Advantage of Navies in War* (New York: Free Press, 1992).

———, *Modern Strategy* (Oxford: Oxford University Press, 1999).

———, *Nuclear Strategy and National Style* (London: Hamilton Press, 1986).

SELECT BIBLIOGRAPHY

———, *War, Peace, and Victory: Strategy and Statecraft for the Next Century* (New York: Simon and Schuster, 1990).

Grieco, Joseph M., 'Anarchy and the Limits of Cooperation', in David Baldwin (ed.), *Neorealism and Neoliberalism: The Contemporary Debate* (New York: Columbia University Press, 1993), pp. 116–40.

———, *Cooperation Among Nations* (Ithaca, NY: Cornell University Press, 1990), pp. 40–9.

Handel, Michael I., *Masters of War: Classical Strategic Thought* (London: Frank Cass, 1992).

Hanson, Victor Davis, *A War Like No Other: How the Athenians and the Spartans Fought the Peloponnesian War* (New York: Random House, 2005).

———, *Warfare and Agriculture in Classical Greece* (rev. edn) (Berkeley, CA: University of California Press, 1998).

———, *The Western Way of War* (New York: Alfred A. Knopf, 1989).

Hornblower, Simon, *A Commentary on Thucydides* (2 vols) (Oxford: Clarendon, 1990–6).

Howard, Michael, *The Causes of War* (London: Temple Smith, 1983).

———, *Clausewitz* (Oxford: Oxford University Press, 1983).

———, *The Lessons of History* (New Haven, CT: Yale University Press, 1991).

Jaffe, S.N., *Thucydides on the Outbreak of War: Character and Contest* (Oxford: Oxford University Press, 2017).

Jervis, Robert, 'Cooperation Under the Security Dilemma', *World Politics*, 30, 2 (January 1978), pp. 167–214.

———, 'Hypotheses on Misperception', *World Politics*, 20, 2 (1968), pp. 454–79.

———, *Perception and Misperception in International Politics* (Princeton, NJ: Princeton University Press, 1976).

Jomini, Henry de, *Summary of the Art of War* (ed. Brig. Gen. J.D. Hittle, abridged edn) reproduced in *Roots of Strategy, Book 2* (Harrisburg, PA: Stackpole Books, 1987).

Jones, A.H.M., *Sparta* (Oxford: Blackwell & Mott, 1967).

Kagan, Donald, *The Archidamian War* (Ithaca, NY: Cornell University Press, 1974/1990).

———, 'Athenian strategy in the Peloponnesian War', in Williamson Murray, MacGregor Knox and Alvin Bernstein (eds), *The Making of Strategy: Rulers, States, and War* (Cambridge: Cambridge University Press, 1994), pp. 24–55.

———, *The Fall of the Athenian Empire* (Ithaca, NY: Cornell University Press, 1987).

———, *On the Origins of War and the Preservation of Peace* (New York: Doubleday, 1995).

———, *The Outbreak of the Peloponnesian War* (Ithaca, NY: Cornell University Press, 1969/1994).

SELECT BIBLIOGRAPHY

———, *The Peace of Nicias and the Sicilian Expedition* (Ithaca, NY: Cornell University Press, 1981/1992).

Kallet-Marx, Lisa, *Money, Expense and Naval Power in Thucydides' History 1–5.24* (Berkeley, CA: University of California Press, 1993).

Kautilya, *Arthasastra* (trans. R. Shamasastry, 2nd edn) (Mysore: Wesleyan Mission Press, 1923).

Kennedy, Paul, 'The First World War and the International Power System', *International Security*, 9, 1 (1984), pp. 7–40.

———, 'Grand Strategies in War and Peace: Toward a Broader Definition', in Paul Kennedy (ed.), *Grand Strategies in War and Peace* (New Haven, CT: Yale University Press, 1991), pp. 1–7.

———, *The Rise and Fall of the Great Powers: Economic Change and Military Conflict from 1500 to 2000* (New York: Random House, 1987).

Kirshner, Jonathan, 'Handle Him with Care: The Importance of Getting Thucydides Right', *Security Studies*, 28, 1 (January–March 2019), pp. 1–24.

———, 'Offensive Realism, Thucydides Traps, and the Tragedy of Unforced Errors: Classical Realism and US–China Relations', *China International Strategy Review*, 1 (2019), pp. 51–63.

———, *An Unwritten Future: Realism and Uncertainty in World Politics* (Princeton, NJ & Oxford: Princeton University Press, 2022).

Klein, Yitzhak, 'A Theory of Strategic Culture', *Comparative Strategy*, 10, 1 (January–March 1991), pp. 3–23.

Knorr, Klaus, 'Threat Perception', in Klaus Knorr (ed.), *Historical Dimensions of National Security Problems* (Lawrence, KA: Kansas University Press, 1976), pp. 78–119.

Lebow, Richard Ned, *Between Peace and War: The Nature of International Crisis* (Baltimore, MD: Johns Hopkins University Press, 1987).

Lebow, Richard Ned and Barry S. Strauss (eds), *Hegemonic Rivalry from Thucydides to the Nuclear Age* (Boulder, CO: Westview, 1991).

———, 'Thucydides, Power Transition Theory and the Causes of War', in Richard Ned Lebow and Barry S. Strauss (eds), *Hegemonic Rivalry from Thucydides to the Nuclear Age* (Boulder, CO: Westview, 1991), pp. 125–65.

Lee, Christine and Neville Morley (eds), *A Handbook to the Reception of Thucydides* (Malden MA: Wiley Blackwell, 2015).

Lendon, J.E., *Song of Wrath: The Peloponnesian War Begins* (New York: Basic Books, 2010).

Levite, Ariel, *Intelligence and Strategic Surprises* (New York: Columbia University Press, 1987).

———, *Offense and Defense in Israeli Military Doctrine* (Boulder, CO: Westview, 1989).

Levite, Ariel and Athanassios Platias, 'Evaluating Small States' Dependence on Arms Imports: An Alternative Perspective', *Peace Studies Program Occasional Paper No. 10* (Ithaca, NY: Cornell University, 1983).

SELECT BIBLIOGRAPHY

Levite, Ariel E., Bruce W. Jentleson and Larry Berman (eds), *Foreign Military Intervention: The Dynamics of Protracted Conflict* (New York: Columbia University Press, 1992).

Lewis, David M., *Sparta and Persia* (Leiden: E.J. Brill, 1977).

Liddell, Hart B. H., *The British Way in Warfare* (London: Faber, 1932).

———, *Strategy* (2nd rev. edn) (London: Meridian, 1991).

Luttwak, Edward N., *The Grand Strategy of the Roman Empire from the First Century A.D. to the Third* (Baltimore, MD: Johns Hopkins University Press, 1976).

———, *Strategy: The Logic of War and Peace* (Cambridge, MA: The Belknap Press of Harvard University Press, 1987).

———, 'Toward Post-Heroic Warfare', *Foreign Affairs*, 74, 3 (May/June 1995), pp. 109–22.

Mahan, Alfred Thayer, *The Influence of Sea Power Upon History, 1660–1783* (London: Sampson Low, Marston, 1892).

———, *The Influence of Sea Power Upon the French Revolution and Empire, 1793–1812* (2 vols) (London: Sampson Low, Marston, 1893).

Mearsheimer, John J., *Conventional Deterrence* (Ithaca, NY: Cornell University Press, 1983).

———, *The Fate of Nations* (Cambridge: Cambridge University Press, 1988).

———, *Liddell Hart and the Weight of History* (Ithaca, NY: Cornell University Press, 1988).

———, *The Tragedy of Great Power Politics* (New York: W.W. Norton, 2001).

Meiggs, Russell, *The Athenian Empire* (Oxford: Clarendon Press, 1972).

Michell, Humphrey, *Sparta* (Cambridge: Cambridge University Press, 1952).

Nichols, Mary P., *Thucydides and the Pursuit of Freedom* (Ithaca, NY: Cornell University Press, 2015).

Novo, Andrew R. and Jay M. Parker, *Restoring Thucydides: Testing Familiar Lessons and Deriving New Ones* (Amherst, NY: Cambria Press, 2020).

Nye, Joseph S., *Soft Power—The Means to Success in World Politics* (New York: PublicAffairs, 2004).

Olmstead, A.T., *History of the Persian Empire* (Chicago, IL: The University of Chicago Press, 1948).

Organski, A.F.K. and Jacek Kugler, *The War Ledger* (Chicago, IL: The University of Chicago Press, 1980).

Paret, Peter (ed.), *Makers of Modern Strategy from Machiavelli to the Nuclear Age* (Princeton, NJ: Princeton University Press, 1986).

Platias, Athanassios, 'Thucydides on Grand Strategy: Periclean Grand Strategy During the Peloponnesian War', *Thucydides: The Classical Theorist of International Relations, Etudes Helleniques/Hellenic Studies*, 6, 2 (Autumn 1998), pp. 53–103.

Platias, Athanassios and Constantinos Koliopoulos, 'Grand Strategies Clashing: Athenian and Spartan Strategies in Thucydides' "History of the Peloponnesian War"', *Comparative Strategy*, 21, 5 (October–December 2002), pp. 377–99.

SELECT BIBLIOGRAPHY

———, 'Thucydides on Grand Strategy II: Spartan Grand Strategy During the Peloponnesian War', *Etudes Helleniques/Hellenic Studies*, 8, 1 (Spring 2000), pp. 23–70.

Posen, Barry, *The Sources of Military Doctrine* (Ithaca, NY: Cornell University Press, 1984).

Powell, Anton, *Athens and Sparta: Constructing Greek Political and Social History from 478 B.C.* (London: Routledge, 1988).

Quester, George, *Offense and Defense in the International System* (New York: Wiley, 1977).

Rahe, Paul A., *The Grand Strategy of Classical Sparta: The Persian Challenge* (New Haven CT, & London: Yale University Press, 2015).

———, *Sparta's First Attic War: The Grand Strategy of Classical Sparta, 478–446 B.C.* (New Haven, CT & London: Yale University Press, 2019).

———, *Sparta's Second Attic War: The Grand Strategy of Classical Sparta, 446–418 B.C.* (New Haven, CT & London: Yale University Press, 2020).

———, *Sparta's Sicilian Proxy War: The Grand Strategy of Classical Sparta, 418–413 B.C.* (New York & London: Encounter Books, 2023).

———, *Sparta's Third Attic War: The Grand Strategy of Classical Sparta, 413–404 B.C.* (New York & London: Encounter Books, 2024).

———, *The Spartan Regime: Its Character, Origins, and Grand Strategy* (New Haven, CT & London: Yale University Press, 2016).

Romilly, Jacqueline de, *Alcibiades* (Greek trans., 2nd edn) (Athens: Asty, 1995).

Schelling, Thomas C., *Arms and Influence* (New Haven, CT: Yale University Press, 1966).

———, *The Strategy of Conflict* (Cambridge, MA: Harvard University Press, 1960).

Schwarz, Benjamin, 'Strategic Interdependence: Learning to Behave like a Great Power', in Norman Levin (ed.), *Prisms and Policy: U.S. Security Strategy After the Cold War* (Santa Monica, CA: RAND, 1994), pp. 79–98.

Snyder, Glenn H., *Deterrence and Defense* (Princeton, NJ: Princeton University Press, 1961).

Starr, Chester G., *The Influence of Sea Power on Ancient History* (New York: Oxford University Press, 1995).

Ste. Croix, G.E.M. de, *The Origins of the Peloponnesian War* (London: Duckworth, 1972).

Strassler, Robert B. (ed.), *The Landmark Thucydides: A Comprehensive Guide to the Peloponnesian War* (New York: Free Press, 1996).

Strauss, Barry S. and Josiah Ober, *The Anatomy of Error: Ancient Military Disasters and Their Lessons for Modern Strategists* (New York: St. Martin's Press, 1990).

Summers, Harry, *On Strategy II: A Critical Analysis of the Gulf War* (New York: Dell, 1992).

Sun Tzu, *The Art of War* (trans. Samuel B. Griffith) (Oxford: Oxford University Press, 1963).

SELECT BIBLIOGRAPHY

Van Evera, Stephen, *Causes of War: Power and the Roots of Conflict* (Ithaca, NY & London, Cornell University Press, 1999).

Walt, Stephen M., *The Origins of Alliances* (Ithaca, NY: Cornell University Press, 1987).

Waltz, Kenneth N., *Theory of International Politics* (Reading, MA: Addison-Wesley, 1979).

INDEX

Note: Page numbers followed by "*n*" refer to notes, "*t*" refer to tables and bold refer to maps.

Adolphus, Gustavus (King), 17
Aegean Sea, 33, 35, 62, 145
Aegina, 33, 35
Aegospotami, 92, 98, 118
Aegospotami, Battle of, 84
Afghanistan, 124, 126, 136
Alaska, 113
Alcibiades, 62, 75, 82, 131, 134, 147, 197*n*39, 210–11*n*98
Alcidas, 81
Allison, Graham, 142–4
al-Qaeda, 124
Alsace-Lorraine, 114
American Civil War (1861–5), 118
Americans, 111–12, 113–14, 120–1, 124–6
Amphipolis, 64, 108
Anglo-American treaty (1850), 113
appeasement, 101, 104, 108–9, 110, 112, 113–14, 115, 120, 139, 152
Arcadians, 32
Archidamian War (431–21 BCE), 88
Archidamus (Spartan king), 44, 45–6, 66, 72–3, 74, 76–7, 79, 85–6, 88, 96

Arginusae, 91, 92
Arginusae, Battle of, 110
Argives, 89, 118
Argos, 32, 38, 89, 109, 132, 186–7*n*39
arms control, 112, 148, 152, 187*n*48
Art of War, The (Tzu), 1, 48
Art, Robert J., 10
Asia Minor, 26, 30, 33, 84, 102, 110, 145
Asia, 14
Asian Minor Greeks, 91
Athenian Empire, 26–8, 30, 31, 47, 60–1, 73, 88, 119
Athenian navy, 26–7, 33, 53, 55, 57–60, 91–3
Athens/Athenians, 14, 28, 46–7, 51–2, 52–4, 54–8, 59–61, 59*t*, 61*t*, 65–6, 68–9, 74–6, 78–84, 88–93, 95–8, 97*t*, 105, 110, 118, 119, 122, 127, 130, 144–9, 152, 153–5, 157, 159–60, 165
  applicability of the Theory, 110–17
  bilateral balance between Sparta and, 44–6, 72–4

229

INDEX

causes of war, 35–40
early phase of conflict, 30–5, 34
issue of legitimacy, 58–61, 84–7
political objectives setting, 46–8
rivalry between Sparta and, 23–30, 27, 29
treaty, 108–9
Attica, 34, 55, 58, 66–7, 77, 80, 81–2, 85–6, 88–9, 97, 146
Austria, 16, 115, 119
Austria-Hungary, 114
Austrian Empire, 16, 114
Austrians, 17

Baghdad, 124
balancing, 44–6, 72–4, 103–4
  external, 109, 114, 153
  internal, 109, 114, 120, 153
Baldwin, David, 65
Balkans, 112
Baltic states, 112
Barnett, Correlli, 206n52
Beijing, 116–17
Biden, Joe, 127
Bismarck, 118
Black Sea, 145
blackmail, 203n23
blockade, 92, 121–2
bloodletting, 203n23
Boeotia, 33, 34, 78, 180–1n54
Boeotians, 64
Bolshevik revolution, 134
border disputes, 113, 153
Bosnia, 121
Bosnian Croats, 121
Bosnian Muslims, 121
Brasidas (Spartan general), 64, 81, 85, 196–7n32
Britain, Battle of (1940–1), 119
British Guyana, 113
'British way of warfare', 119
British, 17

Brodie, Bernard, 47
Bull Run II (1862), 118
Byzantine Empire, 17
Byzantium, 30, 145

Canada, 113
capabilities, 15, 100, 136
Carthage, 100, 111
Carthaginian Empire, 100
Catana, 131
Cavalry, 130, 131–2
Central America, 113
Central Committee of the Communist Party of the Soviet Union, 135–6
Central Europe, 16
centre of gravity, 97–8, 119, 123, 124
Chancellorsville (1863), 118
China, 116–17, 127, 142, 145, 148
Chios, 51
Christianity, 17
Cimon (Athenian general), 31
Clausewitz, Carl von, 3, 6–7, 12, 116, 123
Clausewitzian approach, 97
Coercive diplomacy, 154
Cold War, 9, 42, 118–21
Concert of Europe, 111
Connor, W.R., 42
Copenhagen, 115
Corcyra, 24, 35, 42, 43, 51
Corcyreans, 35
Corinth, 32, 35, 38, 57, 130
Corinthian Gulf, 33
Corinthians, 30, 35, 36, 38, 82
Coronea, 34, 108
Crawley, Richard, 143
Crimea, 126
crisis, 118
  Cuban Missile (1962), 39
  Fashoda, 39
  Sarajevo (1914), 39
Cuban Missile Crisis (1962), 39

INDEX

Cyprus, 31, 84, 105, 145
Cythera, 78, 88, 122
Cyzicus, 91, 92
Cyzicus, Battle of, 109–10

Dardanelles, 30, 33
Darius II (Persian king), 79
Dayton Agreement, 121
Decelea, 82–3, 91, 92, 197n37
Decelean War (413–04 BCE), 90
decisive battle, 117, 123
defence planning, 154
Delbrück, Hans, 18, 59, 61, 144
Delian League, 31, 60
Delium, 64, 108
Deng, 5, 169n20
Diaoyu/Senkaku Islands, 116
Diocletian, 114
Dipaieis, 32
diplomacy, 16, 63, 77, 84, 87, 116
direct approach, 97–8, 117, 118, 122–4
domino theory, 154
Donetsk, 126
Doyle, Michael, 28–9
Druze, 136
durability, 22, 62

Ecclesia, 24, 86
efficiency, 21–2, 62, 63
Egypt, 31, 33, 100, 105, 145
Eleans, 90
11 September 2001 (terrorist attack), 124
ephors (overseers), 25
Epitaph, 59–60
Euboea, 34, 78, 92, 180–1n54
Europe, 111, 113, 118, 147
European Commission, 116
Europeans, 17
Eurymedon River, Battle of the, 31
expected utility theory, 147–8

'Fabian strategy', 54
Fashoda Crisis, 39
fear, 99, 132, 143
Ferrill, Arther, 64
Five Years' Peace, 33, 105
France, 4, 39, 111, 113–15, 119
Franco–Danish naval alliance, 115
Frederick the Great, 17
French Revolution, 16, 21
French, 17

Garst, Daniel, 146
Gelon, 130
Georgia, 112
Georgians, 126
German Empire, 114, 118
German troops, 4
Germans, 7, 10, 11, 13–14, 101, 112–14, 175n4
Gerousia, 26, 37
Gilpin, Robert, 1, 36, 38, 139
Golan Heights, 11
Gorbachev, Mikhail, 115
grand strategy, 6–7, 11f, 59t, 95–8, 97t, 139
 annihilation and exhaustion, strategies of, 117–28
 applicability of theory, 110–17
 Athenian, 49–50, 74–6, 88–93
 determinants of, 99–102, 101t
 military and non-military components, 14–17
 Periclean, 51–8, 61–4, 64–8
 planning and evaluation, 20–2, 21t
 Spartan, 44–6, 72–4, 74–6, 75, 76–84, 84–7, 88–93
 Thucydides and determinants of, 105–10, 106–7t
 typology of, 17–19
 underestimating enemy, 128–37
 See also strategy
Grant, Ulysses S., 118

231

INDEX

Gray, Colin, 68
Great Britain, 10, 17, 19, 39, 53, 101, 111, 113–15, 119, 185n20, 205n47
Greece, 14, 32–3, 35, 55, 76, 90, 93, 105, 109, 131, 145
Greeks, 28, 30–1, 43, 61, 85, 87, 90
Gylippus, 131

Halder, Franz, 134
Handel, Michael, 1
'hard power', 17
Hegel, Georg Wilhelm Friedrich, 38
hegemonic war, 147
hegemony, 113, 142, 144
helots, 25–6, 28, 32, 38, 56, 60, 177n14
Hermocrates, 132, 147–8
Herodotus, 38
Hetoimaridas, 37
History of the Peloponnesian War (Thucydides), 1, 2, 142–3
Hitler, Adolf, 7, 50, 101, 114, 134–5
Hobbes, Thomas, 38, 143
horizontal
 dimension of strategy, 3, 5, 6t, 71, 76, 96
Hussein, Saddam, 122, 124

Iapygia, 132
Iapygia, promontory of, 132
imperialism, 157
indirect approach, 85, 86, 97, 98, 123, 124, 211–12n115
Industrial Revolution, 111
Infantry, 128
intelligence, 125, 135
intentions, 37, 47, 100, 101
inter alia, 1, 122
internal coherence, 22, 62, 63
international
 economy, 6, 102
 environment, 6, 7, 10, 20, 42–4, 62

 relations, 1–2, 36, 38, 42, 141, 142
 system, 6, 24, 37, 40, 119
Ionia, 30
Iraq War (2003–11), 13
Iraq, 122–3, 124
Israel, 22, 136
Italian peninsula, 16
Italy, 132

Japan, 13, 111, 116, 134

Kabul, 136
Kagan, Donald, 43, 178n25, 193–4n9
Kennedy, Paul, 53, 173n58
Korea, 133
Kosovo Liberation Army (KLA), 123, 208–9n80
Kosovo War (1999), 12
Kosovo, 123–4
Kuwait War (1991), 124
Kuwait, 122

Laconia, 25
Lebanon, 136
Lebow, Richard Ned, 38–9
Lee, Robert E., 118
legitimacy
 domestic, 120, 121, 157
 international, 124, 157
 issues, 58–61, 84–7
Lend-Lease Bill, 114
Leotychidas (King), 30
Lesbos, 51
Liddell Hart, Basil, 13, 15, 19, 48, 56, 98, 211n115
London, 114
loss-of-strength gradient, 157
Lugansk, 126
Luttwak, Edward, 121–2
Lysander (Spartan admiral), 92, 98

Macedonia, 81

INDEX

Madrid, 113
Magna Graecia, 42
Manchuria, 133
Mantinea, 118
Mantinea, Battle of (418 BCE), 89–90, 109
Mantineans, 32
Marx, Karl, 38
Megara, 32, 47, 49, 78, 108, 143, 180–1n54, 186n30
Megarian Decree, 49, 77
Megarians, 34
Megarid, 33, 57
Melian Dialogue, 104
Messenia, 25, 30, 38
Metternich, Clemens, 16
Middle Ages, 12
Middle East, 13
military, 14–17, 105, 117, 119–20, 121, 122–6, 131, 133, 136, 148
  strategy, 7–12, 8t, 63, 78–9
Moltke, Field-Marshal Helmuth von, 118–19
Monroe Doctrine, 113
Moscow, 13, 112, 114, 126
Munich Pact (1938), 50
Mycale, 30
Mytilene, 80–1
Mytilenians, 80

Napoleon, 7, 17, 111, 115, 117, 123
Napoleonic campaigns, 18–19
Napoleonic Wars, 16, 17
Napoleonic/Clausewitzian model, 116, 118
national interest, 101, 103–4
NATO, 112, 116, 121, 123–4, 208–9n80
Naxos, 131
Nazi Germany, 111, 114
Netherlands, 111
New York, 124

Nicholas, Czar, 133, 136
Nichols, Mary, 144
Nicias, 130–2
Nicias, Peace of, 108
North America, 113
Northern Alliance, 124

Ober, Josiah, 52
objectives, 124, 149
  policy, 2, 5, 13, 46–8, 74
  political, 74–6
Oenophyta, Battle of, 33
On War (Clausewitz), 1, 2
Operation Barbarossa, 135
Ottoman Empire, 114
overextension, 20, 21, 50, 62, 68, 117, 141

Pacific Ocean, 11
Pamphylia, 33, 102
Panama Canal Zone, 113
Pausanias, 30
Peace of Callias, 33–4, 79, 109, 180n50
Peace of Nicias (421 BCE), 64, 71, 82, 89
Peloponnese, 28–30, 89–90
Peloponnesian League, 28, 32, 34–5, 38, 72–3, 82, 93
Peloponnesian navy, 79, 91–2, 98
Peloponnesian War (433 BCE), 23, 35, 36–40, 82, 117–18, 119–20, 122, 127, 142–3, 167n1, 215n14
Peloponnesian War I (460–45 BCE), 32, 37–8, 77, 84–5, 145–7
Peloponnesians, 34, 50, 54, 56, 57, 64, 68, 79, 87
Pentecontaetia, 23, 26
perception, 38, 40, 117
Periclean Athens, 60
Periclean grand strategy, 96, 97, 121–2

233

INDEX

Pericles, 43–5, 48, 49–50, 52–3, 54–7, 59–61, 64–9, 86–7, 96, 119, 146–7
Persia, 37, 68, 83–4, 102, 105–8, 147
  treaty, 108–9
Persian Empire, 146
Persian Wars, 23, 53–4, 85, 194n10
Persians, 14, 28, 37, 66, 73–4, 79, 84
Phalerum, 52
Pharnabazus, 84
Phocis, 33, 34
Piraeus, 52, 93
Pisander, 73–4
Plataea, Battle of (479 BCE), 14, 30
Pleistoanax (Spartan king), 34, 58, 87
political leadership, 5, 6, 36, 99–102, 117
  Spartan, 34, 67, 92, 97, 109–10
Port Arthur, 134
Potidaea, 24, 80
Power, balance of, 99–102, 103, 104, 152, 202n13
Prague, 101
Prasiae, 56–7
pre-nuclear era, 7, 39
prestige, 105, 162–3
Principle of concentration of force, 164
Principle of unity of command, 164
Prussia, 115
Putin, Vladimir, 112, 136
Pylos, 56–7, 78, 88, 92, 122, 148
Pyrenees, Treaty of the, 113

Red Army, 14, 134
Rome, 100, 111
Rundstedt, Gerd von, 134
Russia, 7, 114–15, 126, 136–7
Russian Federation, 112
Russians, 4, 126
Russo-Japanese War (1904–5), 133

Sadowa, 118
Samos, 92
Sarajevo Crisis (1914), 39
Schlieffen Plan, 4, 11
Schlieffen, Alfred von, 4
'scorched-earth policy', 55
security dilemma, 164
security, 99, 114, 115, 139, 160
Sedan, 118
Serbia, 121
Seven Years' War (1756–63), 115
'Si vis pacem, para bellum', 3
Sicilian expedition (415–13 BCE), 71, 76, 97, 109, 128–9, 133
Sicilians, 152, 162
Sicily, 54, 62–3, 68, 73, 75, 79, 83, 90–1, 109–10, 127–9, 130, 131–2, 145
Silesia, 115
Sino–American relations, 142
Slavs, 134
'soft power', 17
Somalia, 136
South China Sea, 116
southern Italy, 79
Soviet Union, 7, 8, 17, 39, 42, 112, 134, 148, 169n20
  factors of exhaustion, 119–20
  Hitler's invasion of, 114
  invasion of Western Europe, 9
Soviets, 11
Spain, 113, 115, 205n47
Sparta/Spartans, 14, 47–8, 52–4, 54–8, 59t, 61t, 65–7, 95–8, 97t, 105, 108, 109, 127, 145–6, 148–9, 152, 155, 157, 158, 159–60, 162–3
  bilateral balance between Sparta and, 44–6, 72–4
  causes of war, 35–40
  early phase of conflict, 30–5
  evaluation, 88–93
  issue of legitimacy, 84–7

INDEX

political objectives, 74–6, 75
rivalry between Athens and, 23–30
strategy during Peloponnesian War, 117–18
See also grand strategy
Spartan Assembly, 45, 72–3
Spartan Empire, 30, 179n30
Sphacteria, 56–7, 64, 78, 88, 122
Sphacteria, Battle of, 108
St. Petersburg, 134
Stalin, 5, 13, 169n20
Star Wars, 120, 187n48
status quo, 110, 111–12
Sthenelaidas, 72–3, 78, 88
strategy
  annihilation, 18, 19, 41–2, 48, 71, 74, 117–28
  applicability of theory, 110–17
  Athenian and Spartan Grand Strategies, 95–8, 97t
  determinants of, 99–102, 101t
  Economics and, 154–5
  exhaustion, 18, 41–2, 71, 117–28
  levels of, 4–14, 6t
  military, 7–12, 8t, 63, 78–9
  nature of, 3–4
  Thucydides and determinants of, 105–10, 106–7t
  underestimating enemy, 128–37
  See also grand strategy
'subhumans', 7
Sun Tzu, 48, 185–6n28
surprise, 101, 115, 134, 148, 163, 164–5
Sweden, 115
Swedish army, 17
Sybota, 35, 36–7
Syracusans, 109, 131
Syracuse, 83, 130, 131–2, 147, 152
Syria, 100

tactics, 4–5, 11–13, 158, 165
Taiwan, 116

Taliban, 124–6
Tanagra, 33
Taras, 132
Tegea, 32
Terrain, 165
territorial expansion, 101
Thebans, 152
Thebes, 42
Themistocles, 52
theory of victory, 143–4
Thirty Years' Peace, 34–5, 46, 89, 145, 186–7n39
Thrace, 81
threat, 99, 100—2, 103–4, 105, 109–10, 110–17
Thucydides, 1–2, 26–8, 35–40, 41–4, 51, 63, 68–9, 80–1, 83, 85, 86, 89, 104, 139, 141–9, 177n13
  applicability of theory, 110–17
  Athenian and Spartan Grand Strategies, 95–8, 97t
  determinants of Grand Strategy, 99–102, 101t, 105–10, 106–7t
  underestimating enemy, 128–37
Tissaphernes, 84
Total war, 119, 207n69
Trans-Siberian Railway, 134
'tributary cities', 51
Trump, Donald, 116, 127
Tsushima Strait, 134

U.S. Air Force, 124
U.S. Congress, 114
Ukraine war, 127
Ukraine, 112, 126–7
underestimating the enemy, 128–37
United States, 13, 39, 42, 110, 112, 113, 119, 124, 125, 127, 142, 145, 147–8, 197–8n40, 205n47
  China's strategic relationship, 116–17
USSR (Union of Soviet Socialist Republics), 119

235

INDEX

van Creveld, Martin, 40
Venezuela, 113
Verdun, Battle of (1916), 119
Vietnam, 22, 58

Waltz, Kenneth, 38
War of American Independence (1775–83), 111
Washington, DC, 112, 116, 124
Waterloo, 111
Western Europe, 9

'wolf warrior' diplomacy, 116
World War I, 7, 39, 53, 114, 115, 135, 143, 175n4
World War II (1815–45), 7, 11, 118

Xerxes (King), 14, 172–3n55
Xi Jinping, 116

Yanukovych, Victor, 126
Yom Kippur War (1973), 11, 22
Yugoslavia, 123